THE
LEGEND
OF
SAFED

Raphael Patai Series in Jewish Folklore and Anthropology

General Editor
Dan Ben-Amos
University of Pennsylvania

Advisory Editors
Tamar Alexander-Frizer
Ben-Gurion University of the Negev

Haya Bar-Itzhak
University of Haifa

Simon J. Bronner
Pennsylvania State University, Harrisburg

Harvey E. Goldberg
The Hebrew University of Jerusalem

Yuval Harari
Ben-Gurion University of the Negev

Galit Hasan-Rokem
The Hebrew University of Jerusalem

Rella Kushelevsky
Bar-Ilan University

Eli Yassif
Tel Aviv University

THE LEGEND OF SAFED

Life and Fantasy in the City of Kabbalah

ELI YASSIF
Translated by Haim Watzman

WAYNE STATE UNIVERSITY PRESS
DETROIT

Copyright © 2019 by Wayne State University Press, Detroit, Michigan 48201. All rights reserved. No part of this book may be reproduced without formal permission.

Published with support from the fund for the Raphael Patai Series in Jewish Folklore and Anthropology.

ISBN (hardcover): 978-0-8143-4110-0
ISBN (paperback): 978-0-8143-4684-6
ISBN (ebook): 978-0-8143-4111-7

Library of Congress Control Number: 2019930070

All photographs by Shoshi Yassif.

Wayne State University Press
Leonard N. Simons Building
4809 Woodward Avenue
Detroit, Michigan 48201-1309

Visit us online at wsupress.wayne.edu

Contents

Acknowledgments   vii

Introduction   1

1. Voices Rising from Safed
- Wonderful, Wretched Safed   11
- Voices from Outside   18
- Discord and Strife   19
- Halakhists and Kabbalists   31

2. The Myth and Its Disenchantment
- Of Oxen and Beards   39
- Spirits, Reincarnations, and Other Visions   51
- From the Beards of the West to the Sidelocks of the East   58
- The Procession of the Dead   71
- "Toro muerto, vaca es" (A Dead Ox Is a Cow)   77

3. In Fields and Wilderness
- Safed Stories as Local Legends   85
- The Axis of the World   87
- The Galilee as a Semiotic Space   94
- A World Full of Souls   100
- A Mythical Space   108
- The Place as an Ideal and a Rupture   128

4. And He Woke and It Was a Dream
- The Dream and the Fairy Tale   133
- Shmuel Vital, Master of Dreams   137
- Hayyim Vital's Nightmarish Dreams   148
- The Enchanted Garden   155
- Turning Distress into Legend   159

5. Sin Crouches at the Door

From Birth to Death	161
Nothing Is Hidden from His Eyes	169
Reality Is Unintelligible, but Its Signs Are Open	175
From the Erotic to the Demonic	180
A Spirit Entered Her	185

6. And He Had Knowledge About Everyone

Our Own Eyes Saw Terrifying Things	197
Luria Exorcises a Spirit	202
The Hidden World	203
Concealment, Mystery, and Charisma	208
Between Visible and Invisible	210
Were All the Seas Ink and All the Sky Parchment	214

7. Life and Legend

Inconsistency Is in the Eye of the Beholder	221
Existential Tension Resolves Opposites	224
Family or Messiah?	227
The Messianic Age Is Here and Now	231
The Legend Speaks	239

Notes	243
Bibliography	267
Index	287

Acknowledgments

This book is based on research I carried out over many years, during which I also applied myself to other projects on other subjects. I would like to thank my translator, Haim Watzman, for the careful and exemplary work he did here.

I also had the help of friends for whom Safed has always been at the center of their scholarly endeavors, unlike me—I applied myself only relatively recently to the study of one of the most complex periods and phenomena in Jewish studies.

I want to thank Mordechai Pachter, Joseph Hacker, Abraham David, Ronit Meroz, and Yaron Ben-Naeh for reading, commenting on, and correcting parts of this book. I should stress that I am solely responsible for any errors that remain.

Further thanks are owed to the Bahat Prize committee at the University of Haifa, which found this book worthy of its very important award. I also thank two institutions without which this book would never have been published: the ISF (Israel Science Foundation), which provided the basic funding for the translation, and Tel-Aviv University, which provided me with the academic resources to work and publish this book. Thank you also to the Wayne State University Press experts for the fine work they did with this book.

I dedicate this book to my children, Naama, Efrat, and Yinon, who were teenagers when I began this book and are now fine young people of whom my wife and I are very proud.

Introduction

A LITTLE MORE THAN a century ago, Solomon Schechter, explorer and earliest scholar of the Cairo Genizah, president of the Jewish Theological Seminary in New York, and one of the founders of Conservative Judaism in the United States, was the first to draw the attention of scholars in the field of Jewish studies to Safed in its golden age. That was in 1908, when he published his seminal essay, "Safed in the Sixteenth Century." Schechter's study remained hugely influential for many years and spawned many studies of the city's rich culture. Ahead of his time, Schechter took what we would today call an interdisciplinary view of the relationship between Safed's history (the Spanish expulsion, Ottoman policy, the fabric industry, and the tax system) and its spiritual life (halakhic literature, the Safed revolution in Kabbalah, ethical theory, social tensions, and the city's singular ambiance of asceticism, prayer, Torah study, and repentance). He was the first to stress the importance of the Safed fellowships and their rules. He described pilgrimages to the graves of saints and the relations between the different communities in Safed and pointed out the importance of the legends that developed and spread there, legends that form the center of the current book.

In light of the fact that the centennial of Schechter's article some years ago was not adequately commemorated, I dedicate the present study to that exemplary work of scholarship.[1]

However, Schechter's study is not without its weaknesses. It contains some inaccuracies, a result of the limited knowledge available to him about the place and era of which he wrote. His hermeneutic approach led him astray in some of the areas he addressed, including my primary interest here, the Safed legends. Schechter was certainly aware that these were legends—indeed, that is the word he used to describe the narrative texts he addressed. But his general approach is strongly positivistic. In general, Schechter recounts the contents of the stories and relates to them as though they provide factual information about actual events, disregarding their artistic character and their complex and layered meanings. In retrospect, "Safed in the Sixteenth Century" obscured the great disputes and rivalries in Safed, and in doing so reinforced the impression that the milieu of the town at that time was one of idyllic harmony among halakhists, mystics, ethicists, and the socioeconomic elite.[2] This harmonious picture is one of the principal elements of the myth of Safed; it clearly evinces the mystification that lies at the heart of every myth and makes it a formative influence on any given society.

My intention in this work is to use tools developed largely by the New Historicism school to penetrate the mystification of the Safed myth and identify some of the forces acting on and driving it. New Historicism rejects naïve historicism, which views literary texts as an extraneous element to reality that makes no real contribution to the perception of history. Instead, the new school views literary texts as one component of the network of forces that act in the world. Historical context is thus vital for interpreting literary texts, and the texts in turn illuminate and deepen our understanding of historical events. With this in mind, New Historicism seeks out non-canonical materials in the culture under study—letters, rituals, folktales, rumors, and gossip. It also examines everyday customs, dreams, travel journals, and folk beliefs (popularly known as superstitions). By listening to the voices of individuals and groups who have been excluded from the social canon, we gain a more profound understanding of the place and time under study.[3]

Safed's folklore and legends—central genres in its culture—are by their nature anticanonical. They were created by broad strata of the Jewish community and thus convey an anti-establishment discourse that can illuminate unfamiliar aspects of social mentality.[4] Safed's history within the Ottoman Empire, the wide-ranging halakhic literature produced there, its huge contribution to the development of Kabbalah, and its economic and moral life have all been studied intensively. But, although noncanonical materials have been addressed here and there, their importance for understanding the Safed phenomenon has not been adequately recognized.

The magnificent Jewish culture that emerged in Safed around 1600 produced innovations in nearly all branches of that era's religious scholarship:

Halakha, midrash, Kabbalah, customs and rituals, liturgical poetry, and moral teaching. Each of these areas has been the subject of detailed studies, and they have practically become fields of study in their own right.[5] Yet another area, no less important, has received nearly no real scholarly attention: the legends produced by the people of Safed at the time. In fact, a large part of what we know about Safed circa 1600—everyday life, the cast of characters and the relations between them, customs and beliefs, hopes, and tensions—comes from these stories. Safed's legends serve as bridges that connect Halakha, Kabbalah, moral teachings, everyday life, the geographic environment and historical circumstances, the biographies of individuals, and relations within the community, but they have not been studied in their own right as literary texts or as folktales.[6]

True, one of the innovations produced in Safed, the genre of saint legends (the term *shevakhim*, "praises," was used for the first time in Safed), has been noted by writers on the Hebrew story. These cycles of legends, which center on a sacred character, did not originate in Safed. An important example of this literature, a cycle of legends about Rabbi Judah ben Samuel of Regensburg (Judah the Pious), dates to no later than the fifteenth century, and similar cycles of legends about Rashi, Maimonides, Rabbi Avraham ibn Ezra, and Nachmanides appear in Rabbi Gedaliah ibn Yahia's *Shalshelet haKabbalah*, from the mid-sixteenth century. But the first integral and cohesive collections of stories about a celebrated figure from his birth to his death, called *shevakhim*, seem to have appeared first in Safed.[7]

Meir Benayahu studied legends of Rabbi Isaac Luria (Ashkenazi) (known to his followers as the Ari [ha-'Ari], or "the lion") in his comprehensive bibliographic survey *Shivkhei ha-'Ari* (Praises of the Ari) and in particular in the exemplary edition of that work he offered in his book *Sefer Toldot ha-'Ari*. I do not intend to address again the widespread criticism of this work, in particular Benayahu's claim that the source for the material found in the letters of Rabbi Solomon Shlumil of Dreznitz, which he sent from Safed to his family and teachers in Central Europe in the first decade of the seventeenth century, was *Sefer Toldot ha-'Ari* itself and so are merely a forgery. The argument over this point has turned emotional and personal. Benayahu is simply wrong on this point, and there is no point rehashing the entire debate here.[8]

Another weak point in Benayahu's basic work, however, relates to the fact that his edition of *Sefer Toldot ha-'Ari* contributes to scholarship only on the philological-textual level. He does not address the hundreds of stories he published in this edition as texts of literary, cultural, or human value. Benayahu sought out the "earliest" versions of the stories, compared them, and examined their historical "accuracy," but he evinced no curiosity about their meaning, nor did he interpret them as cultural artifacts. His somewhat naïve positivist historical method led him to consider these stories as "testimonies" about Luria and his students, some of them reliable and some fabricated. A historian could use the reliable ones and reject the others.[9]

Benayahu ends up achieving something he had not intended to. He sets out to prove the precedence of *Sefer Toldot ha-'Ari* over the haphazard and emotional collection of oral narratives that Shlumil of Dreznitz had collected on Safed's streets. He definitely does not prove that. It cannot be true according to any criteria. In seeking to do so, however, Benayahu establishes a philological infrastructure and textual foundation on which any future study cannot do without.

The legends of Safed, especially those surrounding Luria, have been taken to have been produced by a small group of Luria's students and admirers during his life and soon after his death. If these legends were indeed produced within Luria's circle, they should be seen as "sectarian" literature. In this book, however, I define and treat them as folk legends. Two observations in this regard should be made here, one in the theoretical context and the other in the historical context. The field of folklore studies, as theorized and elaborated over the last two centuries, claims that what defines a folktale as such is its social reception, not its authorship. Any story, even if written by a philosopher such as Plato, a historian such as Josephus Flavius, or a playwright such as Shakespeare, becomes folk literature if it is taken up by society at large—that is, if it is told and retold in a society that comes to see the legend as a cultural asset, through which it expresses its wishes and fears. The source from which the legend came is but the initial stage in its development. Because it is prior to the story's adoption by the public, it offers almost no information about what the story meant to that public and why it became popular.

The person who discovered and documented the Safed legends in their earliest form was Solomon Shlumil of Dreznitz, who immigrated to Safed more than thirty years after Luria's death. By his own account, Shlumil collected the legends in part from Luria's students who were still living there, but mostly he collected them from women and men in the town's marketplaces, streets, synagogues, and houses of study. Historical inquiry has proven that, immediately following Luria's death, almost no legends about him were known. If there were stories of this sort, they were known only to a small circle of his students.[10] These two facts indicate that the legends Shlumil encountered had metamorphosed and spread outside Luria's coterie of students during the thirty years after his death. During this time, some of the legends, those that indeed originated among his students, were transformed from sectarian legends to folk ones. Other legends, apparently the great majority of them, took form during this period or a few years later. In Chapter 2 of this book, I address the Tale of the Oxen, which offers a notable example of this apparent process. This legend was almost certainly crafted by Rabbi Hayyim Vital, the leading disciple of Luria, who took older medieval legends and applied them to Safed. Over the years, the legend became severed from the limited interests of Luria's immediate circle and came to express the feelings and perceptions of a much broader social and religious public. Thus, even though the Tale of the Oxen was composed by Luria's close student, under the influence of the mind-set of his close associates, it turned into a folktale, and it is as such that I present its literary character and social significance.

The principal importance of the Safed legends is that they express the thoughts and feelings of the people who lived in Safed, not just the great halakhists, mystics, and ascetics. These legends, unlike other folk genres, such as myths and fairy tales, deal with human beings, not gods, kings, or beautiful princesses. Because these legends took form over a long period and were disseminated orally and in writing over an even longer period, they explicitly or implicitly voice the feelings and thoughts of the society that created and told them. They give expression to that society's longings, anxieties, and tensions. Folk literature is generally born of tension—personal, social, or existential—and one of the important means of identifying these tensions is thus through understanding and interpreting the legends created by the Safed "folk."

The myth of Safed, which has developed continuously since around 1600, depicts it as a city of spirituality, Torah, and mysticism. But it does so by diminishing and hiding the flawed human and disappointing aspects of life in Safed, which contrasted sharply with the ideal aspired to by the society that created the myth. Joseph Hacker has pointedly remarked, "The community of Safed was composed of human beings—flesh and blood—and its history and society are not exhausted by the stories of the saints and righteous men who float in the clouds."[11] But, whereas Hacker meant that historians should focus on texts that are not legends or mysticism but rather historical documents offering information about day-to-day life in Safed, I, as a folklorist, take a different approach. I use these legends to achieve the same goal Hacker aimed at; I want to understand Safed's individuals and society through the legends that they created and told. That is the essence of what New Historicism seeks to do: to identify the human beings, the human voice behind the "great" historical and spiritual events. Indeed, the human aspect of life in Safed is better expressed in legends than in any other genre in the wealth of material produced in Safed, as I will attempt to show.

In keeping with this approach, the true hero of this book is Hayyim Vital, not Isaac Luria, despite the fact that Luria is the traditional symbol of Safed and its saintly representative. Vital was ostracized. He lacked leadership abilities and charisma, was plagued by anxiety, and suffered severe mental crises. He spent the last part of his life in Damascus, holding no position and receiving no honor, as full of disappointments as a pomegranate is full of seeds. Yet it is Vital who penned the works that are the fundamental texts of the Safed school of Kabbalah: *Pri Etz Hayim*, *Sefer haHezyonot*, *Sha'ar Ruach haKodesh*, *Sefer haGilgulim*, and dozens of others. It is through these works that we know of Luria and his circle. Although Luria is generally painted as a mythical hero, what might be called in literary terms a "flat character," Vital comes across as a full human being. His humanity, vulnerability, anxieties, and hidden wishes emerge from nearly all his writings. He is a person who lives in a constant state of nerves bared to all; this is his most salient trait. In literary terms, he is a manifestly "round character," whole, full of contradictions, varied, and real. Vital also shows himself to be a renaissance man; he is at home in nearly all fields of knowledge of his day—Halakha and Kabbalah, ethical theory and the theory of the soul, dreams and their interpretation, learned and natural medicine, astrology and geography (of the sacred type, i.e., the description of tombs and routes for pilgrims). He also engaged in practical Kabbalah, that is, magic. He delved into the science of his day and even took an interest in cooking—he left us a considerable list of recipes. He wrote about plants and animals and was blessed with a naturally keen and uncommon curiosity. In this and other ways Vital, with his complex and neurotic personality, was an embodiment of the atmosphere of Safed and its characteristic mentality. The fissure that ran through his soul between what he thought he ought to be—a leader of messianic qualities—and his marginal and miserable life in Safed and Damascus not only typified him but also was the basis of the tension that was Safed's most striking feature.[12]

My purpose is to propose a different way of scholarly examination of the legends of Safed, one that can open a discussion of one of the most vital and fascinating chapters of Jewish culture that came into being at the beginning of the modern age. This book is based on a fundamental and unitary assumption: that legends, perhaps more than any other literary genre, express a basic tension that was characteristic of Safed's actuality, spirituality, and mentality at the time in question. The individual chapters are thus inseparably tied to one another. Each chapter builds on the conclusions of the others and on the texts the other chapters examine. That being the case, I suggest reading this book as an integral work, not as a collection of essays on different topics. The specific focus that each chapter focuses on is one facet of a single subject and derives from the same perspective on life and thought.

Here is the place to confess a lacuna in my earlier book, *The Hebrew Folktale: History, Genre, Meaning* (1994; English translation, 1999). In that work, I surveyed the history and development of the Hebrew folktale from its origins in the Bible through oral-communal tales in the State of Israel. However, I skipped from the Middle Ages to the Hasidic story at the end of the eighteenth century, leaving out the tales of the Safed period. It was not because I did not know of the Safed legends or think them unimportant. On the contrary, I believed that Safed had produced some of the most important material in the long and rich history of Hebrew storytelling. But the lack of a solid foundation of research on that oeuvre meant that I could not properly place the Safed legends in their historical and literary context in that historical survey.

Here and elsewhere in this book I write of "the period," or "era," or use other such terms. When I use them, I mean the time period in and around 1600. I do not offer a study of that year alone, just as studies of the year 1000 by medievalists do not address only a single year. Rabbi Isaac Luria arrived in Safed in 1570 and died there in 1572. Hayyim Vital died in Damascus in 1620. These two figures are the principal protagonists of this book, and the period I examine stretches between them. The "Praises of the Ari" legends began to emerge only after Luria's death, although some of them had originated already in his lifetime. Rabbi Shlumil of Dreznitz, Moravia, the most important discoverer and documenter of the legends, arrived in Safed in 1602. He sent his four famous letters to Europe during the five years after his arrival. Vital's important works that are of interest to this book, primarily *Sefer haHezyonot*, *Sha'ar haGilgulim*, and *Sha'ar Ruach haKodesh*, were composed during this period. The Kabbalah of Safed began to influence the Jewish world after 1620, as kabbalistic works such as *Emek haMelekh*, historical works such as *Sefer Divrei Yosef*, and ethical ones such as *Sefer Haredim* and *Reshit Hokhmah* disseminated the mystic, narrative, and moral message of Safed throughout the Jewish exile. The year 1600 lies in the center of this decisive fifty-year period in which the legends that are the subject of this work took form and were disseminated.

In addition to these matters, the chapters of this book present a rich variety of texts: legends and myths, dreams and fantasies, gossip and rituals, moral instructions and mystical visions. They were spoken, created, and practiced 400 years ago, and they collectively reflect one of the richest, most interesting, and most dynamic cultural phenomena that the Jewish people ever produced. All these texts were written and preserved in Hebrew (although, orally, they might have been told in other Jewish vernaculars). They were translated here into English with an attempt to preserve their original style and atmosphere.

The book spans two planes. The text is intended for the general reader with an interest in the history of Jewish culture in general and in the early modern period in particular. I have thus avoided, as much as possible, the use of scholarly jargon. The other plane lies in the footnotes, which offer both bibliographical information and specialized comments, including my differences with previous scholars—all that is to be expected in professional scholarly literature.

The seminal tension between the material life and the spiritual life of Safed around 1600 ("reality and fantasy") is best seen in the opposing perspectives on Safed as presented by inside and outside spectators. The opening chapter of the book is, it seems, the best introduction to this long journey into one of the most vital periods of Jewish history and culture.

1

Voices Rising from Safed

> Voices upon voices, frenzied and frightening . . . quarrels and clashes.
>
> —Rabbi Moshe Alsheikh

WONDERFUL, WRETCHED SAFED

SAFED SITS ON A mountain, enveloped in nebulae of mysticism and mystery. It had this magical aura also during its great golden age more than 400 years ago. The aura was so potent that a simple Jew from a town in Moravia divorced his wife, liquidated his assets, and set off alone, on the intermediate days of the Sukkot holiday in October 1602, for the Safed of his dreams. Solomon Shlumil of Dreznitz,[1] who sought to immerse himself in the town's kabbalistic milieu, would become one of the major shapers and disseminators of the myth of Safed. He describes his first encounter with the town in one of the letters he sent to his family and teachers in Europe,

> And I found a holy community here in Safed, because it is a great city of God, a city full of wisdom [or Torah], close to 300 great rabbis, all men of piety and action. And I found eighteen yeshivot in Safed, may it be built and established quickly in our day, and twenty-one synagogues, and a great house of study with close to 400 boys and young men. . . . And on the eve of every new month, until midnight, they act as on Yom Kippur, imposing on themselves a prohibition against work, and all the Jews gather in the one large

synagogue . . . and pray an awe-inspiring prayer to God until noon, and sometimes devote the entire day to God in prayer and sermons. And the Gentiles who live on the soil of Israel are all submissive and subservient to the holiness of Israel. . . . Other than this, I found the entire Holy Land full of God's blessing and plentiful and inexpensive food beyond measure and estimation and telling . . . which even in its destruction produces fruit and oil and wine and silk for a third of the world, and [men] come in ships from the ends of the earth, from Venice and Spain and France and Portugal and Constantinople, loaded with grain and olive oil, raisins and figs and honey and silk and soap, good as the sand on the beach. We buy wheat as clear as the sun . . . and olive oil . . . and sesame oil and sesame that is as sweet as honey and has the taste of manna . . . and wine, whoever buys grapes at the time of harvest and stores them in the press . . . as well as spirits of mead . . . and bee honey . . . and grape honey . . . and raisins . . . and dried figs, chickens, very cheap eggs . . . and fish . . . sometimes very cheap. And inexpensive rice and many varieties of legumes and lentils like you have never seen and which taste like nuts, cheap. And all kinds of jams and countless good vegetables that taste like nothing you have ever tasted can be found all the time, throughout the year, in the summer and winter, almost at no cost, in addition to good fruit, carobs, oranges, lemons, melons, and watermelons that taste like sugar . . . and also healthy and clear air and healthful water that lengthen one's days. For this reason most inhabitants, almost all of them, live long lives, eighty, ninety, even one hundred years. . . . And this is the sign, overseas almost all people and small children are full of boils on the knees and thighs, and in the Land of Israel, thank God, there is not even one person suffering from boils, neither children nor adults; instead all are as clean as gold, thank God.[2]

Shlumil's letter, dated July 19 (24 Tammuz), 1607, was copied and printed and reprinted. Texts of this sort are fine tinder for feeding the fire of myth. Shlumil provides details of Safed's full and intensive religious life, which puts aside the chores of the everyday and makes life into an ongoing sacrament. Safed's Jews live lives of profound religious experience that overshadows the practical and the material. Shlumil underlines the security they feel as a result of the respect and admiration they receive from the town's Gentile inhabitants. He portrays the flourishing economy, which benefits not only the wealthy but also all levels of society—all enjoy plenty. Even more important for Shlumil is the difference between the dark, disease-ridden, ugly Exile and the purifying light of Safed, a clear sign of God's special favor for the city and its inhabitants.

Safed's marvels and ideal life of Torah are also described by the Yemenite traveler and poet Zechariah (Yahya al-Dahiri), who visited the Land of Israel forty years before Shlumil, in 1567. He offers a different account of life in Safed at that time.

> And I came to that city [Safed]
> And within it the Divine Presence dwelt
> For within it is a great community far from falseness
> Fourteen thousand
> In eighteen yeshivot
> Stationed at the study of Talmud
> There I saw the light of the Torah
> And the Jews had light . . .
> And they made a breach in the boundary of wisdom
> Never have ignorants been found among them . . .
> In synagogues and houses of study
> Hearing preachers
> Preaching in many methods
> For they know every secret
> From the ceiling to the foundation
> Especially the great light the sage Joseph Karo
> Whose yeshiva the sages of Safed never leave
> Because the Talmud is deposited in his heart . . .

> And I went one Sabbath to his yeshiva
> To see his glorious greatness
> And I sat at the door, at the doorposts
> And my ideas were turbulent with ignorance
> And the elderly sage sat on a chair
> And held forth on the subject at hand
> In his speech removing man from the yoke of time
> To bring him close to the faithful God . . .
> And he spoke both the simple meaning and the Kabbalah
> This precious and sublime sage
> Some 200 valued and superior students
> sat on benches
> And when he ceased to speak his wisdom
> He signaled to one student facing him
> To speak of the soul and its powers
> And its purpose and about it
> And he stood before him
> Chanting his thoughts[3]

Those who heard Zechariah's account of his long journey through the Holy Land or read of it generations later in his written account, *Sefer haMusar* (Book of Ethics), cannot but be impressed by the wonderful atmosphere of Jewish religious learning that he experienced in Safed. The full force of the world of Torah was concentrated in this small patch of the Upper Galilee. Hundreds of students, dozens of houses of study, and the greatest scholars of the era could be found within the narrow bounds of Ottoman Safed. Zechariah's account is completely devoid of the everyday life evoked by Shlumil—the marketplace, merchandise, regular people, material existence. Perhaps he thought such details so inconsequential that he did not bother to mention them. More likely, however, he simply saw them as entirely subsidiary to Torah study. That seems more likely because the connection between the two can be felt in Shlumil's letter, as it could be heard in the voices of Safed's Jews many years later. So, for example, Eleazar Azkari, one of Safed's leading ethicists and a member of the fellowship of Luria's students, writes:

> Here in Safed we established a holy fellowship and gave it the name *Sukat Shalom*, and many have gathered to return [to God] with a full heart. From time to time the head of the court also preaches to each community on repentance. Also in each single fellowship the comrades listens together. The material days are sealed, and pound like the sea on the Torah and on the service [of God].[4]

Like Shlumil, Azkari does not ignore the mundane, the material days. He also knows that not all hours and days are sacred. But even on these days, the mundane is "sealed" or limited, and even they "pound like the sea," meaning that they are drowned out by the sound of the sea of Torah and the service of God. That is the significance of the wondrous and ideal life of Safed. Everyday life and weekday activities are not placed outside the pale but rather become an inseparable part of the closed circle of the life of Torah and piety. Zechariah, a traveler coming from the outside, sees only spiritual activity, but Safed's inhabitants—Shlumil writes some five years after his arrival in the city and Azkari is a native—point to the complexity, a town in which there are weekdays as well as days filled with Torah and service of God (as in every Jewish community) but in which the sacred overshadows the mundane and poses an impossible tension between the two. It is this complexity that makes Safed unique but that is also the source of the considerable tension, signifying its life and being.

Diametrically opposed to these ideal depictions, which were major factors in establishing the myth of Safed, come other voices, resentful and angry about the city's economic and spiritual plight. In 1592 one of Safed's great scholars, Rabbi Moshe Alsheikh, set out on a fundraising mission to Jewish communities in Turkey and Italy. That year, in Constantinople, he penned a missive, "Hazut Kashah" (Difficult Vision), in which he coins the idiom, "Because of Safed, may it be built and established quickly in our day, all the Land of Israel is maintained, and if there is no Safed, there is no Tiberias or Jerusalem or Hebron and there is no city in the Land of Israel, God be with me."[5] He immediately follows these praises, which are consistent with what Shlumil and Zechariah wrote, with the following plaint:

And before we tremble and shout our wounds on the land that God has cursed, we will tell just one of the thousands of evils and sorrows that have raged on us, because they are uncountable, only one evil out of many, because they are more than the locusts. . . . God and Israel knows, and Israel knew, that we have declined from the beginning, all earlier days were better than these. . . . For there is not even a bit of relief in the Land of Israel, which God gave us through tribulations, sustenance for the hungry and to pay the poll tax to those who hate us, and all sorts of cataclysms and disasters and false charges by wayward officials, small and large, and all sorts of taxes they afflict us with, legitimate and illegitimate, to the point that the Hebrews has been depleted of people; they have gone down to the roads and gates, broken, both the rich and the poor destroyed in Zion . . . for we are wearied by the many tribulations and evils and can no longer withstand them, but the land is miserable, the land has crumbled, the graceful land roars like a lion, because its mourners has become frequent, its agony doubled. . . . A very heavy famine [has befallen us], unlike any before; there is no sustenance. . . . There are no buyers and no sellers, the currency no longer buys anything, the poor have no work, and the penniless seek employment but there is none . . . hungry and thirsty, beaten, weeping and screaming, dragged, hidden and imprisoned, because the city is wretched, its sons impoverished within it these many days . . . and all the people weep from end to end, these weep and those weep, the rich weep and cry out that the middle ones who ate up all their money and impoverished [them], and the middle ones cry out from the multitudes who have plundered them and thus become poor, as if they were dead, and the poor who always perished in the city as eternal dead. . . . The leaders and wealthy have left the city in full view of all, and the ears ring in the streets and roads voices upon voices, frenzied and frightening, between one man and another, between man and wife, between father and daughter, *quarrels and clashes* on behalf of their obligations and accounts . . . and in their bitterness they seize and drag them and raise a deadly hand against them and interrogate [them], and one beats the other with a stone or a fist. . . . Because they have walked the streets of Safed, may it be built and established quickly in our day, and all those who knew it from ancient times and have turned to it and were ashamed [because of its situation], alas, lonely sits the city once great with people, how has it been overthrown. Because from such a multitude a fissure could have opened up between the walkers on its streets, but now it is reviled and ravaged, bereft of its children, sitting bereaved and forlorn. . . . Because but a few have remained in the city and there is no counting their tribulations, their faces are blacker than soot, they are not recognized in the streets, none comes or goes because those who go out and those who come in have no respite from troubles . . . for there is no bread throughout the land, and even if God were to endow the land with bread, in our house there is no bread, because there is no business, as the clothing trade has ceased, which was the mother of all life, from which both rich and poor lived, and without it we are all dead. . . . Then all wept. . . . And in their horror, as they wept, they turned their faces to the city's sages and said to them, your eminences, why did you leave your honor, for do we not remember the God-fearing sages who came before you, with all their troubles and their age on the troubles of their flocks and cast their souls before them to save them from thunder, and you are all silent on your watches.[6]

Even taking into account that the letter was written to compel well-off communities in Turkey and Italy to contribute to the support of the Safed community, the sense of desperation in Rabbi Moshe's letter rings true.

The letter's depiction of Safed could not be more different from that of Shlumil of Dreznitz. Shlumil trumpets Safed's prosperous economy, the abundance of food and its low price, attainable by all. In contrast, Alsheikh paints a picture of grinding poverty and famine. Shlumil lauds the harmonious relations between the Jews and Gentiles in Safed and its environs. Alsheikh writes of oppression, disturbances, and mortal fear of the Arabs and Turks. Where Shlumil, like Zechariah, speaks of a flourishing spiritual life and a sense of holiness under the leadership of great and learned rabbis, Alsheikh speaks of a great religious crisis, with the community losing faith in its spiritual leaders.[7]

Voices from Outside

Outsiders can offer a view from a distance that may be more objective, free as it is of the heavy burden of Jewish history. In 1600 an English traveler, William Biddulph, visited Safed and wrote of his visit, "When we came to the top of the mountains, we saw Saphetta [Safed] on the right hand a universitie of the Jewes, where they speake Hebrew and have their synagogues there." This English traveler, acquainted with the venerable universities of Oxford and Cambridge, each a collection of individual residential colleges in which young students studied and lived, perceived Safed in that light. He understood the scattered houses of study, the city's pride, to be colleges of a single university. At Oxford and Cambridge instruction was offered in a sacred language, Latin, so it was logical that the holy tongue of the Old Testament, Hebrew, would be the language of instruction and speech at the putative University of Safed. That this traveler paralleled the ascetic spiritual character of the British universities with the sacred milieu of Hebrew Safed shows how the idealization of Safed had seeped into the world of Christian travelers who passed through and made brief visits.

But other visitors came away with other impressions. A Portuguese traveler, Pantaleão de Aveiro, visited Safed in about 1565. He met many Portuguese Jews who had found a haven in the Galilean town after their expulsion from the Iberian Peninsula. "One night several Jewish women of Portuguese extraction came to me with tears in their eyes," he wrote of one such encounter, "lamenting that their sins had taken them out of Portugal not to the Promised Land, as they had believed, but to the Land of Despair, as they had seen with their own eyes and as they had experienced in their plight."

Another voice is that of a German traveler, Ludwig von Rauter, who visited Safed in 1568. He relates that "the city sits on a mountain and is inhabited by 2,000 Jews, most of them elderly, and they come here from all lands when they are already old, both men and women, their desire being to die in the Holy Land." According to von Rauter, Safed's streets were lined with indigent refugees who had fled religious persecution in their own countries but then greatly regretted it. Some were old and ill, with their lives already behind them, whose expectations were to die and be buried in the soil of the Holy Land. In other words, von Rauter did not see Oxford and Cambridge but rather a poor Levantine village full of misery and affliction, dejection and death.[8]

Discord and Strife

How can the polar contradictions between these accounts of Safed be explained? Most likely, the contradictions are illusory and the accounts simply portray different facets of a single multifaceted reality. The opposing impressions and disputes about Safed testify to its unique position in Jewish cultural history. As with every culture, the most profound understanding of its life and mentality emerges not from agreements about it but rather from the disparate voices that tell of clashes between ideas and values, between social groups, and between religious beliefs. Safed's culture has been depicted, since Schechter's 1908 essay, as almost monolithic, where groups of different backgrounds, customs, and social standing live together in harmony. On this account, Safed's different religious currents accepted each other without suspicion or envy. In fact, however, Safed was replete with disputes, perhaps more than other Jewish communities of other places and times. That may be because of the relatively plentiful documentation that has come down from Safed at the cusp between the sixteenth and seventeenth centuries, produced by the large number of Torah scholars and writers who lived there. But it might also be a product of the huge social, religious, and economic tensions, which had both internal and external causes, that prevailed in Safed.

These disputes occurred throughout almost the entire second half of the sixteenth century. They did not all break out at once, of course, and not all ended a short time after they began. Some lasted for decades. Even though the beginning and end of this era certainly differ on this score, I take Fernand Braudel's *longue durée* approach here. The disputes I recount are rooted in the distant past and grew out of historical, social, and economic developments, and they affected Jewish communities over the long term. For these reasons, and because this study focuses primarily on the cultural implications of historical occurrences, I do not offer a chronology of events. Rather, I use large brushstrokes to bring out cultural significance on a large scale.

Social tension was a primary factor in Safed. The town was home to a multifarious Jewish community of a wide range of origins. There were Sephardim (Spanish Jews, refugees after the expulsion), North Africans, Ashkenazim (Western Europeans), Italians, Portuguese, Musta'arabim (the local native Jews who had lived in Palestine for centuries), Hungarians, and Provençals, to name just a few. Each group sought to maintain its particular identity, which led to endless arguments and disputes. They argued over prayer customs and religious study, the understanding of what was "authentic" Judaism, ethnic identity, and tax payments. Minna Rozen offers a typical example in her study of a dispute between the Musta'arabim, the native Jews who lived in Safed before the Spanish expulsion, and the Sephardim who arrived after it.

> In the middle of the sixteenth century, there was a constant struggle over preserving the prayer customs of the Musta'arabim in Safed. . . . One such dispute had to do with Purim customs. The Musta'arabim observed the second day of Purim like the first, taking out a Torah scroll, on the assumption that all cities in the Land of Israel had been walled in the time of Joshua. The Sephardim claimed that this was not at all certain and thus did not take out a Torah scroll [on the second day, which according to Jewish law is observed instead of the first day in cities that were walled at the time of Joshua's conquest of the land]. . . . R. Isachar ibn Susan, the Musta'arabim community's most important rabbinic authority, who recorded an account [of the dispute] claimed that the Sephardim did not void the custom of the

Musta'arabim and that the two customs were practiced side by side, and that he believed that the Musta'arabi custom was better because it had been, he believed, the custom of our forefathers in the Land of Israel. In 1599 . . . on the second day of Purim, the prayer leader in the Musta'arabi community refused to take out a Torah scroll because he saw that that [the Sephardim did not do so] and explained that he did so, so as to not make a doubtful blessing [on the reading of the Torah, as the Sephardim claimed it would be]. In the meantime, the community sat impatiently, waiting for the Torah scroll to be taken out. That being the case, Rabbi Isachar ibn Susan rose and directed the prayer leader to take out [the Torah] because there was no reason to fear that the Sephardi custom [was correct]. The prayer leader was convinced to take out a Torah scroll. But that was not the end of the affair. Some of the Musta'arabim wanted to adopt the Sephardi custom, and one of them went to Rabbi Joseph Karo and told him about the incident and how Rabbi Isachar had compelled the prayer leader to take out the Torah scroll. This man thought that perhaps Rabbi Joseph Karo would make a big scandal, but to his surprise he said, "He did well and it is a good custom to say Al haNisim [the Purim addition to the Amidah prayer] today and to take out the Torah scroll, but our Sephardi communities, may the Rock guard and sustain them, did not practice [this custom] and I, finding these practices to have been practiced for a long time, let it be."[9]

The incident gives us an idea of how tense Safed was during the late sixteenth century. The members of the two communities were separated by language (Arabic and Judeo-Spanish), customs, dress, cuisine, and different versions of the standard prayer services. They looked different, sounded different, and behaved differently. But they also influenced each other. In the case at hand, the local community was induced to change its customs by the strong and educated Sephardic community but discovered that its own ancestral custom had the support of the greatest Sephardic authority in the city, Rabbi Joseph Karo, even if Karo and his community did not adopt the local custom. This interplay of acceptance and rejection was the most salient symptom of the social and religious tension that pervaded Safed at the time.

One reason for this ethnic tension was the economic structure of the communities and the heavy taxes imposed on them by the Ottoman regime. The tax burden was imposed equally on each community, meaning that larger and better-off communities, or those that enjoyed generous support from donors in their home countries, could bear the taxes much more easily than the small and poor communities that lived side by side with them. This economic inequality quite naturally caused the poor communities to resent the wealthier ones.[10]

One dispute that caused conflict among Safed's Jews along all these dimensions—ethnic, spiritual, and socioeconomic—was the Eberlein controversy, which had to do with a tax exemption enjoyed by Torah scholars. In the beginning of the sixteenth century, the court presided over by Rabbi Isaac Shul'el, the leader of the Egyptian community, ruled that "from this day onward no penalty or taxes or levies will be imposed on full-time well-off Torah scholars except for the poll tax [imposed on non-Muslims] without their consent." All of Safed's authorities, Rabbi Joseph Karo and Rabbi Moshe Mitrani among them, stood solidly behind this ruling.

One of the reasons for the great Jewish migration to Safed was the Ottoman tax system, which favored the city's Jews. Because each community was assessed a fixed sum, the more a community grew, the less each of its members had to pay. The same method later prompted Jews to abandon Safed, when the Ottomans raised the tax rate just when the city was in the midst of an economic crisis—the textile industry was shifting to Western Europe, shipping lines in the Mediterranean were suffering from piracy, and overland travel had also become less secure. At the same time, an increasing number of residents called themselves Torah scholars, and even those who were well off and owned businesses refused to pay any tax (except the compulsory personal tax). As a result, a greater burden fell on everyone else, and they, quite naturally, were outraged. Rabbi Yehuda Eberlein, the leader of the Safed Ashkenazic community, sought to rescind the exemption for scholars who engaged in commerce and could afford to pay taxes (but not for those who only engaged in Torah study). Rabbi Joseph Karo, the senior scholar of his generation and the spiritual leader of Safed, responded:

> As the transgressions of this generation have multiplied, Satan has grown envious [of the Jews' return to the Land of Israel] and has put it into the heart of Yehuda Eberlein to ascend [immigrate] himself to the Beautiful Land. And he has thought thoughts in his heart to engulf and destroy the ramparts of the Torah and to cast its yoke off him, and the fear of the sages will not be on the wealthy, rather the fear of the wealthy will be on the sages.[11]

Karo here raises a socioeconomic dispute on a mythological level: God versus Satan, Sons of Light versus Sons of Darkness, scholars (i.e., Karo and his colleagues) versus the wealthy. This rhetorical style, which we know well today, was used in an ugly campaign against Eberlein and those who supported his position, waged by the very Torah scholars whose purses were endangered by Eberlein's initiative. At the height of the dispute, these scholars placed Eberlein under a comprehensive ban. Their unrestrained language and the social persecution they engaged in are typical of a class of zealots that sees itself as an aristocracy, unobligated by the rule of social equity and economic cooperation.[12]

This sort of economic strain is typical of all societies, but what made Safed a special case was the involvement of its sages. Supposed to be devoting themselves to matters of the spirit alone as professional scholars, they were in fact up to their necks in the economic dispute. They involved themselves in other controversies as well, in which their economic concerns were accompanied by struggles for power and authority.

From the beginning of the Safed period, during the 1520s and 1530s, Rabbi Ya'akov Beirav and his school fought a fierce battle over ordination with the rabbis of Jerusalem. Ostensibly, religious claims overlaid what was really a dispute over authority. The polemic over Beirav and his standing continued beyond his lifetime, carried on by the students he ordained, Mitrani and Karo.[13]

The most interesting dispute that Safed's rabbis were involved in was over the nature of Judaism itself. The traditional view was that Jewish religious law, Halakha constituted the center of the religion. This view was challenged by a new religious sensibility, centered on the Kabbalah in its unique Safed guise. By the beginning of Safed's golden age, during the lifetime of Rabbi Ya'akov Beirav, an attack was being led by Rabbi Menachem Habavli, a well-known rabbinic judge and sage from Greece who spent time in Beirav's school in 1537. Habavli condemned the claim made by the Safed kabbalists that they had received the gift of prophecy. Mitrani, a student of Beirav and one of the leading sages of the golden age, was known as an opponent of the groups of pietists who detached themselves from society and, by adding strictures and customs to established law, in particular in matters of food and sex, set off a storm in the Safed community. Mitrani condemned these extreme and separatist customs, which he and other religious leaders saw as bordering on sacrilege and as having a negative effect on Safed society.[14]

The legends of Safed, first set down by Shlumil of Dreznitz and later collected in *Shivkhei ha-'Ari*, were the most notable folk evocation of the city's atmosphere at the time. As I have already noted, they seem to have originated in the small and elitist circle surrounding the Ari (i.e., Luria), only to be adopted in the 1590s by a broader public, as testified to by Shlumil. In the process, they underwent changes and adjustments, just as all legends do. Whereas the disputes mentioned earlier were documented in travel literature, letters, halakhic rulings, and rabbinic responsa, this later dispute, between the halakhists and the kabbalists of Safed, finds expression mostly in legend. To put it another way, this particular dispute, which would seem to belong to the scholarly class, caught the imagination of a much larger group.

To prevent misunderstandings, two things should be stressed, once again. First, these legends would not have become accepted as folk legends (i.e., they would not have been disseminated in writing and by word of mouth in different versions) had they not been meaningful for large parts of the community. It was not the identity of the author (or narrator) of the legend who determined its character but rather the legend's propagation and the role it was assigned by the society that told it. The legends are not historical documents, nor do they reflect reality. The second, interconnected issue is that we know that most of Safed's sages, led by Rabbi Joseph Karo, were in fact men of both Halakha and Kabbalah (as was proved recently, in much detail, by Altshuler [2016]). The divide in the rivalry was not between halakhists and kabbalists but was rather largely a social and generational divide. Nevertheless, the legends are not beholden to facts. They express social worldviews and cultural issues with complicated relations with the truth that are never direct or unambiguous.

My purpose in this book is not to reexamine historical documents but rather to use legends to reveal social and psychological worlds that those documents do not know. Take, for example, one legend of much interest.

> Again, one day they [Luria and his students] were studying, and the Rabbi [Luria] said to the companions, "Know that the rabbis have gathered in their assembly and want to cancel the *hilula* [festival] of Rashbi [Rabbi Shimon bar Yohai on Mt. Meron, near Safed], saying that adorned women should not go to Meron, and if they go in everyday clothes they should not sleep there, except for elderly women. And if they [the assembly of rabbis] do that [prevent the traditional festivity, as it was always celebrated], they will, God forbid, bring on a great plague and both good and bad will be destroyed." And Rabbi Hayyim Vital responded, and said, "Why do you not inform them of this so as to save Israel?" The Rabbi told him, "They do not believe in me." Said Rabbi Hayyim Vital, "I will go and notify them." He said to him, "Go." He went there [to the assembly of rabbis] and informed them. Some did not believe, and some said, "Have the Rabbi [Luria] come here and we will see what he has to say." And they sent for him and he came, and they spoke with him there, that they did want to [hold the festival] since at that time there are celebrations and joy with eating and drinking, and even though they might be saved from actual transgression, they would not be saved from thinking about it, and it would not be proper in this holy place to do it [such sins]. And he responded to them, "The truth is with you.

And what can we do that Rashbi is pleased with it, and it has been celebrated for many years and God forbid that he be angry with us and a plague come on the people [because of the cancellation]. But I will tell you something if you believe me, that at this time at Meron there is no mutual responsibility, but each sinner will die himself." And when they heard that, they counted themselves and resolved to revoke their agreement [to cancel the *hilula*] and it was revoked.[15]

The narrative structure of the story suggests a confrontation between two camps. The first camp consists of Luria and his chief disciple, Rabbi Hayyim Vital; both are identified and visible. Against them stands a camp of "rabbis," whom we hear only as a collective voice. In other words, not only does the end of the story represent the point of view of Luria's circle, but so does the basic narrative structure. Not only is the story not objective—folktales never are—but it also bears a clear and trenchant message about the Safed milieu and the power struggles within it. First, it reflects Luria's standing in Safed: He is a recently arrived merchant from Egypt (less than two years elapsed between his arrival and his death) and faces off against the venerable and established community leaders. He is not invited to the rabbinic council that makes the decision about the festival at Meron, but he also knows that if he were to tell the rabbis what he knows, they would not believe him. So he sends his student, a native of Safed, who had also been a valued student of those same rabbis, and he persuades them to heed his master.

Note the cautious formulation of Luria's response to the rabbis. He justifies their decision, but claims that Rashbi is "angry with us and a plague [will] come on the people." But how does Luria know this? One possibility is that he knows divinely, thanks to his wondrous ability to know what lies beyond, as we will see in the following chapters. But he does not dare say that to the rabbis, to whom he offers a different argument: Because the celebration at Rashbi's tomb has taken place for several years and because the saint has accepted it as a celebration in his honor, Rashbi will see its cessation as an insult to him, as stated in *Sefer Hasidim*: "He who is accustomed to a precept and stops observing it—they will be angry with him."[16]

Furthermore, Jewish ethics does not favor collective punishment; rather, each person should be punished for only his own sins. For that reason, it is not right to punish the entire community and to forbid it to celebrate the saint simply because some individuals sin at the celebration. The rabbis are likely to see the logic in Luria's claim, which is in the spirit of accepted tradition. Luria makes no claim to prophecy (although Karo himself, the leading Safed religious authority, made such a claim about himself), which the rabbis would utterly reject. It is clear to Luria that, despite his short time in the city, if he wishes to be accepted by Safed's religious leadership, he needs to speak in its language and use its logic, which is fundamentally different from that of his fellowship and which he and his students sought, with no little success, to bequeath to generations to come.

But the confrontation between Luria's fellowship and the Safed religious leadership has another aspect. It is clear that the celebrants of Rashbi's festival on Mt. Meron—those who dance and sing, eat and drink, who sleep there out in the open—do not belong to the social or spiritual elite. They are Safed's common people, its craftsmen, beggars, lower-class women, and children. Most of them, apparently, are Musta'arabim, Jews native to the region, whose voices we heard in the previous section. We may presume that the *hilula* at Mt. Meron in those days attracted much the same social strata as it does today. Standing against this popular festival and all it stands for are "the rabbis." They see the festival as wantonness and sacrilege and thus seek to forbid everything that is likely to attract the masses—camping out overnight, eating and drinking, dancing and singing—especially with women present. In other words, they want to get rid of exactly those elements that constitute what Bakhtin would term the carnivalesque character of the *hilula*.

Such constraints would, for all intents and purposes, put an end to the festivities and cause the masses to cease to make this annual pilgrimage to the tomb of a great rabbi of the Mishnaic period. Clearly, the rabbis fear that the religious event that occurs around the tomb on Mt. Meron is one that they have no control over. Its rules are determined spontaneously, from below, rather than through an institutionalized halakhic process. So as not to lose control of this observance, they act in the way the story describes. Why did Luria get himself involved in this controversy? The answer would seem to be that both the fellowship of students around Luria and other such fellowships that took form in Safed and its environs operated outside the control of the "rabbis." They fashioned their own frameworks and ritual rules and did not attend, in general, to institutional halakhic rules. Luria viewed himself, rightly, as belonging to those rituals celebrated on Mt. Meron, as part of outside and liminal activities. Even though Luria's fellowship was manifestly elitist, closed to outsiders, it was part of that religious action that undercut Safed's powerful religious establishment, and mysticism and magic were central to its identity.[17]

This folkish aspect of culture, beyond the control of the establishment and the leading players of its society, behaves according to norms that challenge accepted boundaries. A fascinating testimony to this reverses the roles in the previous narrative on Mt. Meron.

> This event happened in the days of the Wondrous Light, Luria of blessed memory: there was a sage then, Israel Najarah, may peace be with him, who had a sweet voice. And once on the night of the holy Sabbath this sage sang at his table as was his good custom, and the Rabbi of blessed memory saw the angelic hosts dancing their way to his home to enjoy his songs. And the Rabbi, may his memory last forever, immediately saw that one angel came and cleared the entire troupe of angels who was there, because his [Najarah's] arms were bare, and he did not have a hat on his head, at the table before God. And when the Rabbi of blessed memory sensed this, he sent for our teacher Rabbi Hayyim Vital and our teacher Rabbi Joseph Hacohen to tell him that the angels on high had been enjoying themselves with him there at his table but had gone, because he did not place himself in fear and awe before God. And when the said sage Israel heard the words of the Rabbi's students, he was overcome with trembling and stood shaking and sat in great respect wrapped in his cloak and a hat on his head and returned to his singing in joy and trembling, and immediately the angels of God were climbing up and down to him as at

the beginning, joyous and happy as if at the love making of a groom and bride. And the Rabbi of blessed memory and our teacher Rabbi Hayyim Vital of blessed memory saw this wondrous deed.[18]

Israel Najarah, the greatest Hebrew poet of his time, who made a major mark on sacred Hebrew poetry in the generations that followed, was in fact a Turkish poet. He worked in the Ottoman cultural context, was influenced by the contents and form of Turkish poetry, and borrowed from there popular tunes of his time. Seeing himself as part of the glorious Ottoman tradition, he permitted himself considerable freedom in his personal life, dress, and public behavior. He thus presented two faces: As a Safed poet, he composed hard-core liturgical works in Galilean synagogues and other communities in the Ottoman Empire, but as an Ottoman poet, he led a somewhat bohemian and permissive life. Notably, in this story about him, Najarah, not Luria, is the carnivalesque figure who does not observe social norms of dress and manners. On the contrary, Luria pushes himself, uninvited, into Najarah's private life and asserts his authority over the poet's mores, the opposite of the position he took in the tale about Mt. Meron.

Two factors explain these diametrically opposed portrayals of Luria. First, the Meron story addresses a subject close to Luria's heart: the cult of sacred graves. When the rabbinic leadership sought to eliminate it, Luria did everything in his power to avert the "evil decree." The second reason is that these legends seem to indicate a shift in religious power and authority from the older generation of rabbis, headed by Rabbi Joseph Karo, to the new generation of kabbalists, headed by Luria. Because these legends were related decades after Luria's death, they show how his students and his students' students viewed the revolution that Safed's culture had undergone, from halakhic rabbis to kabbalistic visionaries.

But this is not the end of the story between Israel Najarah and Luria's school. In the years that followed Luria's death, most of his disciples left Safed. Rabbi Hayyim Vital eventually settled in Damascus. During his time there, that city's Jewish community was rocked by a famous case of possession. A spirit entered the daughter of one of the community's leaders, Rabbi Raphael Anaf. The incident, known as the Dybbuk of Damascus, will be dealt with in detail in Chapter 2. In the present context, what concerns us is that the spirit speaking through the girl's mouth accuses the Damascus Jewish community of engaging in shocking sexual behavior. (Najarah could take comfort in the fact that he was not the only one to be slandered so rudely and insulted. The spirit denounces many of the other leading Jews of Damascus in similar terms.)

> And here is R. Israel Najarah. The truth is that the ditties that he has written are good in and of themselves, but it is forbidden to speak with him or to allow the ditties he wrote to emerge from one's mouth, because his mouth always speaks wickedness and he is always drunk. And one day, which was between the straits [the days of mourning between the fasts of the seventeenth of Tammuz and the ninth of Av], he sat down to eat a meal at a certain time at the home of Ya'akov Mundash, and placed his hat on the ground and sang songs loudly and ate meat and drank wine, and got drunk, and how can he declare shifts in Gobar and speak to them of repentance [be a moral teacher]?
>
> And I, Hayyim, told him of this matter and he confessed that this indeed happened. Now also, as he fled the plague, he was so drunk that he lay with a man. And on the Sabbath he committed two transgressions: the first, he fought with his wife and expelled her from his house, and the second, after that a Gentile woman came to his home and lighted fire in the oven on the Sabbath and afterward he lay with her. It is therefore forbidden to benefit from him and forbidden to give him a marriage contract or divorce to write, and it would almost be proper to void [those he has written]. His younger son has also had sex with a Gentile and is an utter reprobate, may his bones grind down [in the grave]. But his older son is not a sinner.[19]

The story has two parts. In the first, the spirit speaks through the girl, and in the second Vital speaks. It should be noted that it is this second passage that contains the crudest gossip. This has to be seen in the context of Vital's life in Damascus, when he clashed with members of the community over their refusal to recognize him as Luria's heir and grant him the rabbinic status befitting a scholar of his stature. It might well be that Najarah was one of his opponents and that is why Vital brings this outburst against him. In any case, even if we restrict ourselves to the first part of the passage, it is clear that the poet was an exceptional figure in the community, both in Safed and in Damascus. His colorful character is manifested in the multifarious and even contradictory nature of his activity: on the one hand, his poetry, the greatness and cultural status of which not even Vital can deny, and, on the other, his permissive and unrestrained behavior, which violates the mores of his time and place.

Halakhists and Kabbalists

Safed's unique culture, with its wealth, variety, and difference of voices, emerges in a fascinating way in the tension between masters of Halakha and those of Kabbalah,[20] as expressed in legends, if not in historical reality. In these legends Safed's great halakhists are depicted as avid admirers of Luria and his doctrine, though they are not worthy of being numbered among his students. Rabbi Hayyim Vital offers a fascinating testimony to the dialogue between his two great teachers, Rabbi Moshe Alsheikh, who taught him Halakha, and Luria, his master in Kabbalah.

> In that year, my teacher, Rabbi Moshe Alsheikh, established his school in the yard of an Ashkenazi woman. And one day she saw him sitting in sorrow. And she asked him, "Why are you sad?" And he said to her, "How can I not be sad about my student, R. Hayyim, who does not want to teach me the wisdom of the Kabbalah?" And she said to him, "And is your student greater than you?" And he told her how when my teacher [Luria] of blessed memory was alive, he went to him one day and wept and pleaded with him to teach him the wisdom of the Kabbalah, he himself, not by me. And he told him that he did not come into the world except to teach me alone and that this wisdom could not be revealed except by

me. And he [Alsheikh] told him, "How could it be that after I was his teacher that I will be his student?" And he [Luria] said to him, "May you have the merit to be his student, because had not our rabbis, of blessed memory, said that, one may envy every man other than his son and student, I would myself envy him for the potency of the merit, that [he] will raise something immeasurable."

It hardly needs to be said that this testimony of Vital's needs to be treated with great caution. In the chapters that follow I show just what levels of exaggeration he rose to in praising himself and in speaking of the divine qualities he attributed to himself. The passage at hand suffers from that same weakness. But, disregarding Vital's conceit for the moment, we can see that his placement of Alsheikh, one of Safed's most celebrated teachers of Halakha, in a position inferior to that of Luria and his disciple, Vital himself, is carefully calculated. It places kabbalists on a much higher level than halakhists. That statement is reinforced by another narrative about Alsheikh that also originated in Luria's circle.

> The soul of Rabbi Moshe Alsheikh of blessed memory desired this wisdom [Kabbalah]. He went back and forth until he came to the Master [Luria], and kissed his feet. He said to him, "Sir, what is my crime and what is my sin that you, sir, do not want to bring me in to be one of your students?" . . . The rabbi said, "Because his [your] soul did not come into this world except to write those books that you wrote according to the simple meaning [of the Torah, meaning Halakha]." . . . And our rabbi and teacher Moshe Alsheikh pleaded, saying he thought that the reason [Luria] rejected him was because he was not worthy of that wisdom. And Luria of blessed memory said to him, "This is the sign, that tomorrow you will go to a certain place that we always pass that way to welcome the Sabbath. If you see us walking on that road, know that I reject you in those things [it is only I that do not want to teach you Kabbalah, not a divine will],

but if not, know surely that your soul did not come into this world to learn the wisdom of Kabbalah."

And when our rabbi and teacher [Alsheikh] heard this, it seemed good to him, and he rose early on Friday and prepared his needs for the Sabbath, and at noon he donned Sabbath clothes and sat on the main road to wait for the rabbi to pass there with the companions, and he tarried and waited for the Rabbi's arrival. When that same hour arrived, a great weariness came upon him and he slept. And the rabbi with the companions passed by and he did not see them, until on the way back the Rabbi said [to the companions] that they should waken [Alsheikh from his slumber] to go to his home because the sun had already set, lest the villagers kill him for being there, God forbid. And then the companions wakened him, and he stood on his feet in alarm and said, "What have I done, the whole day I waited, and at this hour sleep overcame me?!" The rabbi said to him, "Did I not tell you that your soul did not come this time to learn Kabbalah, therefore do not preoccupy yourself with this matter further. Be strong and gird yourself, do not leave your craft, which you do in the writing of books of simple interpretation, for they will become known throughout the world and the generations that come after you will make use of them." And from that day on he thought no more of studying Kabbalah.[21]

This story explicitly presents the central spiritual dispute in Safed's cultural life. But it is not the explicit message and the mortifying humiliation suffered by one of Safed's great teachers that are so impressive. Rather, it is the symbolic means by which it is expressed here. The central motif in the story is sleep, around which the story's narrative tension and mystery is ranged. The enigmatic slumber that overcomes Rabbi Alsheikh is a manifestation of a divine message. He cannot join the companions walking the road on their way to sanctify the Sabbath, because he cannot achieve their spiritual level. As they are deep in holiness, he is deep in sleep, a physical activity that contrasts with their spiritual state. He is thus doomed to spend the rest of his life in the material world, addressing the simple meaning of the Torah, Halakha, while they address Kabbalah, the divine world.

Even the authority and leadership of Rabbi Joseph Karo, which was seemingly unchallenged by the members of this generation, does not seem that way from the point of view of the folk legends that grew out of Luria's fellowship and the widening circle of his supporters at the beginning of the seventeenth century. The shift in the center of authority to Luria's students and their worldview is loudly and clearly heard here.

In his second letter about the forces beyond this world that were revealed by the Safed sages, Shlumil of Dreznitz quotes a testimony from Karo's journal *Maggid Meisharim* and, having mentioned him, goes on to relate:

> And nevertheless, he was as if insignificant before the wisdom of Luria of blessed memory. And he himself sat before the wisdom of Luria of blessed memory and learned secrets of the Torah from him, and Luria of blessed memory did not want to teach him and said that his soul was not capable of accepting more wisdom, except in the way of Rabbi Moshe Cordovero of blessed memory. And a mark of this is that each time that our teacher Rabbi Joseph Karo sat down to study, immediately when he was on the verge of discovering a secret, our teacher Rabbi Joseph Karo, may peace be with him, began to sleep and doze off, until he himself saw and recognized that he was not worthy of it, and stopped studying. And I, the young Shlomo, testify that I spoke with the widow of Rabbi Joseph Karo of blessed memory and she told me that [he] had a fine son and betrothed him to the daughter of Luria of blessed memory. And when he returned to his home, Rabbi Joseph Karo of blessed memory said to his wife, "My wife, my wife, what can I say to you and what can I tell you of the secrets and reasons of the Torah and commandments, what knowledge I gained from him at this meal from the holy mouth of Rabbi Isaac Ashkenazi. Where is there power in flesh and blood to obtain from him what

he knows. There is no power even to an angel to know what knows He. It is clearly a soul from one of the early prophets, not even a *tanna* [one of the sages of the Mishnah] can say what he told [me]. But I am afraid that because of our great sins, this evil generation cannot tolerate his great sanctity, and he will be taken from them and lost by cutting short his years because of the sins." And so it was.[22]

I see no reason to doubt that Shlumil indeed met with Karo's widow and asked her about the relations between the two great men when they were alive, more than thirty years earlier (Luria died in 1572, Karo in 1575). One thing that can be learned from this story is that Shlumil engaged in intensive "fieldwork" on Safed's streets in his efforts to hear and collect stories of the city's golden age. He neglected no one who could offer first-person testimony. The homes of famous men such as Karo and other men of stature were sites of pilgrimage during their lifetime, but they were empty immediately after their deaths. Their widows thus tended to live in and glorify the past by telling stories to anyone prepared to listen.

What, though, did Karo's widow really tell Shlumil thirty years after the events, and were they stories she really heard from her late husband? The style and content are much like the stories told by Luria's disciples about their master in the years following his death, such as the claim that his soul was that of a biblical prophet, placing him on a level above the sages of the Mishnah, and that his early death was caused by the sins of his generation. It is hard to believe that Karo himself said such things. There is more than an air of anachronism here. It may be that Shlumil shaped the story in this fashion, seeing himself as one of Luria's followers, and that in his letter to Europe he assumed their language and attitude. But it is also possible that Karo's widow, speaking of a reality in which Luria's stature was growing and his doctrines were taking center stage both religiously and socially, put the story in a form close to this, her purpose being to underline the harmony that prevailed between her husband, the greatest scholar of his generation, and a man now seen as being the holder of that position. Similar stories about Safed's great halakhists—Rabbi Moshe Alsheikh, Rabbi Moshe Galanti, and others—pleading with Luria and his students to teach them Kabbalah were also created in that tense environment.

But the principal importance of this legend lies not in its agreement with the facts but rather in the way it reflects the rivalry and dissent between Luria's fellowship and the halakhic leadership in Safed just before the death of both luminaries. The interesting part of the story is Shlumil's framing of it, not the widow's testimony. The claim that Rabbi Joseph Karo "sat before" Luria is no more than wishful thinking. We should remind ourselves here of Zechariah's report of Karo's social and religious position, with the inhabitants of Safed thronging at the door of his seminary, thirsty to hear him speak. We have no reason to doubt the reliability of this testimony, which recounts the situation in the city many years before Luria arrived there. In this account, Karo was considered the senior scholar, the greatest authority of his generation. Luria, in contrast, when he seemingly met with Karo much later, was an anonymous merchant from Egypt who had just recently arrived in Safed.

Years ago, scholars discovered that Karo was not just a halakhic authority, the label Luria's disciples attached to him with no little success. He was hugely interested in the hidden world. As Shlumil hints, Karo accepted the kabbalistic system of Rabbi Moshe Cordovero, who was Jewish mysticism's leading spokesman in Safed before Luria's arrival. Studies of Karo have demonstrated the great significance of mystical ideas in Karo's hugely influential halakhic works, most prominently *Beit Joseph* and *Shulkhan Arukh*. We can reconstruct an event in which Luria, a while after arriving in the city, went to present the new kabbalistic theory he had developed in Egypt to Safed's great personage. Karo, who was at the time quite elderly, still spent his days and nights in study and writing, on top of which he bore the burden of leadership of the Safed Jewish community and its environs. As Luria spoke, the great scholar fell asleep, as elderly men are wont to do. He may even have spoken out in favor of Cordovero's kabbalistic theory, which he knew and valued. Luria took offense, as is evident from Shlumil's account. Karo is not worthy of the new and bold theory of Kabbalah, Luria told his disciples. He is still frozen in the world of yesterday, in the outmoded system of Cordovero. The slumber that fell over Karo during Luria's presentation was a divine indication of Karo's spiritual inferiority. The deep voice of the insult felt by a small group that saw itself as a spiritual avant-garde but was actually shunned by the mainstream led by Karo is clearly voiced through the years that passed since the incident and is evident in Shlumil's account.

The brief passage from Shlumil's letter that I have quoted here contains within it a microcosm of the Safed myth and its shattering. It offers the voice of Karo's widow, who expresses the harmonistic view of later generations: There was no dispute between "my chosen one, Joseph," and the "divine Rabbi Isaac." They admired and recognized each other's greatness in their chosen field of expertise, confirmed by the symbolic marriage of their descendants. In this account, Safed's halakhists and kabbalists lived together in an ideal society of mutual esteem and recognition. In contrast, the first part of the letter presents the full depth of the break between them: Karo dismissed Luria's new theory, to the point that he dozed off listening to its author's presentation. Luria, for his part, viewed the greatest scholar of his time as an inferior soul unworthy of the great divine events taking place in Safed at the time. This fascinating cultural process, in which a harmonizing myth seeks to cover over an internal fissure and silence the richness of the voices emerging from it, is the subject of the next chapter.

2

The Myth and Its Disenchantment

Regarding the wonders of Luria of blessed memory ... none of those stories of what he did ever happened.... Luria spent most of his day dealing with his merchandise.

—Leon of Modena, *'Ari Nohem*

OF OXEN AND BEARDS

AT THE CLIMAX OF the mythic age—Isaac Luria's era in Safed (1571–1572)—one of the city's residents, Rabbi Ya'akov Abulafia, set out to solicit donations from the generous and well-off Jewish community of Egypt. Such donations were the common and accepted means by which the Jewish communities of the Holy Land sustained themselves. A wonder tale about his trip offers solid testimony about Luria's firm and central position in Safed at the time—and of his exceptional mystical powers,

> And I found in the sacred writings of the community trust in Egypt a wondrous story about this in the days of our master, the wondrous light Luria of blessed memory, and I include it in my admonishment so as to make the hair on the skin of criminals and sinners stand on end. And here it is, word for word: One day the sage Rabbi Ya'akov Abulafia came before my teacher [Luria] of blessed memory. And my teacher of blessed memory greeted him and said, "Your eminence wishes to go to Egypt and requests that I write him a letter [of authorization to show to the Egyptian community]." And he said to him, "Yes, sir." He said, "Sir, go in peace and God

will be with you on your way, and your visit there will be a great boon, because it is a great necessity." He said to him, "What is the necessity, since it is an elective trip [a casual trip, of a personal nature]." He said to him, "Upon your return you will know why I am telling you these things." And my teacher immediately wrote him the letter and handed it to him and again cautioned him on the matter of traveling quickly. And he rose and went to Egypt, and they received him with great honor in his own and his rabbi's honor. Afterward he turned his feet back to his home in Safed, may it be built and established quickly in our days. And a caravan set out and he did all that they did. And one day the people of the caravan [stopped to] rest, as they were accustomed to do, and the aforementioned rabbi did the same. And when he dismounted his donkey, a deep sleep immediately fell upon him and he slept for a full hour. And when they all rose to go, and they woke the sage from his sleep and he rose and undid his donkey and the donkey went [following the caravan], and once again a deep sleep fell on him and he slept a full two hours, and when he rose he did not see anyone. And the man was frightened and startled and began to run following the road, in fear and great trepidation. And as evening approached he saw plowmen coming toward him and was relieved and said, "I will go with them." And he ran over to them and came to [their] place and sat there a bit. And he saw that the plowman was brutally beating the oxen, and soon saw the plowman turn into an ox and the ox became a man, and they hitched him to a yoke and began to deal him many blows, and they did this again and again. And the sage was alarmed and he had nowhere to flee to because he did not know which way the light dwelt, and he was in great sorrow because his intention [to go to Safed] was not done. And the sun set and all three became human beings and cried out and wept and spoke with him, saying, "Welcome, is your eminence from Safed?" He said to them,

"Yes." They fell before his feet and wept, and the sage wept with them. "Does my lord see our matter and our sorrow?" And he said, "Yes." And they said to him, "In the name of the Holy One of Israel, have mercy on us, for we are of the Children of Israel. And when you go to return to Safed, quickly go before the Rabbi and fall before him and plead with him to rectify [*letaken*, literally 'repair'] our souls, for you will see that [we are] helpless and incapable and abandoned." And the sage said, "I will do as you say." And they had him take a severe oath to confirm and carry out any rectification [*tikkun*, here in the sense of penance] that the Rabbi would tell him to do. And then they instantly took him and placed him in the caravan, and his spirit was restored. And when he arrived in Safed, he immediately set his eyes to go to the king [Luria] and plead with him in the matter of those wretches. And he came before the rabbi, and the rabbi welcomed him and said to him, "You came, sir, in the matter of the oxen—I know. Come to me tomorrow." And so he did. And my teacher of blessed memory said to him, "Know now the necessity I told you regarding this trip? And it is because your eminence is of the root of their soul. And their names are so-and-so the son of so-and-so from someplace." Then the sage asked what their transgression had been. He said to him, "For the sin of cutting off their sidelocks." And he said to him, "And what is the connection between sidelocks and oxen?" He said to him, "Have you not read [it in Scripture]?" He said to him, "My lord, this thing is not written, not in the Gemara or in the Midrash." He said to him, "It is a full [explicit] verse [in the Torah]." He said to him, "There is no such verse in the Torah." He said to him, "It is written, 'You shall not round off the side-growth on your head, or destroy,' and the acronym [of the first letters of the Hebrew words] is *parot* [cows]. Saying that, anyone who rounds or destroys his sidelocks or beard is reincarnated as a bull. And you must rectify them and afflict yourself tomorrow and intend this and this in the name of this person," and in this form he wrote down for him all the rectifications and mortifications he needed to do until those people were rectified. And they came to the sage in a dream and said to him, "May God bless you, may your thoughts be at rest just as our souls are at rest, from that day that you began to do the rectifications that the rabbi told you. Because the one rectification you did removed us from that hard labor which you saw and brought us into Gehenna, and the same way each rectification you did removed us from a heavy yoke to an easier one until they brought us into our intended place [in the eternal world]."[1]

This strange story seems to be somehow rooted in historical reality. It was common for well-known figures in the Safed community to make fund-raising trips; in the seventeenth century, funds obtained in this way seem to have been the primary support of the community in Safed, as it was in the other holy cities in the Land of Israel.[2] Abulafia's connections in Egypt are known from other sources, which sometimes refer to him as "the sublime sage, the honored teacher and Rabbi, 'Jacob the Egyptian' Abulafia."[3] It is also quite reasonable that Abulafia would have approached Luria before leaving for Egypt, because Luria was considered an authority on Egypt. After all, Luria had lived in that country for fifteen years, from his youth to adulthood. He studied there under its great Torah scholars and had engaged in local and international trade, mostly in spices and fruit. He served on the Cairo Ashkenazic community's religious court, devoted himself to philanthropic activity for communities and individuals in the Holy Land, and married the daughter of a wealthy member of the Cairo community. Asking for the help or advice of a person, indeed an expert, so involved in the Egyptian Jewish milieu before a fund-raising trip would have been natural and unremarkable.[4]

However, Meir Benayahu, who republished this story in his edition of *Toldot ha-'Ari*, suggested another reason: "It seems to have been well-known in Safed that anyone who wished to travel went to Luria." In other words, Abulafia approached Luria before his trip not because of Luria's expertise on Egyptian affairs but because his authority was so great that anyone who left Safed on a communal or private mission went to Luria to receive his blessing and sanction. That is, in fact, the point that this story seeks to stress. Abulafia, one of the most central figures in Safed of the time, was a scholar of Halakha and, as far as is known, did not take an interest in Kabbalah. He was the student of Safed's greatest halakhists and was sanctioned to teach and issue rulings thanks to his ordination there, under the system of certifying rabbinic authorities that Safed took pride in. He was a scion of a famed rabbinic dynasty of sixteenth-century Palestine, being the grandson of Rabbi Ya'akov Beirav. His grandfather was the reviver of the institution of ordination in Safed (1538) and one of the dominant figures in establishing Safed as a center of religious learning. The story's argument, which Benayahu accepts on its own terms, is that as central a personage as Abulafia presents himself to Luria before setting out on a trip, not just to get advice about Egypt but to receive his blessing for the trip. That places Luria in a position of exceptional authority. Perhaps it should not be surprising that several other stories included in *Shivkhei ha-'Ari*, the famous collection of legends about Luria, depict the most senior of Safed's rabbis and its greatest sage, Rabbi Joseph Karo, as well as another great figure, Karo's successor as head of Safed's yeshiva, Rabbi Moshe Galanti, doing the same. Both of them submissively plead with Luria to teach them Kabbalah or for spiritual rectification (*tikkun*), as we saw in Chapter 1.

The story thus reflects a certain type of harmony between Safed's halakhic authorities and kabbalists while ascribing absolute superiority to the kabbalists. Such harmony between communities, religious currents, and different approaches to Judaism is one of the important components of the Safed myth. The figure of Rabbi Joseph Karo stands out prominently in all stories about Safed, as evidence of such harmony.[5] But this wonderful concord between the law and secret lore, as embodied in the figure of Karo, is in fact a smoke screen intended to cover up an agonizing fissure in this great rabbi's personality and intellectual activity, a dissonance that brought on a severe neurotic crisis. This profound internal conflict paralleled that of Safed's Jewish society as a whole. As the accounts of Safed circa 1600 presented in Chapter 1 show, Safed was a place of argumentation and diverse voices.

The Safed myth emerged and began to crystallize at the end of the sixteenth century. Its central component was the figure of Luria and the wondrous deeds attributed to him. The numerous writings sent from Safed to Jewish communities of the East and West, among them the letters written by Shlumil of Dreznitz that were discussed in Chapter 1, were the agents and disseminators of the myth. But these writings probably played a role secondary to Luria's disciples and their students who left the city, taking Luria's teachings with them. Among these were Rabbis Israel Saruk, Yedidya Galanti, and Shmuel Vital, who wandered among the large and wealthy communities of Turkey, Italy, and Egypt spreading word of Safed's wonders and greatness. One of Italy's greatest scholars of the early seventeenth century, Leon of Modena (Judah Aryeh), was a witness to the construction of the myth. His book *'Ari Nohem* (Roaring Lion), published in 1638, tells of Rabbi Israel Saruk's activity in Venice, where Leon lived at the time.

> And this belief [in reincarnation] is so central among them [Safed's kabbalists] that one who denies it is [considered to] deny every [tenet of Judaism]. And [regarding] the wonders they tell of Luria, the basis of most of them is that he knew of every person what his soul had been in [previous] incarnation[s]. Similarly, his student Rabbi Israel Saruk, whom I knew and spoke with thousands of times during his stay here in Venice, was renowned for knowing what the soul of each person had been at other times. I will not name those about whom I heard from him in private, to whom he ascribed [previous noble incarnations] according to their wealth or importance, and enough said.[6]

In other words, Saruk offered public demonstrations of divining people's previous incarnation, a skill he learned from Luria. It sounds as though his services in this regard were in demand and popular among Venice's Jews. Jews were not the only ones fascinated by magic and supernatural phenomena. It was a feature of European culture at this time. People all over Europe were conversing with the spirits of the dead through mediums, and wonder workers offered displays of cosmic powers and sorcery. They brought magical objects from distant and exotic climes as well as human "monsters" that they put on display. Safed's mysticism was part of this more general fashion. Through it, the Jews of Central and Western Europe discovered a world of wonders and mysticism that was "theirs," without needing to have recourse to the alien phenomena that played such an important role in the consciousness of Christians of that era.[7] The deeds performed by Israel Saruk before his audiences and the stories he told of the even greater feats performed by Luria before him served as fodder for the dissemination of the myth of Safed at the beginning of the seventeenth century. But Leon of Modena, a sharp and critical scholar, saw that the incarnations that Saruk claimed to reveal were highly dependent on the current class affiliation of the subject and that there was more than a little flattery involved. Apparently, Saruk told the wealthy and respectable that their previous incarnations had also been worthy and reputable. The more pleased they were by the pedigree of their previous incarnations, he apparently reasoned, the more willing they would be to offer him material compensation. Leon's report continues:

> The sage Rabbi Israel Saruk of blessed memory, who was one of his [Luria's] greatest students, was here with us, coming and going over the space of more than six years. And they said of him that he did fearsome deeds [by invoking the] names [of God]. What can I say except that I discerned what he really was! And [the tales told by] the grandchildren and great-grandchildren [of those for whom he supposedly performed wonders], and people he was in debt to for the benefits they gave him—not one of the things they spoke of really happened!

This is the second stage in the development of the myth. Years after the death of Rabbi Israel Saruk, people in Venice were still talking about the wonders he performed, just as he told about the feats of his own teacher, Luria (in fact, there is doubt as to whether Saruk was indeed Luria's disciple).[8] Barely half a century had gone by since Safed's golden age of the 1570s, but the myth of Safed, now being told to a second and a third generation, was gaining force. However, Leon of Modena tore off the veil of mystification. He himself had been a witness to Saruk's conduct over the space of six years, and he did not witness a single deed of those attributed to him. He fought a desperate rearguard action against the ever-growing mystification of Jewish life, in which the myth of Safed played such an important and central role. Leon's courageous book was devoted to this hopeless battle. Surprisingly, the hero of our story, Rabbi Ya'akov Abulafia, offered support to the Venetian rabbi's campaign. According to Leon,

> It is impossible to tell you what happened more than twenty-five years ago.... The sage Rabbi Yedidya Galanti of blessed memory came here, an emissary from the Land of Israel.... Galanti told [us about] the miraculous deeds and wonders of Luria, of blessed memory . . . and I will not hide from you that one great sage and pious man from our yeshiva.... While this man [Galanti] was speaking of the wonders of Luria of blessed memory, before we commenced our studies, [this local sage] said that several times Rabbi Jacob Abulafia of blessed memory, *who was a companion and brother to Luria,* said to him that none of those stories of what he did ever happened . . . such actions as those related in the story had ever happened! And that even he [Luria himself] said to him that the things said about him were not honest . . . and he further said in the name of that sage [Abulafia] that Luria spent most of his day dealing with merchandise.

Here the demystification goes back from the generation of the disciples to the source itself. According to Leon of Modena, Abulafia knew Luria well and was so close to him that Luria would disclose to him his most intimate secrets. Abulafia testified several times that Luria had never performed miracles and wonders. Furthermore, the spiritual figure of Luria reflected with such force in the praises and writings of his students was no more than an illusion. Luria had been a merchant in Egypt, and he remained one in Safed, a man who spent most of his time in the material, not the spiritual, world. We can only imagine the huge damage that such testimony, coming from such a central figure in the Safed community, could do the consolidation and dissemination of the myth. Abulafia thus became the worst and most dangerous enemy of Luria's disciples and the other "impresarios" of the myth of Safed at the beginning of the seventeenth century.

The impresarios of the myth dealt with such testimonies in two ways. One was to fashion counternarratives that presented these accounts as representing Luria's modesty and reluctance to advertise his greatness.

> And they heard [of Luria's fame] throughout the city until it was heard by two great [local] sages who did not believe what they heard. And they came and said to him, "What is it, Isaac, that they are saying about you, that you predict the future, please tell us." *And his modesty was so great that he denied these things and said, "I am not a prophet and I am not the son of a prophet and I know nothing."* And as he was speaking to them, a man passed before them and his garments touched the garments of Luria of blessed memory, and he [Luria] said to this man, "God will forgive you for having made it necessary for me to immerse myself several times" [ritually, to remove the impurity the man caused by the contact of their clothing]. When the sages compelled this man who touched Luria's garments to confess before them, the man was frightened of them and said to them, "What can I say and what can I declare, and God has discovered your servant's iniquity, and the Evil Impulse caused me to have intercourse with my wife tonight in an unnatural way."[9]

The story goes on to relate that, from that point on, these sages accepted Luria as their master. Luria's response to the disdain of the two sages of Safed is quite similar to the response he made in Abulafia's account, and the story sounds very much like a direct response to his testimony as cited by Leon of Modena. That testimony is here countered by acknowledging that Luria indeed said what the testimony claims he said, but that he did so out of humility, whereas his personality and actions proved the opposite. Why should we not dare to conjecture that one of the two "great sages" in this story was Abulafia himself? On this account, Abulafia indeed heard what he said he heard, but after comprehending how great Luria was, he accepted him as his master, just as the Tale of the Oxen relates!

Another way of coping with Abulafia's damaging testimony was to malign the witness harshly and violently. This is a strategy that extreme Orthodoxy has always been prone to adopt. It can be seen in another version of the Tale of the Oxen.

> He [Abulafia] said to him [Luria], "Sir, what is the connection between the bulls plowing on a weekday and [shaving one's] sidelocks?" He [Luria] said to him, "Did I not tell you that he [Abulafia, speaking of him in the third person] thinks himself a scholar and does not know anything." He [Abulafia] said to him, "Such a thing is not hinted at in the Gemara or in any book." He [Luria] said to him, "It is a complete verse, and your honor does not know it? Have you not read [in the Torah], 'You shall not round off the side-growth on your head, or destroy'? And the acronym [of the first letters of the Hebrew words] is *par* [bull]." And then he acknowledged the rabbi's [wisdom] and said to him, "The truth is that we know nothing."[10]

This version of the story is much sharper than the previous one. Here Luria scathingly humiliates Abulafia and makes one of Safed's greatest scholars out to be devoid of knowledge. How can this be reconciled with the previously mentioned testimony by Abulafia regarding his friendship with Luria? One possibility is that the story portrays their relations as that of rabbi and student, with the rabbi fondly teasing his student for his ignorance. But such an interpretation is not really possible, given Abulafia's personality, not to mention his social and religious standing in Safed during Luria's time.

Another possibility is suggested by Gershom Scholem. Scholem views this story as a "fabrication" that seeks "to transform the sworn opponent of Rabbi Haim Vital and the noted denier of Luria's miraculous deeds into an active partner in one of Luria's miracles and wonders."[11] It is not clear what Scholem means by "fabrication"; no one disputes that this text is a legend, not a historical document. It may be that this is consistent with Scholem's and Yeshayahu Tishbi's (Isaiah Tishbi) portrayal of the entire book of *Hemdat Yamim* as a fabric of falsifications, as we will see. But it seems that Scholem uses the claim of fabrication principally to dismiss the possibility that Abulafia was really humiliated by Luria. After all, the story does not really make Abulafia a participant in one of the praises of Luria but rather humiliates him, and in doing so presents his testimony as unreliable. This is consistent with Luria's disciples' interest in preserving the myth of Luria in Safed in the face of slanderers and opponents like Abulafia and Leon of Modena.

I adduce the Tale of the Oxen from *Hemdat Yamim* because it is the only version told in the first person: "One day he came before *my* teacher of blessed memory, the sage Rabbi Jacob Abulafia, and *my* teacher greeted him . . . and *my* teacher immediately wrote him this letter . . . and *my* teacher of blessed memory said to him." In other words, the narrator of this version is Rabbi Hayyim Vital, a disciple of Luria's and the most important disseminator of his teachings. Scholem may have seen this as a fabrication; Benayahu would certainly not have had a problem with Vital as the narrator, because this would have supported the story's authenticity. But, like Scholem, he also rejects the possibility that the legend was told by the closest person to Luria, although without conviction. The most important authority on *Hemdat Yamim*—Tishbi, who ferreted out all the work's sources in a comprehensive and unprecedented fashion—concludes that *Hemdat Yamim* was composed in the first quarter of the eighteenth century in Izmir (Smyrna). Furthermore, Tishbi shows that the book, while presenting itself as the primary source for the stories it contains, is in fact a compilation of hundreds of quotations from earlier works. In other words, *Hemdat Yamim* is by and large one big fabrication. Tishbi's study that relates directly to the matter at hand is his article "The Genealogy of the Fictitious Terms 'My Teacher' and 'My Master and Father' in *Hemdat Yamim*." But Tishbi does not address every passage containing these terms, only those whose source he is able to trace. More important, the instances of these terms in passages that *Hemdat Yamim* takes from Luria's and Vital's writings have been shown to be reliable. However, Tishbi's ire is directed mostly at the fact that the book's author claims that Luria, who had died 150 years previously, had been his teacher.

That is not the only way of looking at it. It may well be that the author of *Hemdat Yamim* quoted his sources as he found them, without any intention of making himself out to be Luria's student. I see no reason to doubt the testimony offered by the book, which is one of the most important mystical-ethical books to be written under the influence of Safed and its rituals. The story, attributed here to "the sacred writings in Egypt," is not connected in any way to the author of *Hemdat Yamim* but is rather quoted from this stated source, almost certainly accurately, as Tishbi shows in the case of dozens of other quotes. In the story at hand the situation is reversed—the author of *Hemdat Yamim* states explicitly that he copied it from other sources and that he himself did not compose it. Because the principal redactor of Vital's work was his son, Rabbi Shmuel Vital, who worked for the most part in Egypt and from there disseminated his father's writings, that may well be the source of the Tale of the Oxen. I thus see no reason to have any qualms about attributing the story to Hayyim Vital.[12]

Furthermore, studies of the way oral folk legends develop in a variety of cultures show that legends undergo transformation. They begin as first-person testimonies, called *memorats*, and transmute into *chronicats*. A chronicat is a story in a form that is told by other members of the community, who, after hearing the memorat, retell it as a historical story in the third person, changing it to fit their milieu.[13] This can explain the metamorphosis of the Tale of the Oxen: Hayyim Vital told the story in the first person, as he recalled it many years after Luria's death. Those who heard the story from him or from others who heard the story from Vital retold it in the third person, as a chronicat, the form in which it has been preserved in most versions. But the author of *Hemdat Yamim* seems to have used the version told by Vital himself and thus quoted it accurately, without making any changes at all. I view Vital as the first teller of the tale and perhaps as its author. This has critical implications for the story's interpretation and its contribution to understanding the Safed myth.

In addition to the extremely important testimony of Leon of Modena regarding the early stages of consolidation of the Safed myth, Rabbi Hayyim Vital's journal, *Sefer haHezyonot* (Book of Visions), is the most important literary-personal document of this early period. In this diary Vital recorded his thoughts, fears, hopes, and dreams in an extremely open and intimate way. It is hardly surprising that his great opponent, Abulafia, would also play a central role in the work.

Spirits, Reincarnations, and Other Visions

On 29 Tammuz 5369 (July 31, 1609), Damascus was rocked by a sensational incident that lasted for several weeks. This incident became known as the Dybbuk of Damascus. The daughter of one of the members of the city's Jewish community, Rabbi Raphael Anaf (or Anav), began to display severe signs of distress. She was wracked by spasms, lost consciousness, and "lay like a dead body with no sensation at all." Eventually she began to speak in an alien voice, which identified itself as the sage Jacob Pisso. The voice claimed, "I am not like other spirits, because I am a sage and saint and I came [in this form] only because of a minor sin that I still must rectify, and to be an emissary to you, to bring you back in repentance for the multitude of transgressions among you." After recounting in great detail his reincarnation as a fish, Pisso demanded that "R. Hayyim the kabbalist" be brought to him. The girl's father and the others who witnessed the event refused to comply "until he issued a ban against them."

When Rabbi Hayyim Vital arrived, he entered into a mesmerizing conversation with the spirit. Their exchange centered on repentance, which the spirit had disparaged during his lifetime. It was for this, apparently, that he was being punished. Vital acknowledged that he had been unsuccessful in his efforts to induce the Damascus Jewish community to repent its sins and change its ways, because "they do not attend to [my] voice." When Vital returned to his home to eat and pray, the spirit revealed the real reason he had come,

> And here is the entire reason for my mission: It was only for him [Vital], because I was sent by heaven to reveal to him secrets of the highest heavens, which were unknown to his master [Luria] of blessed memory, and also that he bring the world to repent, because the rectification of the world depends entirely on him. And I came to reveal to him

matters [relating to] the Messiah, for he is surely hanging by a thread to come. And here he [Vital] always preaches to them to repent so that the Messiah will come, and R. J[acob] Abulafia, out of jealousy, says to the people, he speaks falsehoods, because the Messiah will not come in this generation, and laughs at him. Woe to him [Abulafia] because his punishment [will be] great, as because of what he says and the great transgressions in this city, and the birth pangs [*hevelei*, which can also mean "ropes"] of the Messiah have been made even heavier, into thick iron bonds.[14]

But Hayyim Vital did not carry out the mission he was assigned.

Because he [Vital] did not want to listen to the words of that spirit and waited for Abulafia to arrive from Safed, and as a result the matter was confounded. . . . Here I [Vital] delayed bringing the people back in repentance because he [Abulafia] was not then in the city [Damascus] and I thought that the matter could be rectified by the both of us, but it was undone because upon arriving he ruined everything. And here he [Abulafia] arrived on the eve of the Sabbath of 15 Av and he spoiled everything in the eyes of the people so that I would not receive any honor from the above-mentioned words of the spirit.

When Abulafia arrived at the site of the incident with his students, the spirit humiliated him and commanded him to speak with it only from outside, through the window.

Because you are a sinner, and the Messiah is angry with you, as you always joke about the subject of the arrival of the Messiah, and say, the Messiah will not come in this generation. And when R. Hayyim the kabbalist preaches repentance to the people regarding the Messiah, you make fun of him and spoil his words out of envy of him. . . . You should

> have listened to the secrets of the Torah from R. Hayyim. And here he wanted to preach and admonish the people on the Sabbath day and you held him back and thwarted the repentance of Israel.

The spirit, which had just intimated those "great transgressions" that spread through the Jewish community of Damascus, went on to enumerate the sins: adultery with married women, siring bastards, sexual relations with Gentile women, homosexual acts. It also explicitly named the sinners: the leaders and pillars of the community, R. Jacob Abulafia among them.

> And here there are many homosexual acts in this city, also there are many delays of justice and injustices in this city. R. Abulafia responded to him, "And how am I supposed to know all that?" It [the spirit] said to him, "But look at your son Moshe. He and Menahem Romano brought a Gentile woman from a house on the last Shavuot holiday, before he went to Tzuba, and lay with her." He said to him, "Could it be that my son committed this sin?" He said to him, "Sons inherit the acts of their fathers! And did you not do things that were not good in your youth?" He said to him, "If so, I will go to Safed." He said to him, "You have destroyed Damascus and [now] you will go to destroy Safed as well?! . . . But what you say out loud is different from what is in your heart, because you do not believe in these things . . . but you are not a believer at all."[15]

What we see here is the ugly relationship between Vital and Abulafia, which no doubt had its roots in Safed's golden age, thirty years earlier. A reconstruction of the interaction between these two individuals from the story of the Dybbuk of Damascus would look something like this: Raphael Anaf's family and friends viewed his daughter's symptoms as a clear indication that a spirit had taken over her body. It was natural for her father to call in an expert on such cases, a kabbalist. The preeminent kabbalist in Damascus was Rabbi Hayyim Vital. But Anaf refused, preferring to wait for the arrival of a different sage whom he liked better, Rabbi Ya'akov Abulafia, who was not in Damascus at the time. Vital nevertheless arrived at the site of the incident, whether by his own volition or because others asked him to. He realized that the case of possession was a sign, one of many others, that had been given to him previously in his dreams and visions telling him to reassume the central role that had been his during his years in Safed. He was to exhort Damascus's Jews to repent their evil ways and return to the Torah, in preparation for the coming of the Messiah. But Vital knew that he lacked the strength and social standing to take on such a heavy task and, perhaps, was no longer certain of his ability to act on his own. He needed the help of a central figure, one who had (perhaps, as we saw from the testimony of Leon of Modena) been a friend and close associate of Luria, Ya'akov Abulafia. He thus awaited for Abulafia to arrive, but this turned out to be a mistake, because Abulafia "spoiled [hehevil] him"; in other words, he mocked him and told the people around the affected girl that anything Vital said was no more than empty air (hevel). What recourse did Vital have as an elderly man, nearly blind, miserably poor, and rejected by the community? He could only repeat gossip about the alleged sins of Abulafia, members of his family, and the community leaders who supported him. We can only guess the extent to which such gossip "contributed" to raising Vital's standing in the Damascus Jewish community.

The fierce rivalry between Vital and Abulafia is also on display in other parts of Vital's memoir. In one place he argues that the community's prayers to God offered at the synagogue were not acceptable to heaven, because heaven itself had banned Abulafia for the injustice he caused to Vital. In another place Vital describes a strange dream that a close associate of his, Rabbi Nisim Cohen, had on 2 Shevat 5370 (February 13, 1610). In it he saw "a ruddy Gentile stalwart with a book in his hand, written in Ishmaelite letters." When asked, the Gentile said that he was the "son of the daughter of Mohammad the prophet of the Ishmaelites [who says], and I am a Jew and five companions are with me, disciples of Rabbi Jacob Abulafia, and we think that he is a greater sage than our teacher Rabbi Hayyim the kabbalist." They later realized their error and became Vital's disciples.[16] An exceptional accusation is leveled at Abulafia—that he and his disciples have close ties to Muslim groups, a charge that would be made again in connection with the sin of the Jews who cut their sidelocks and were reincarnated as oxen. What is clearly reflected here is contention over disciples, a rivalry in which Abulafia had the upper hand, as we know from the story of the Dybbuk of Damascus. It may be that the dream had its source in an actual incident in which some of the students in Abulafia's yeshiva, a converted Arab among them, were not content to study only Halakha and, seeking kabbalistic knowledge as well, found their way to Rabbi Hayyim Vital, a sage not often sought out by students.

Vital's attempts to approach and reconcile with Abulafia show that he was in the inferior position. He wanted to teach Kabbalah to Abulafia, but Abulafia rejected his overtures; he waited for him to return from Safed before exorcising the spirit that had entered the body of Raphael Anaf's daughter because Vital did not dare do so without Abulafia. Binyamin Saruk, a close associate of Vital's in Damascus, recorded a dream he had on 19 Adar (March 14, 1610) of that same year, in which Vital was summoned to the vizier (apparently the governor of Damascus) to report to him on omens indicating the Messiah's arrival. In the dream Vital explains to the vizier that the greatest obstacle to the Messiah's arrival is that there are "two sages, R. Hayyim and R. Jacob Abulafia, between whom there is discord, and one speaks badly of the other, my teaching has been demeaned by the common people. . . . And they administered all sorts of oaths to the dreamer, to tell this dream to me and to R. Abulafia . . . and it would connect the two of us and make peace between us. And then he woke up."[17] This account shows that the relations between the two men were painfully one-sided. *Sefer haHezyonot* offers no account of any attempt by Abulafia to approach Vital (if such a thing had happened, Vital would certainly have highlighted it in his book). In fact, it sounds as though Abulafia is utterly indifferent to Vital and everything he does. Such disregard explains Vital's inferiority complex in relation to Abulafia, which turned into an obsession that took on mythic dimensions.

On the night following the Sabbath, 29 Tammuz 5368 (July 12, 1608), Eliahu Amiel, apparently a close associate of Vital's, had a dream in which Vital and his disciples make a pilgrimage to holy graves near Safed. They take along the most important of Safed's sages (Rabbis Joseph Karo, Moshe Cordovero, Moshe Alsheikh, Shlomo Alkabetz, Eleazar Azkari, and Moshe Galanti) and enter a cave under the Temple (of Jerusalem), where they find Luria.

> And my teacher of blessed memory said, "Bring Jacob Abulafia before us." And they went . . . and brought him there. And all these saints were dressed in white, and I also was dressed in a white worsted wool [garment]. And this Jacob came dressed in black clothes, and he also had a black covering over his head and face and beard. And my teacher commanded the two sages who had brought him to remove his black clothing and to dress him in a small white coat that reached only to his thighs.[18]

The motif relates to one of the stranger stories to emerge from the Middle Ages, the Tale of the Radiant Robe, which appears in an eleventh-century book by Rabbi Nissim ben Jacob of Kairouan, *Hibur Yafeh min haYeshua'* (An Elegant Compilation Concerning Relief After Adversity). In this story two sages have a vision that the robe of a secret saintly man, meant to be his garment in paradise, is not whole. Although the robe is finer and more beautiful than that accorded to others of the righteous, it lacks a collar. The saint must perform one more great good deed to complete the garment. This saint consults with his wife and with her consent sells her into slavery. He gives the money he receives from her sale to charity and thus completes the collar of the garment designated for him in paradise. The story is based on a well-known Muslim narrative of the time. In its original form the great figures of Islam are clothed in splendid garments in paradise, the length of which reflects the good deeds they did during their lifetimes. The garments of the less righteous reach down only to their loins, so as to chasten them.[19]

The story in *Sefer haHezyonot* is also a paradise for the righteous. The sages all gather in the Temple, are dressed in white, and engage themselves in Torah study. Abulafia's black clothing presents him as an antithesis to these saints, as a person whose life and deeds are blacker than black. Even when he is saved, perhaps by Luria, who was his friend during his lifetime, he receives only a short garment, which reaches down to his thighs only, just like sinful scholars do in the Muslim tradition. In other words, he is publicly humiliated in the eternal world. Hayyim Vital may well have heard a version of the story from Muslims in Safed or Damascus and used it for his own purposes.

The mythic dimensions of the rivalry between Vital and Abulafia climax in a dream attributed to another acquaintance of Vital's, on 27 Av of that same year, 5368 (August 9, 1608). The Saklein community (synagogue) in Damascus rejected Vital's candidacy to be its spiritual leader (perhaps under pressure from Abulafia). Using complex games with letters, the dreamer proves to the community that rejected Vital that the Messiah's name is Hayyim. He also proves this from the Talmud, "where it is written 'in the footsteps of the Messiah insolence will increase,' meaning that the name of the Messiah is Hayyim also . . . while Ya'akov [Abulafia] will delay his coming, as an outcome of his insolence toward Hayyim."[20] This means, in mythic terms, that, although Vital is the Messiah, his great opponent, Abulafia, who delays the coming of the Messiah, is no other than Armilus, the Jewish Antichrist.

Thus we are aware of the huge dimensions of the rivalry and animosity that form the psychological foundation on which the story of Abulafia and the oxen is built. The story involves a classic transference of Abulafia's animosity from Vital to Luria, even though there is no record of any rivalry between Abulafia and Luria. According to Leon of Modena, the two men were personally close. But this turned into a clash of mythical proportions between Abulafia and Vital, and perhaps some of Luria's other disciples, who were interested in promoting the name of the master. The story's claim, that Abulafia was sent to the men who had been reincarnated as oxen because he belonged to the same root of their soul and that he must rectify himself before their souls can be rectified, can only be understood against the background of the intense enmity revealed by the dreams and visions I have just recounted. These dreams and visions are the product of Vital's conflicted and unstable mind. The claims regarding Abulafia's sins, about him holding back the arrival of the Messiah, about a ban on him in heaven, have been transformed into the language of the Tale of the Oxen. Corroboration of this is provided by the spirit who spoke through Anaf's daughter in Damascus, who accused Abulafia and the other respected members of the Damascus community of serious sexual transgressions. The spirit also accuses two Egyptians of such sins, and thus "anyone who now goes to Egypt, even to do business, is banned from heaven, and in the end he will lose all his money because of the evil things there."[21] It can hardly be a coincidence that in the Tale of the Oxen Abulafia goes to Egypt to trade with members of that country's Jewish community and, on his return, encounters the Jews who had sinned and received a severe punishment.

All these reinforce my hypothesis that the version of the story in *Hemdat Yamim* is the original version and that Rabbi Hayyim Vital is its narrator and creator. It may well be that Vital told this story during the same period and atmosphere in which the visions and dreams I have adduced were experienced: during the first two decades of the seventeenth century. The protagonist of the story, Abulafia, whom Luria sends out like a delivery boy and who is humiliated before the master's other disciples for his great sins, is the same Abulafia who appears in Vital's visions, where he is humiliated by Luria in a cave under the Temple by appearing in a garment that reaches only to his thighs. *Sefer haHezyonot* is thus as critical to deciphering the story as it is for understanding other Safed stories, as we will see in the chapters to follow. By touching the frayed edges of nerves, it opens a window through which we can see, on the one hand, the interdependence of Vital's fears and neuroses and, on the other, the construction of narratives of mythical character, such as the dream of the cave and the Tale of the Oxen.

From the Beards of the West to the Sidelocks of the East

The story that immediately follows the Tale of the Oxen in *Hemdat Yamim* is another story about mutilation of the beard. It tells of Rabbi Judah the Pious (d. 1217), a leader of a mystical and ascetic movement in the Rhineland in the twelfth and thirteenth centuries, reproaching one of the wealthy men of his city for shaving his face. The author of *Hemdat Yamim* presents the story as further proof, in addition to the Tale of the Oxen, of the severe prohibition against shaving. He does not know, or perhaps simply ignores, the possibility that the story about Rabbi Judah is not an independent tale but rather, almost certainly, the source of the story that precedes it. It appears in a work called *Sefer haGan* (Book of the Garden), attributed to Rabbi Eleazar of Worms, a relative of Rabbi Judah's (there is no evidence to support the attribution). The story in *Sefer haGan* is quoted from a manuscript by Rabbi Moshe Zaltman, Rabbi Judah's son, which testifies that Zaltman heard the story from his father.

> When I was studying in Speyer before Rabbi Yedidya [writes the author of *Sefer haGan*] of blessed memory, I found in his house of study a manuscript in the hand of Rabbi Zaltman which said: My father and teacher The Pious, told me that in his time there was a matter of a wealthy man of Speyer who would shave his beard with scissors, and my father and teacher rebuked him, but he [the wealthy man] paid no attention to his words, because the wealthy man said, "I am a fastidious man and I cannot tolerate a beard." My father and teacher said to him, "Know that your end will be severe, as after your death demons in the form of cows will trample the side-growth of your beard—that is the fate of those who destroy the side-growth of their beard. And know that this is so, for the acronym of 'You shall not round off the side-growth on your head, or destroy' [Leviticus 19:27] is 'cows.'" And when that wealthy man died, all the great men of Speyer sat [in mourning in his home] and my father and teacher was there. And he wrote a Name [of God] and cast it on that dead wealthy man and he [the dead] stood up, and all those sitting there fled. And the dead man began to pull at his head and tear out his hair. My father and teacher said to him, "What is the matter?" He said to him, "Woe, had I only listened to you." My father and teacher said to him, "Please tell, what we must do to save your soul?" He said to him, "When my soul left [my body] a demon came, who looked like a large cow, and brought a vessel full of tar and sulfur and salt and put my soul in it and it could not get out. And the Divine Judgment came and took that vessel with the soul from the demon and brought it before the Creator of Souls. A divine voice came and said to me, 'Have you studied and repeated [the study of scripture and Talmud]?' I said to him,

'I have studied and repeated.' Immediately He [the Creator of Souls] ordered a book to be brought and said to me, 'Read from it.' As soon as I opened The Book I found it written: 'You shall not round off the side-growth on your head, or destroy,' and I did not know how to respond. I immediately heard a voice proclaiming, place the soul of this [man] on the lowest rung [of hell]. As they were bearing my soul to bring it to the lowest rung a divine voice appeared, [saying], 'Wait a bit for this, my son Judah is more righteous than he, and now plead for mercy and his soul will not descend to hell.'" Here concludes his [my father's] words.[22]

The combination of seeing the word *cows* in the acronym of the words of the Torah's commandment, the punishment in the afterlife, the warning from the saint, and the proof he was right are all persuasive evidence of the connection between this story and the Tale of the Oxen. There is no reason to believe that Rabbi Hayyim Vital did not know the story—*Sefer haGan* was printed in 1606 in Venice, in a cultural space well connected to Safed and Damascus. We also know that the acronymic reading of the verse as *cows*, and perhaps the story connected to it, was familiar to the sages of Safed even before Luria's sojourn in the city.

The shaving of the beard is a central subject in both stories. In both, this prohibition is portrayed as so severe that punishment for it is meted out after death, making it more severe than many other transgressions. The question of cutting the hair on one's face has preoccupied Jewish sages since biblical times, and medieval authorities were sharply divided on the subject. The issue has been studied by Louis Ginzberg, Yitzhak (Isaac) Zimmer, and Elliot (Elimelech) Horovitz, who have provided the historical, social, halakhic, and mystical background for the severity of the prohibition.[23] Beyond the theological question and the commandment in Leviticus, the polemic focuses on the socionational issue of the beard as a distinguishing mark between Jews and Gentiles. The writings of many authorities on the subject give the impression that they were fighting an almost Sisyphean battle, waged by religious leaders against the members of their communities who were seeking by a variety of means to circumvent this explicit biblical prohibition against removing facial hair, so as not to look different from the Gentiles among whom they lived.

This state of affairs is the background to Rabbi Judah's story and to the explicit statement in his book *Sefer Gematriot* that "any man who has a forelock on his head and whose beard is shaven, even with scissors, or whose garments are like the Gentiles', may not be called up [to read from] the Torah scroll. . . . And you must not follow the ways of the Gentiles who beautify themselves for harlotry . . . as it is forbidden to shave, even with scissors."[24] In other words, Rabbi Judah made more than a theological claim that the Torah's commandment had to be complied with. He also took a strict view of the prohibition against looking like the Gentiles and adopting their ways. The polemic was still alive during Safed's golden age. *Hemdat Yamim*, which offers the two stories one after the other, devotes a long discussion to the prohibition against shaving, focusing on the social aspect.

> But the Children of Israel are holy and arrived at this transgression and to destroying the side-growth on their heads and their beards only by mingling among the Gentiles in this terrifying Exile and by learning their ways, and in particular in the Frankish lands in which this plague has spread among many members of our nation, who cannot be distinguished [from the Gentiles] on the streets. . . . And in these lands this plague has spread among some of the rebellious members of our nation to the point of destruction, some rebelliously and in violation [of the covenant], to follow the laws of the Gentiles.[25]

The main problem, then, is not transgressing a Torah commandment but the failure to observe a *visual* distinction between Jews and Gentiles, which the author sees as the root of all evil, a sin that might induce Jews to adopt other Gentile customs as well. However, why does the author of *Hemdat Yamim* point his finger specifically at the Jews of France—that is, Western Europe—right after having told the Tale of the Oxen, in which the sinners live in the Land of Israel or Egypt?

In fact, the two stories differ in a significant way. In the earlier story about Rabbi Judah, the wealthy man of Speyer is guilty of shaving his beard with a scissors. But the Tale of the Oxen says that the two victims are punished for destroying the side-growth on their heads. The beard and the side-growth (or sidelocks) are not the same. The difference is of great importance because it points to a profound difference between the communities of the Mediterranean, who lived among Muslims, and the Jews of Western Europe. The esthetic-cultural norm in Europe was a shaven face (as most visual depictions from the Middle Ages show), but the opposite fashion prevailed in Islamic lands, where a thick and magnificent beard was a badge of male honor. Thus, in Europe, a Jew who wished to look like the Gentiles had to remove his beard (or cut it very short), whereas in the Orient Jews grew and tended their beards in order to resemble the most respected Gentiles. Both Christians and Jews who traveled from Europe to the Levant reported that the Muslims and Jews there looked much the same, because all wore beards.

But the Tale of the Oxen does not accuse the men reincarnated as oxen of having shaved their beards. They stand guilty of having "rounded off the side-growth" on their heads. Notably, *Hemdat Yamim* and other works that came out of Luria's circle offer detailed descriptions of the growth of sidelocks.[26] Jacob Tzemach quotes Hayyim Vital as saying, "In the matter of sidelocks, my teacher [Luria], may he be remembered forever in the next world, was accustomed to leave alone the entire width of the sides, which is all the hair from the ear to one-third of the forehead . . . and he would also allow the hair of the sides of his head to grow to the point that they actually extended below the place of the beard." In other words, Luria's sidelocks were broad, long, and prominent. We can presume that the veneration accorded to him by his disciples and his broader group of followers included imitating his personal customs, including his sidelocks. As it happens, this custom was not a personal whim of Luria's. It was in fact the prevailing custom among the Jews of Egypt, where Luria lived and studied for many years. According to a manuscript laying out Luria's penitential rule,

> The holy community of Egypt. Penitence for one who shaves his sidelocks. . . . For in this time the Gentiles circumcise [their sons] and our dress is largely like their dress and

nothing remains [to distinguish the Jew] with even a bit of difference, such as the cap and so on, and thus if a man is naked in the bathhouse or [clothed in regular cloths] on the road, anyone who sees him thinks he is a Gentile, and all the more so if he dies on the road he might be buried in a Gentile grave, but by means of *the large sidelock such as the holy community of Egypt leaves*, the Jews are a slave [recognized] in life and death, and in this is observed "and I have set you apart from other peoples" [Leviticus 20:26]. And this actually happened, that because of the sidelock, a certain Jew who died was buried in a Jewish grave.[27]

Thus the role played by the beard among the Jews of Western Europe—a badge of identification and distinction from Gentile society—was played by sidelocks among the Jews of the Islamic world. If the Jews who were reincarnated as oxen indeed came from Egypt, as seems to be the case from their location in the story space, it might even be possible to apply the last part of the quotation to them. In other words, they died in the desert, where Ya'akov Abulafia found them, and were not buried in a Jewish grave because they could not be identified as Jews. They had beards but not sidelocks, just like the Gentiles around them. That is why they must tell Abulafia that they are Jews—he could not have identified them as such from their appearance—and inform him of their plight. By the rule of measure for measure, characteristic of religious legends, the sinners in both stories, about Rabbi Judah and Luria, sought to obscure their Jewish identities. In punishment, after their deaths, their human identities (their place in the next world) were taken from them.

Even though the two stories are much the same, there is a profound difference between them. The punishment meted out to the sinner in Rabbi Judah's narrative is the common one in popular medieval belief, both Jewish and Christian. The dead person returns to the land of the living to report what happened to him. But the dead person returns to this world in his own form, without any changes in him or his body that transform him into something else. Furthermore, his punishment is not wandering or suffering in this world, as the men-oxen suffer—the sinner returns only to report—but rather affliction in the next world. In this case, demons in the form of cows beat him mercilessly, and he is cast down to the bottom rung of hell in a way reminiscent of Dante's *Inferno*. The difference between this episode in the story of Rabbi Judah and that of Luria expresses the transition between two periods, two views of the world, and the two cultural realms that produced those views.

The sinners in Luria's story are not punished by demons in the form of oxen. *They themselves* are transformed into oxen. In Judah's story the dead man's return to this world is "a reminder of his wonders" (Psalms 111:6), miracles (*mirabilia*) that medieval people, both Christians and Jews, searched for everywhere so as to provide backing for the existence of another reality that proves the presence of a divine power that rules our world. One of the common and classic manifestations of such *mirabilia* is the return of the dead to this world. Medieval people viewed the existence of such dead individuals and their ability to wander between the worlds as solid proof of the immanence of the godhead. These dead people who return to life have generally been endowed with an unusual capacity for speech, which they use to testify in detail and at length about what they have seen in the other world. They principally speak of the hierarchy of God and the angels and of the rigid and cruel system of reward and punishment, thus confirming the truth of the theological principles accepted in their culture.[28]

A different worldview is expressed in the Tale of the Oxen and in Luria. The principles involved are laid out in Gershom Scholem's great essay, "*Gilgul*: The Transmigration of Souls." In pre-Lurianic Kabbalah there are few examples of the reincarnation of human souls in inferior entities, such as animals, plants, or inanimate objects. The purpose of reincarnation is to purify the soul, and that is difficult to accomplish in the body of an inferior being. Lurianic Kabbalah had a different view of reincarnation: A Jew's soul could be reincarnated in a lower entity, just as the divine sparks fell among the shells to rectify them and raise them up again to their source. Ronit Meroz has pointed to sermons given by Luria about how human souls were implanted in animals (and plants and inanimate material) and then transferred to other humans who ate the animals. This was a way for pure souls to find their way into sinful bodies in order to rectify them, or to rectify flawed sparks (the souls of sinners) by their reincarnation in pure bodies.

Another motif that appears here is Abulafia's connection to the souls reincarnated in the oxen. Because he is "the root of their souls," as Luria knew even before, he was chosen to seek them out, as only he could rectify them. Scholem writes:

> All the sparks or individual souls belonging to the same root . . . are connected to each other in a special affinity and sympathy. Only sparks of a common root can be connected in incarnation and conception; only they can assist and strengthen each other. The law of sympathy rules all sparks belonging to the same large soul: they suffer together and the good or bad action of each of them affects all the others. A profound and invisible connection between "close souls" determines their fate. Even an utterly righteous man cannot raise sparks that are not from the root of his soul from among the shells. . . . The sparks that are from the same root soul of the individual soul constitute a kind of expanded zone of that soul, and help it: "All are guarantors of the other and all are a single soul" (Vital, *Sha'ar haGilgulim*). . . . In general, a person does not know his previous incarnations; only those reincarnated in low forms of life, especially in animals, have a vague knowledge of the bitterness of their fate.[29]

The identification and rectification of these entities that had a previous existence—that is, their return to the pure source to which they belonged before they sinned—are cosmic processes that will, through many such rectifications, bring about the great and final rectification, the final redemption. "Lurianic Kabbalah," Scholem continues, "placed the Jew within a skein of incarnations from which there is no escape, and in this way was able to connect with an ancient teaching the profound consciousness of those generations, that all things are in exile and that all must wander and reincarnate and prepare the way for the redemption in a common effort."

In this sense, the Tale of the Oxen can be seen as a narrative realization of the process of repentance and rectification developed by Luria's Kabbalah.[30]

The Myth and Its Disenchantment • 65

If Rabbi Hayyim Vital is indeed the first to tell the story in the Safed tradition, based on the medieval tradition of Rabbi Judah, it is clear that the most important change he made in the story was to adjust it to fit Luria's doctrine of reincarnation and thus to make it into a story that demonstrates the process of repentance and rectification.

Another difference between the two stories lies in the nature of the narrative conflict, an element that generally indicates the changes in its meaning and role. The conflict in the medieval story is clearly between the wealthy man who shaved his beard with a scissors and Rabbi Judah, who forbade him to do so. The hints offered by the story are also unmistakable: The rabbi's adversary is wealthy and fastidious, and when he dies, all of Speyer's great men come to mourn him. The wealthy man is clearly one of the pillars of the Jewish community, a man who acts in accordance with his wealth and authority. He shaves because, in keeping with his wealth and status, he wishes to resemble the local Gentile nobility. The clash between Rabbi Judah and the wealthy man is a small-scale version of the contention between the monied aristocracy and the religious leadership. Judah seeks to impose his authority, which is, in his view, the authority of the Torah itself, on the community's leadership, but the leader rejects his authority with no little derision, arguing that he is fastidious, that having a beard irks him, and thus that he is not bound by the rabbi's command. The man's beard is the emblem of the power struggle between the Jewish community's two-pronged leadership, but the use of the beard in this context is not arbitrary. It is an issue on which the spiritual leader can cite an ancient tradition—a verse from the Torah and its application to everyday life—and the lay leader can cite his social position and his close relations with the ruling Gentile elite.

In the Safed story, the focal point of the conflict has shifted. The conflict is not between the spiritual leader, Luria, and sinners who do not accept his authority. In fact, Luria and the sinners never meet. Neither is Luria's emissary, Abulafia, at odds with the sinners. They accept his authority and that of his master. The story's only moment of conflict is when Abulafia returns to Luria and attempts to challenge Luria's all-knowing authority.

> And [Abulafia] came to him [Luria] and said to him, "On my master's life, tell me what this vision [the oxen] means."

He [Luria] told him, "So-and-so the ox is so-and-so the son of so-and-so from a certain place. And more in this way. And they used to mingle among powerful men and rounded off the side-growth on their heads and for this they were dealt this punishment." He [Abulafia] said to him, "Sir, what do oxen plowing sand have to do with the side-growth?" He said to him, *"Did I not tell you that you think yourself a scholar but that you do not know anything."* He said to him, "There is no hint of such a thing in the Gemara or in any book." He said to him, "It is a full [explicit] verse [in the Torah], and you don't know it?!"

The sin of the men reincarnated as oxen is no different from that of the wealthy man in Rabbi Judah's story: "They used to mingle among powerful men and rounded off the side-growth on their heads." In other words, they knowingly committed a religious transgression in order to resemble Gentiles and be accepted into their society. But the conflict, once again, is not between them and Luria but rather between Luria and Abulafia. Even though Luria's disciples would never dare doubt or differ with him, Abulafia's words imply a skepticism about Luria's understanding of the case. The circumstantial connections that Luria finds between the sand-plowing oxen and the cutting of the men's sidelocks seem to Abulafia to be groundless. Even worse, he challenges Luria's knowledge of the Torah, claiming that there is no hint of any such connection in the Gemara or any other source. Luria's curt response expresses contempt for those outside Luria's circle who do not know and understand the special idiom that formed among his disciples and in this ignorance raise logical or textual objections to his doctrines. The axis of the conflict in the Safed story is thus not between the spiritual elite and secular community leaders but rather between Luria's authority as a spiritual leader and the authority of Safed's great Torah scholars ("Did I not tell you that you think yourself a scholar but that you do not know anything"). Abulafia, who was, as we have seen, the grandson of Rabbi Ya'akov Beirav, was authorized to teach and judge by the greatest Torah scholars of Safed and thus clearly belonged to the scholarly elite, as all those who heard the story certainly knew.

Luria writes Abulafia a "prescription," which is confirmed as effective when the sinners appear to him after having undergone rectification.

> "And you must rectify them and afflict yourself tomorrow and intend this and this in the name of this person," and in this form he wrote down for him all the rectifications and mortifications he needed to do until those people were rectified. And they came to the sage in a dream and said to him, "May God bless you, may your thoughts be at rest just as our souls are at rest, from that day that you began to do the rectifications that the rabbi told you. Because the one rectification you did removed us from that hard labor which you saw and brought us into Gehenna, and the same way each rectification you did removed us from a heavy yoke to an easier one until they brought us into our intended place [in the eternal world]."

In other words, Abulafia alone could accomplish such rectifications for the sinners, because he is "of the root of their soul" and, even more critically, because he is a sinner like them. I have already cited the dream from *Sefer haHezyonot* in which Rabbi Hayyim Vital accuses Abulafia of sexual depravity. Abulafia certainly did not wear large sidelocks as Luria did and was thus, in the eyes of Luria's fellowship, guilty of cutting his sidelocks. He thus had to do a rectification for himself with the rectification he did for the oxen-men.

A widespread medieval tradition, from the Gaonic period, is known as the Tale of the Tanna and the Dead Man. In its broad contours, it resembles the Tale of the Oxen. According to this legend, a *tanna* (a sage of the Mishnaic period) encounters a man running through a forest, gathering wood and burning himself with it. In response to a query from the *tanna*, the man explains that this severe punishment was imposed on him for his sins. He relates that he cannot even enter hell (his soul is supposed to wander for eternity) because there is no one who will say a prayer to raise his soul out of the netherworld. The *tanna* discovers that the man has a son who is growing up wild, who does not know how to read and write, and the *tanna* thus takes the son and teaches him to pray. After the son prays to raise his father's soul from hell, the dead man appears to the *tanna* in a dream and thanks him for bringing his soul into the next world.[31]

The two stories clearly resemble each other structurally, and it seems reasonable to suppose that the Tale of the Tanna and the Dead Man, which is pervasive in written and oral Jewish sources, was known in Safed and served as another narrative model that shaped Hayyim Vital's Tale of the Oxen. But note an interesting difference: In the Tale of the Tanna and the Dead Man, the *tanna* does nothing for himself. He simply teaches the sinner's son and thus saves him from his ignorance. In contrast, in the Tale of the Oxen, Luria orders Abulafia to rectify himself, and the change in the world beyond takes place only after the protagonist has undergone an inner transformation in this world. Abulafia is portrayed as a sinner who requires forgiveness and rectification before he can rectify other sinners.

The difference between the two stories underscores the classic Lurianic view that great cosmic rectification that brings about redemption begins with the personal rectification made by each Jew. We have already seen that the principal narrative transformation in the move from Rabbi Judah's medieval story to the Tale of the Oxen is the application of Lurianic principles. The move from the Tale of the Tanna and the Dead Man to the Tale of the Oxen occurs in the same conceptual space and reinforces the claim that the principal changes in the story indeed occur in this area.

However, in the story's broader context, the shaping of the conflict is more complex. In fact, Abulafia's actual rival is Vital, not Luria. It is Vital who tells the story, in the form of a first-person testimony, in the version that appears in *Hemdat Yamim*, and it is Vital who is responsible for the major changes that make the story part of the genre of *Shivkhei ha-'Ari*. I have already noted that we do not know of any actual historical rivalry between Abulafia and Luria; in fact, the evidence we have indicates that the two men were close and friendly. In other words, the Tale of the Oxen belongs to that group of stories, visions, and dreams found principally in *Sefer haHezyonot*, in which Abulafia is portrayed as a nemesis and mythological opponent of the messianic hero, Vital himself. The story is thus the product of a long clash between Vital and Abulafia, fashioned on the medieval narrative model provided by the story of Rabbi Judah and the wealthy man who shaved his beard. The personal, ideological, and psychological confrontation between the two men and their two paths led to a radical change in an ancient narrative tradition and turned it into one of the foundation stories of the Safed myth.

The actual conflict between the two figures extends beyond the bounds of the narrative. Judah's story is one in which he seeks to impose his authority on the community's wealthy people. The fact that this fastidious wealthy man cynically dismissed Judah's threat and that the community's wealthiest and most respected members, including Rabbi Judah himself, gathered around his deathbed indicates that rabbinic authority was being challenged in the community. When spiritual leaders need to use the next world as a means of intimidation and warning, their standing in this world is clearly in jeopardy. In Rabbi Judah's case, we have little information from outside the story about his life and social standing, so we can only presume that the story reflects real life. But in the case of Hayyim Vital, the situation is much clearer,

Following the death of Luria in 1572, Vital, his closest disciple, had one public success: He convinced Luria's other students to sign a document prohibiting them from publicizing their teacher's doctrines and agreeing to make Vital the sole custodian of Luria's legacy.[32] But, to the best of our knowledge, Vital's standing declined from this point. He left his beloved Safed and, for reasons that are not clear, lived in Jerusalem for a brief period and then spent his final years in poverty and social isolation in Damascus. It was there, apparently, that he composed and edited his intimate memoir, *Sefer haHezyonot*, while never ceasing to dream about Safed. Again and again he called on Luria to appear to him and to shore up his hopes of returning to his former home. He assured those around him, and himself in particular, that although returning was difficult and the road was full of obstacles, it would indeed come to pass. Vital's great longing for Safed can also be seen as his yearning for the authority he had lost. In Safed, under Luria's tutelage and even for a short time following his death, it looked as though leadership of the fellowship was passing to Vital and that the promises and hopes that had formed in Luria's fellowship, both personal and national, would in fact come to be. Luria's small chosen group of disciples, so it seemed, would be the vanguard of the new movement. But as

Safed receded, both in time and space, Vital's position grew less secure, as did the force of the promises. It is a classic syndrome of the failure of most messianic movements, both on the personal and social levels.

We can now better understand Abulafia's role in *Sefer haHezyonot* and the Tale of the Oxen. For Vital, Abulafia, by virtue of his personality and social standing in Damascus, symbolized the ruin of his authority and the failure of the great promise presented by Luria's teachings. Abulafia had lived in Safed at the climax of this promise and then lived in Damascus along with Vital, playing a central role in challenging the authority of Luria's teachings, which Vital bore on his narrow and weak shoulders.

The Procession of the Dead

The connection between the Tale of the Oxen and traditions deriving from the Ashkenazic Pietists of the thirteenth century is not limited to the story of Rabbi Judah and the wealthy man who shaved his beard. The Safed legend is also connected to another story told by Rabbi Judah in *Sefer Hasidim*.[33]

> It happened that a man was riding alone at night and the moon rose that night. He rode in the desert and saw a huge multitude, wagons and more wagons, and people sitting on the wagons, and people pulling wagons, and he wondered what they were doing. When he approached them, he recognized some of them who had already died. He said to them, "Why are you are pulling wagons all night and some of you are on wagons?" They said to him, "Because of our transgressions. When we were alive in the same world, we played [had sexual relations] with women and young girls, and now we are pulling the wagons until we become so tired and wearied that we can drive no more, and we take them down from the wagons and we get up and rest and they drive us until they are weary." Afterward they . . . and the righteous ones beat the pullers as if they were pulling the wagon like beasts. . . . He who does a beastly act in his life must work in that world as a beast.

The connection between this story in *Sefer Hasidim* and the Tale of the Oxen in the stories about Luria is not hard to discern, but, surprisingly, it was not noted until it was pointed out by Aryeh Wineman in 1988. The story in *Sefer Hasidim* lacks the narrative frame of the journey to Egypt, the return to Safed, and the act of rectification. But the narrative kernel of the caravan of the dead drawing wagons like beasts, driven by others who exchange places with them from time to time, is the central narrative episode in each of them. The most evident difference is that in *Sefer Hasidim* it is human beings pulling the wagons like beasts, whereas in Luria's story the wagon is drawn by human beings who have been reincarnated as oxen. This shift can be explained without difficulty as an integration of the Safed doctrine of reincarnation with the medieval story.

Had I presented the story as though it were told by Rabbi Judah, the principal author of *Sefer Hasidim*, we would overlook the major reason why it is important. The story that appears in *Sefer Hasidim* is in fact a variant of a legend prevalent in Christian Europe in the twelfth and thirteenth centuries, "The Wild Hunt" (or "Familia Herlechini," after the name of the leader of the troop in several common versions). The French medieval historian and folklorist Jean-Claude Schmitt, who investigated these European traditions, noted that different versions of the story can be found in different areas of the continent and that the medieval public, both scholars and laymen, believed the story to be true.

The monk and scholar Orderic Vitalis (1075–1142), author of a monumental history of Norman Christianity, presents the earliest first-person version of this story. In Book VIII of his history he tells of an incident involving a young monk named Walchelin on the night of January 1, 1091, near the French city of Angers. Walchelin is returning to his monastery after visiting a sick person. He hears the approach of a "great host" apparently returning from battle. The monk hides among the trees and sees a giant armed with a mace marching at the head of a troop of foot soldiers, who are crying out bitterly. Among them, the monk sees, are several acquaintances of his who had recently died. They are followed by men bearing heavy wooden biers, on which are dwarfs with unusually huge heads, as well as two Ethiopians bearing on their shoulders a miserable man in chains, shouting in pain because a horrifying demon is sitting above him and stabbing him unceasingly with burning spikes. The monk recognizes the afflicted man as one who had, two years earlier, murdered a monk and then died without being punished. After them come a group of women riding horses bareback; red-hot nails are scattered over the horses, pricking the women in the genitals each time they bounce on the horses' backs. Among the women, Walchelin makes out young noblewomen who had lived lives of luxury and debauchery. The frightened monk then sees a group of clergymen and monks, led by bishops and abbots, wearing black hats, with hot coals covering their flesh. These victims recognize Walchelin and call out to him by name, pleading with him to pray for them. The monk is terrified when he sees among them a man he had admired in life. He identifies them by their names and their high positions in the church. Afterward comes a group of warrior knights, who are described in great detail. Dressed in black, they spit fire, ride huge horses, and are armed as though they are going out to a great battle. Here, too, the monk identifies several important local rulers who had recently died. They, too, shout at him, pleading for him to tell their relatives that he has encountered them. Only then does he identify the procession as the army of Herlechin. He had heard others tell of seeing this army galloping through the forest, but he had not believed them until now. Walchelin's brother, who had chosen war as his calling, also appears in the procession. He relates how horrible his agonies are and how he has to bear a burden of blood "heavier than Mt. St. Michele," penance for the huge amount of blood he had spilled. He demands of his brother the monk to remember him, to help him with his prayers, and to save him from his agonies. The young monk, who fell gravely ill upon his return to the monastery, gave the historian Vitalis his testimony, and Vitalis wrote it down word for word. The monk even showed the historian a bad burn on his hand, incurred when he tried to touch one of the horses in the procession.[34]

Variants of these stories appeared all over Europe during the following 300 years. What they all have in common is the military character of the convoy. Whereas the participants include representatives of other medieval castes—those who pray and those who labor—the army of heavily armed warriors dominates in most of the testimonies. All the stories are related as reliable testimony, supported by concrete evidence (e.g., items taken from the procession or wounds suffered by the witness during his encounter with the procession). The reason for stressing the reliability of the testimony can be found in the primary tradition summarized here: The monk himself had refused until this point to give credence to such stories and had even derided them. Who could be more believable as a witness to the existence of Herlechin's army than an erstwhile skeptic?

The Hebrew versions of the story are not concerned with the question of credibility, perhaps because the story is related by a religious figure whose trustworthiness derives from his authority (Rabbi Judah and Rabbi Hayyim Vital) or because it is contained in a written source (*Sefer Hasidim* or *Hemdat Yamim*) and is thus not based on oral testimony, as the European parallels are. Another difference is the nature of the procession: wagon riders or drawers of plows, as opposed to a procession of warrior-knights. The change was almost certainly made in the medieval period, as the story in *Sefer Hasidim* relates, and is characteristic of the adoption of European traditions by Jewish communities. Jews had no interest in the warlike nature of Christian society, and thus the protagonists of such stories underwent a transformation into civilian guise. Rabbi Judah, or the tradition that he heard, focused on that group in the procession of the dead that was closest to his own view of the world, as a Jew living in Christian society. From *Sefer Hasidim* the tradition passed into the Safed narrative traditions.

The procession of the dead does not simply fall under the category of *mirabilia* (marvels), which reflect medieval mentality and the then deep-seated belief in a world of the dead and of demons who could return to this world. Its primary importance lies in the role it played at around the time of the year 1000, the millennium, and in the reasons it spread widely. It is the nature of folk traditions of religious and ideological content that they explain themselves. In keeping with this, in the first textual witness, that of Orderic Vitalis, the moral tenor of the story is on display. It is constructed according to the conceptual model of "measure for measure." This is the model of many other stories of this time, the most important of them being depictions of hell, where sinners are punished in accordance with the severity of their crimes—for example, gossips hang by their tongues, adulterers by their genitals, sinful women by their nipples. In the procession of the dead we see the same phenomenon: Those who have spilled blood are punished with blood; those who wore finery are clothed in glowing coals; adulterous women are seated on red-hot nails. Judah's story reflects the same concept: "He who does a beastly act in his life must work in that world as a beast."[35] In all these medieval traditions, the dead have not yet reached hell. They undergo horrible suffering outside the underworld, which like all suffering rectifies and purifies them. Schmitt notes that the procession functions, in many cases, as a "purgatory in motion." Like those two central concepts in medieval mentality, hell and purgatory, the purpose of the procession is to paint in bold colors the fate of sinners and to provide credible "recipes" for sins and the punishments meted out for them.[36]

A highly significant similarity between the European Wild Hunt traditions and the Hebrew story is the plea of the dead men in the procession to the human observer that he take action to rescue them from their plight. In another version of "The Wild Hunt," Count Emicho, who died in or around 1117, appears before a congregation of worshippers in church and explains to them that their prayers and donations can help save him from the procession of the dead. Another monk, who saw his beloved brother in the procession, celebrated masses, and the brother later appeared to him to thank him for rescuing him. The Safed story also posits that the living can affect the fate of the dead in the next world. But here also lies the difference between the two: The dead in the Safed story do not ask Abulafia to pray for them. Instead, he is to conduct a reparation ritual, one involving him personally, to be dictated to him by another spiritual authority, Luria. In other words, he must apply a rectification on himself so that they too can be rectified.[37]

This important difference between the medieval European traditions and the Safed legend is not necessarily a product of the move from Christian to Jewish culture. It can be found in Jewish culture itself. As we have seen in the Tale of the Tanna and the Dead Man, current from the time of the Gaonim, the *tanna* who encounters the dead man is not involved personally in the dead man's fate. He himself does not require rectification or purification of any sort but is simply asked to pray (or to see to it that prayers are said) to save the dead man from his punishment.

The change evident in the Safed tradition seems to be the product of two factors. The first is the fundamental messianic view of Lurianic Kabbalah, which requires every individual Jew to take part in the process of rectification and redemption. The sinners in the story who have been reincarnated as oxen are essentially divine sparks that have fallen among the shells. Thus Abulafia's personal rectification can extricate them. The fundamental Lurianic belief in the duty of each individual to participate in the process of rectification and redemption is almost certainly one of the reasons for the fundamental difference between the Safed legend and its parallels. But there is another reason, one having to do with the figure of Abulafia himself. In the parallel versions the people who saw and reported the procession of the dead were monks, priests, or, in the Jewish case, a *tanna*. All are figures whose merits save the dead from their fate. In contrast, in the Safed story the witness, Abulafia, is a figure little valued by Luria's circle, and the story's demand for him to apply a rectification on himself before the rectification of the dead derives from the story's desire to demean him and accuse him of sins no less serious than those of the dead who require rectification.

Jean-Claude Schmitt and others who have studied the European traditions of the Wild Hunt have noted an interesting historical fact: These stories reemerged and then vanished again over the course of the period extending from the eleventh to the thirteenth centuries in a cycle connected to the strength and stability of the central government in the areas where the stories appeared. When conflict between the king and the feudal aristocracy and knights weakened central authority and undermined confidence in the king's ability to provide security, reports of sightings of the Wild Hunt increased. The more that secular rulers and the church were at odds, the less secure individuals and communities felt and the more current the story of the Wild Hunt became, with witnesses saying that they had seen the leaders involved in these political conflicts in the procession. The stories may well have served, among other things, as a propaganda tool in violent clashes and political skirmishes, or perhaps they functioned as a kind of mental pressure valve for releasing anxieties and uncertainties during times of danger and leadership vacuums, both secular and religious. What this tells us about the Safed tradition is that it has multifaceted meanings.[38]

As I have already noted, the Tale of the Oxen does not appear in the earliest cycle of *Shivkhei ha-'Ari* stories. It is apparently a later tradition, closely connected to the figure of Rabbi Hayyim Vital. I have suggested that Vital created it toward the end of his life, during the first two decades of the seventeenth century. All that remained of Safed's great age then was a memory, which its acolytes, Vital first among them, sought to glorify and extol. Abulafia, a dominant and authoritative figure in the Damascus Jewish community at that time, had lived in Safed as a young man and had participated in its spiritual life. But, as we now know, he challenged the mystification of Safed, including the legends, beliefs, and rituals that Vital sought to transplant from Safed to Damascus in an effort to recreate the Galilean city's ambience and found it again as a myth. For Vital, the wonders of Safed faded into the distance and the sharp lines of what had really happened there blurred. He was almost certainly not alone in experiencing this. His attempts to revive and recreate that experience in Damascus were met by opposition and even derision. Recall his recurring dreams in which Luria appears to him and rebukes him for not persuading the Jews of Damascus to repent their ways and for neglecting his destiny. Vital protested that the Damascenes did not listen to him and that Abulafia was leading the opposition. He felt helpless and unconfident in his ability to carry out the mission to which he had devoted his life. It was a painful dissolution of what Safed had meant to him and to other believers, and it was caused by opponents like Abulafia.

This sense of instability, the challenge to the standing of an authoritative figure—his master and teacher, Isaac Luria—and the loss of personal and social security were shared by Hayyim Vital and the European societies in which the Wild Hunt stories appeared. Folklorists have shown that periods of instability and social crisis produce stories of demonic possession. This is how we should understand the development of the Safed legends and the way they reflect personal and public coping with the Safed myth at the beginning of the seventeenth century.

"Toro muerto, vaca es" (A Dead Ox Is a Cow)

There is another, seemingly marginal difference between the story as it appears in *Sefer Hasidim* and the legend in praise of Luria. In Rabbi Judah's story, the beasts are cows, whereas Abulafia relates that he encountered oxen. Demons in the form of cows trampling the soul of the sinner in hell are an inseparable part of the story, because they fit the acronym taken from the biblical verse "You shall not round off the side-growth on your head, or destroy the side-growth of your beard" (Leviticus 19:27). Their replacement by oxen in the Safed story disregards the ancient acronym but fits its moral content. We have already seen that Rabbi Judah stresses, in connection with the version of the Procession of the Dead story that he offers in *Sefer Hasidim*, that a person who acts like a beast in life should not be surprised to find that his fate in the next world is a beastly one. That being the case, it hardly makes a difference whether the sinners have turned into cows or oxen. The question is the subject of an interesting discussion in one of the ethical books from the Safed period, *Sefer Kharedim* by Rabbi Eleazar Azkari, one of the most influential and important figures of Safed's golden age. In Chapter 7 of *Sefer Kharedim*, Azkari discusses the punishments meted out to sinners after their deaths. Regarding the fate of evildoers who burn in hell, he writes:

> And after spending a set time in hell, in accordance with his sin, God returns his soul in a reincarnation in this world, reincarnated as a worshipper of stars and constellations, who are considered beasts, or as a beast or animal or bird which He, may He be blessed, assigned [man] to rule over them all, as it is written, "You have made him master over your handiwork" [Psalms 8:7]. And he has acted as a beast, and has been brought down to the level of a beast, as it is said, "Let us make man in our image, after our likeness" [Genesis 1:26].... As in his life he did not devote his heart to the honor and glory of his majesty which is the image of the honored and terrible God and marred the image of the king and was like the beasts and did their deeds, after his death he will return him to the world incarnated in the image and likeness of the beasts.[39]

The theological concept at the basis of Azkari's account explains Rabbi Judah's argument and connects the sin to marring God's creation. Because the sinner has done this, God punishes him in kind after his death. The sinner preferred the likeness of a beast to that of his creator, so he returns to the world as a beast. The principal difference between Rabbi Judah's and Azkari's accounts have to do with the concept of reincarnation. Rabbi Judah speaks of the sinner turning into a beast *after his death* (his meaning is not clear, because he does not explicitly state that the sinner took on the form of a beast, only that demons in the form of beasts trample him). In contrast, Azkari stresses that the soul of the sinner is *reincarnated* as a beast and as such returns to the world of the living. In other words, the sinner's soul continues to live in this world, in accordance with the kabbalistic doctrine of reincarnation, but it inhabits a beast in punishment for its behavior in its previous incarnation.

At this point Azkari offers a list of sinners and their reincarnations. A man who has relations with another man is reincarnated as a hare or rabbit; one who has sexual relations with a beast is reincarnated as a bat; one who has relations with another animal or bird returns as a raven; one who has relations with a married woman returns as an ass, and so on. The real sins, in his view, are sexual ones; Rabbi Hayyim Vital accused the people of Damascus of these kinds of transgressions. For Luria's fellowship (but not just for them), these were the really serious offenses, as we will see in Chapter 5. It must be, then, that the sin of shaving one's sidelocks is in the language of Luria's circle a euphemism for another, much more serious sin, one of a sexual nature.

Immediately following his list of sexual sins and reincarnations, Azkari tells another story that, surprisingly, links this topic to the Tale of the Oxen.

> It happened in Castile that an ox was designated for the worshipers of stars and constellations for their sport, in which they were accustomed to beat and torture it. On that day, on that night, a Jewish man had a dream and saw his father, who said to him, "Know, my son, that for my many sins they have reincarnated me after my death as an ox, and it is the ox designated tomorrow for torture and horrible agonies in these people's games. Therefore, my son, redeem and save me, that I might flee through that place before they kill me and before they devour me, and you will redeem me, and

have no thought for your money, and slaughter that ox in a kosher manner, and have poor Torah scholars eat of it. So I have been informed by heaven and they have allowed me to tell you, and by this my soul will again ascend from its incarnation as a beast and be incarnated as a man, and I will have the privilege of serving God, with God's help. And many such stories happened in Israel, ask your father and he will tell you, your elders and they will explain to you" (Deuteronomy 32:7).[40]

It may be that this is the missing link between Rabbi Judah's story of the cows and Luria's Tale of the Oxen. The story told by Azkari belongs to the Spanish period, and just as it was familiar to Azkari, it must have been known to many other Spanish exiles and their descendants in Safed, as the final sentence in the passage indicates. The story describes, perhaps the first time the subject appears in Hebrew literature, a custom still observed in provincial Spain and Provence: the *Encierro*, or the running of the bulls.[41] In this event, bulls are chased through a city's streets until they are slaughtered and eaten in a great ceremony. This short story tells us what the local Jews thought of this popular entertainment of their Christian neighbors. The verbs relating to torture, persecution, and suffering indicate the deeper meaning of the story for the Jews; they tell the story from the point of view of the bull, not of its pursuers. They may perhaps unconsciously have seen themselves in the role of the martyred, pursued, anguished, and slaughtered bull. They did not take part in the joy of the Gentiles who chased the bull down with such relish.

Studies of this element of Spanish tradition claim that the chasing of the bulls should not be seen as a battle or a game but rather as a religious ritual.[42] The running of the bulls (and the bullfight) has its roots in popular religion, originally as a fertility ritual growing out of folk beliefs regarding the bull's great virility. The ritual sacrifice of the bull symbolizes the desire to transfer its virility to the members of the community and its fertility to the land, which is the source of their livelihood.[43] Some scholars make a distinction between the bull (*taurus*), an animal venerated for its virility and fertility, and the ox, which is a bull that has been castrated so that it can be domesticated and used as a plow animal. Most Hebrew texts do not make this distinction, so in Azkari's text the bull being fought is an ox. But even if the terminology is imprecise, it is clear that Hebrew writers have always been well aware of the difference between the bull who fights in the arena and inseminates herds of cows with its impressive virility, and the castrated oxen who are yoked to a plow or a wagon and draw it docilely.

Scholars of the romantic worldview of the seventeenth and eighteenth centuries have noted that the huge bull symbolizes untamed, primal nature as well as the "mythical" ancient civilizations before their emasculation by modern culture. In contrast, the ox is a domestic draft animal that symbolizes the devitalization of nature by humankind. In this sense, the difference between the ox in Azkari's story and the oxen in Luria's story is hugely significant. Azkari's ox is a belligerent creature, full of vigor, whereas the oxen in Luria's legend plow the earth, tamely harnessed to a plow. In other words, they are actually cows, as in the ancient Spanish proverb that serves as the heading for this section. These are the cows that appear in Rabbi Judah's story.[44]

In psychoanalytic terms the bull symbolizes the male and the father. It is a sensual and symbolic expression of the virility that the young boy fears and unconsciously desires, wishing for it to shift from the father to himself.[45] In Azkari's story these unconscious wishes hardly need bold interpretation, given that they are entirely transparent. The bull is indeed the father, and its capture by the son and its slaughter and consumption in a public ceremony explicitly expresses such secret and repressed wishes regarding the father figure. (Keep in mind that, in the Safed context, the consumption, by pure and righteous people, of a beast in which a sinner's soul has been reincarnated has further meaning, connected to the Lurianic doctrine of reincarnation.[46]) How can an enormous bull, galloping through the streets with dozens pursuing it, elicit associations with one's father? Does the bull remind the dreamer of his father's strength, authority, or violence? In the story the father confesses that he has sinned but offers no details. As we have seen, just a few paragraphs before this tale Azkari lists severe sexual sins. They apparently apply to the father's deeds, because the story is related in the same context. In other words, the father in life had been

The Myth and Its Disenchantment • 81

a "bull," violent and engaging in indiscriminate forbidden sexual acts. His son fears him but is also drawn to him and admires his strength and power. It would be hard to find a more explicit example than this story of Freud's claim that dreams are in fact wish fulfillment.[47]

Azkari's story of the running of the bulls can, from another angle, explain Vital's attraction-repulsion and love-hate relationship with Abulafia, expressed so potently on many pages of *Sefer haHezyonot*. Similarly, the symbiotic connection between Abulafia and the oxen he is sent to perform rectification for is clear in light of the Lurianic doctrine of reincarnation, as we have already seen. Abulafia is sent to perform rectification for the oxen because he is of the root of their souls; he too shares that taurine nature of wild power and sexual potency, with all it implies. These two factors—seeing Abulafia as a bull and the uncontrollable fear and veneration he arouses in Vital—lead to the inevitable conclusion that, for Vital, Abulafia was a father figure.

The prime conscious father figure who is the object of Vital's desire is Luria. *Sefer haHezyonot* documents many instances of Luria appearing to him in dreams. At times, Luria reproves him; sometimes he offers support, hurries him, or shows him the way to go. But Abulafia is a more dominant father figure, because he was present in Vital's life for at least thirty years, whereas Vital knew Luria for less than two years. Abulafia was also close to Luria, as an equal, not as a disciple, and almost certainly enjoyed a higher standing in Safed. After the end of Safed's golden age he continued to enjoy that status, making him the true representative of the city's greatness and influence. Vital's attraction to Abulafia, at the same time that he profoundly feared him, is evident on the symbolic level as well. Would Abulafia, who in his person and social standing represented Safed in its greatness, recognize Vital as an equal, alongside him, in the Safed myth? His blunt rejection of Vital's request demonstrates how deep an antipathy Vital developed for him.

In short, what seemed like just another legend of praise for Luria in fact chronicles a harsh polemic of significant personal and social dimensions. As an expressive genre, the legend does not "reflect" historical events, as Benayahu and Scholem thought. Instead, it expresses them, engaging in a keen dialogue and taking a clear position about what happened. If, as I have suggested, this legend was indeed composed by Hayyim Vital during the final period of his life in Damascus, it expresses, on the one hand, the immensity of his personal failure to carry out the great mission assigned to him by Luria: to bring about the repentance of the Jewish people as the first stage in bringing about the messianic redemption, according to Lurianic messianic doctrine. Yet, on the other hand, the legend also shows Vital carrying out a rearguard action to assert Safed's place—that is, the place of the Safed myth—in Jewish national and religious consciousness.

3

In Fields and Wilderness

> And [Luria] disclosed most of his secrets in the fields and wilderness and did not need any book.
>
> —Shlumil of Dreznitz, first letter

Safed Stories as Local Legends

The principal and oldest sources of the legends about Rabbi Isaac Luria, as they have come down to us, are the four letters that Shlumil of Dreznitz sent home to Europe beginning in the summer of 1607 (we know of four; there may have been others that have been lost). By his own account, Shlumil heard of Luria's deeds from men and women in Safed, both learned and lay. Such stories, told and retold, serve as testimonies about incidents surrounding a revered figure; folklore scholars call them legends. A legend has three components: (1) It is grounded in a known and well-defined historical time; (2) it takes place in an identifiable geographic space; and (3) the community that listens to the legend displays a fundamental belief in the events related. The narrative center of gravity divides legends into three principal subcategories: (1) historical legends, in which the story gives prominent place to a significant historical event; (2) local legends, which are centered on a place or an object in a place known to the listeners (e.g., a tree, well, wadi, a rock with an exceptional shape); and (3) belief legends, in which the narrative shape of the story highlights a folk belief important to the community that tells the story.[1]

Legends of Safed, like every other assemblage of legends, exhibit all three of these types. Yet the Safed legends are conspicuously ahistorical. They contain almost no references to social or political events, and not much can be learned from them about the history of the Safed community. The same is true with regard to the belief component. Clearly, the community that related the legends of Safed believed them to be factually true—that was the case at the beginning of the seventeenth century and continues to be the case among broad portions of the Jewish people today.[2]

Nevertheless, no particular belief stands at the center of these legends, such as a belief in demons or folk healing. The legends do not provide a foundation for or disseminate such tenets. They are fundamentally saints' legends—tales of praise—that branch off in different ways from the historical legend subgenre. Instead of focusing on the historical event, they place a saintly figure at their center.[3]

In this chapter I argue that the Safed legends are not fundamentally hagiographic praise stories but rather local-geographic ones. As proof, I submit that the corpus contains dozens of stories about other exceptional figures, among them Joseph Karo, Shlomo Alkabetz, Moshe Cordovero, Hayyim Vital, and Avraham Halevy Baruchin. What all these legends have in common with the legends about Luria is not, of course, their protagonist; nor is it a shared historical moment. Rather, it is a place—Safed. Another piece of evidence is the prominence given to this location in *Shivkhei ha-'Ari* (i.e., the stories collected by Shlumil of Dreznitz in his letters). Although Luria spent most of his life in Egypt and Jerusalem and only two years in Safed, *Shivkhei ha-'Ari* offers only two or three stories about these earlier periods in his life, amid dozens that take place in Safed. Furthermore, the first person to set down these stories, Shlumil of Dreznitz, who came to Safed from Moravia nearly thirty years after Luria's death, was drawn to the city because it was the cradle of Kabbalah he had longed for in distant Europe. On top of this, even a casual reader of the Safed legends, in any of the formats in which they have been preserved, cannot help but note the local elements that are central to the stories: mountains and orchards, caves, springs, tombs, roads, fields, and especially the streets and houses of Safed. Clearly, the Safed legends are primarily *local legends*. Viewing them in this light led me to read them not as they have been read thus far, as saints' legends about Luria, but rather through the prism of the holy place. I seek the ways in which the geographic space and Safed as a location have shaped the stories and what this can teach us about their significance in Safed's life and culture.

The Axis of the World

One of the best-known Safed legends is told by Shlumil of Dreznitz in his first letter. He saw the legend as one of the most important testimonies about Luria, because it exemplifies his moral behavior. I quote it from the initial source of Shlumil's letters, *Kitvei Shevah yekar uGedulat haAri*, which was copied into a book written by Yosef Shmuel Rofe (YaSha"R) of Kandia (Crete), *Ta'alumot Khokhma*, published in Basel in 1629.

> My purpose is to inform you, your eminence, of two great events from among the awe-inspiring deeds that took place during the time of Luria of blessed memory, for they testify to the power of charity, and happy is he who performs his actions in the name of heaven. Once Luria of blessed memory sat in a field near Safed with his ten chosen students, and he preached and revealed secrets of the Torah to them. In the middle of his homily he said to them, "My companions, I hear the voice of a herald who is standing and calling out in the skies above in the court above, and his voice is going through all the heavens and saying these words: 'This sentence is decreed by the Watchers; This verdict is commanded by the Holy Ones [Daniel 4:14] that countless locusts will come to the environs of Safed and eat all the vegetation and all the fruit of their [the people of Safed's] soil, no sustenance will remain for all its inhabitants. This is because of one poor scholar whose name is Rabbi Ya'akov Altaratz who sits and bellows against the Holy One, Blessed Be He, and the Holy One, Blessed Be He cannot hold back any longer about all his bad neighbors who live in Safed who do not take notice of him.'" This is the language of the herald. Said Luria of blessed memory, "My sons, for God's sake, quickly collect from among us a good gift, and we will send it to him. Perhaps God will turn back from the thing he said he would

do to his people." Immediately they collected something like three thalers from among them, and the rabbi sent them with one of his students, whose name was his excellency, our teacher Rabbi Yitzhak Cohen of blessed memory. And his excellency our teacher Rabbi Yitzhak Cohen of blessed memory quickly went and entered the home of the poor man and found him sitting and weeping. He said to him, "Why are you weeping?" He said to him, "I am weeping about my bad fortune, that the clay jugs I always filled with water for the whole week have broken, and now that they have broken, how will I buy more? I sat and wept before God, may he be blessed, why must I be in such great duress, and am I more evil than the rest of the world?!" When his excellency our teacher Cohen heard these words from the poor man, he wondered how correct the words of the rabbi were. And he gave him the coins and said to him, "My wise sir, for God's sake take care from here on out against bellowing against the attributes of the Holy One, Blessed Be He, as was the case." And that poor scholar who was sitting and weeping and, as it were, bellowing against the attributes, thanked him and promised not to do this anymore and prayed before God for him to forgive him and to rescind the evil he had decreed. And Rabbi Yitzhak Cohen returned to the place where the rabbi and companions sat and told them what had happened, and all the companions wondered about the great discernment of their master. Luria, may peace be upon him, said that the decree had been canceled, thank God, and they returned to their study. And they had sat for about two hours when they raised their eyes and saw locusts coming in a great host, very heavy, and all the students were fearful. The rabbi said to them, "Do not fear, for the decree has been canceled and we have reconciled the poor man and from now on there is nothing evil, thank God," and so it was. They [the locusts] were all carried by the wind into the Great Sea and there they drowned, and not one of them reached the land. And from that day onward, all the inhabitants of Safed, may be it be built and established quickly in our day, have seen to that poor man and provided all his needs. And in truth that poor man is a pious man, erudite in all of the Torah, and I know him and today he is the head of the court in Sini, which is called Tripoli, in Syria.[4]

The story's final sentence is a classic example of the way trust is gained in the legend as a literary genre. Shlumil, the narrator, sends his story to readers who are both geographically and mentally distant from Safed. To make it seem reliable, he hangs his story on his personal acquaintance with one of its characters, indicating that he has vetted the story and would not have passed it on had he not been persuaded that it was true.

The legend has a clear spatial structure, which constitutes the basis for understanding it and the principal means for interpreting it. Luria and his quorum of students are sitting outside Safed, on an open plain looking down on the city, in sight of the old wall that still stood at the end of the sixteenth century, and on the city's jumble of densely packed buildings. From a distance the structures look like a single large block made up of a variety of architectural forms with both sharp and rounded contours. Facing it is an invisible space, "in the skies above in the court above," where a divine herald is calling out, "and his voice is going through all the heavens." The text then zooms in for a close-up on a single home in a single alley in which the indigent Ya'akov Altaratz sits. The story offers such a close-up three times: first through Luria's vision, which offers a detailed account of what he saw; second through the story of his disciple Yitzhak Cohen, whom Luria sent to the poor man with the contribution the company had raised for him; and a third time through the disciple's narration to his companions after he returns to them.[5]

Another component that plays a role in the spatial shaping of the story is the motion of the locusts. The swarm appears on the horizon, almost certainly from the east (as in the case of the plague of locusts in Egypt, which serves as a model for the Safed story),[6] and then disappears in the west, over the Mediterranean, which can be seen on a clear day from some of the peaks around Safed.

The narrative space is thus defined by three principal coordinates. One stretches between Luria's fellowship and the city; a second between this world and the heavenly world, with its heavenly court; and a third, which is marked by the appearance of the locusts in the east and their disappearance in the west.

But this provides only the first part of the spatial analysis. As Gabriel Zoran puts it:

> The concept "field of vision," as its name suggests, has a strongly cognitive aspect. It belongs to the plane of the textual organization of the space, a plane that has to do with the space as it is organized linguistically in the text. But opposite this plane stands another, that of the ontological organization. . . . The level of textual organization addresses the space as an object that can be recreated and the recreation process itself; the plane of ontological organization addresses the nature of the space *after* it has been recreated.[7]

The first ontological level is that between heaven and earth. The heavens look down on events on earth and respond to them. The nature of the vertical heaven-earth or God-human axis is one of reward and punishment. God responds to human actions immediately, equitably, and evenhandedly, tit for tat. When a sin is committed on earth, heaven sends down a punishment on the vertical axis. Furthermore, the punishment itself has a vertical nature—locusts appear in the sky and descend on the land. As in the Bible, locust swarms are the rod with which God punishes humanity.[8]

A horizontal axis crosses these two vertical ones—the gaze of Luria's fellowship on Safed. The close-up shot of the city is seen through Luria's eyes, but he does not stop with what can be seen on the outside. He penetrates into the city's moral interior and bids his disciples' gazes to follow. The true Safed is not what we readers see from a distant, external perspective; rather, it is that taken in by the Lurianic close-up. That shot makes Luria and his fellowship aware that Altaratz's "bad neighbors . . . in Safed . . . do not take notice of him."[9] Luria's close-up reveals a fundamental moral flaw in the city that severs the vertical axis. The connection between heaven and earth requires the moral integrity of the horizontal human space. The fellowship, under Luria's guidance, acts to repair the axis that connects the human with the divine. Once it is repaired, the direction of the axis of punishment—that is, the swarm of locusts—also changes. Instead of moving vertically, between heaven and earth, it moves horizontally, from east to the sea.

On the ontological level the story thus structures a sharply contoured *moral space*. The intersection of the vertical and horizontal axes is *the place where Luria and his fellowship are seated*. The axis connecting heaven and earth reaches down to them, and the horizontal axis originates from them and stretches to the city and its sins. It is at this spot that the locusts are diverted from the vertical to the horizontal axis: "a great storm rose and bore the locusts and hurled them into the sea." In other words, Luria's fellowship is the *axis mundi*, the center point of the entire universe, conceived of as a moral space. They receive the message of God and put it into operation in the human space. This is what Luria tells his disciples at the end of the story: "Then the rabbi said to the comrades, 'Blessed are you as for your sake the decree was revoked.'"[10]

This spatial analysis of the story shows that Luria's fellowship placed itself at the intersection of the principal axes that define Safed's space. Although they are part of Safed society (the horizontal axis), they are also exceptional, inasmuch as they also belong to the divine reality (the vertical axis). This special status grants them the power to repair flaws and the key to changing the world. The story's ostensible purpose is, as Shlumil declares, to advertise the power of charity. But it is actually a powerful expression of the way Luria's disciples see their position in Safed society and their role as a vanguard in the most profound sense of the word.

The same fellowship stands at the center of another story, one of the best-known tales from *Shivkhei ha-'Ari*. In Shlumil of Dreznitz's first letter, it appears just a few sentences after the Tale of the Locusts (in the fourth letter, the two stories appear one right after the other). Shlumil of Dreznitz there claims that Luria is the Messiah ben Yosef.

> And he is seen as such in another story. Once, on the eve
> of the Sabbath, close to the arrival of the bride [i.e., the

beginning of the Sabbath], he went outside the city of Safed with his disciples dressed in four white garments: a robe and capote and shirt and pants to welcome the Sabbath. They began the psalm "Ascribe to the Lord O divine beings" [Psalm 29] and the song sung for welcoming the Sabbath, and "A Psalm, a song for the Sabbath day" [Psalm 92] and "The Lord is king" [Psalm 93] with pleasant melodies. And as they sang the Rabbi said to his students, "My companions, would you like us to go to Jerusalem before the Sabbath and do the Sabbath in Jerusalem?" And Jerusalem is more than twenty-five parasangs [about 100 miles] from Safed. Some of the students responded, "We would like that." Some of them responded by saying, "We will first go and inform our wives." Since they said they would go first to their homes, the Rabbi was overcome with a great fear and clapped his hands and said, "Woe to us that we did not have the merit to be redeemed, had you all responded unanimously that you want to go with great joy, all of Israel would immediately have been redeemed, as this was the hour of redemption, and because you turned it down the Exile has returned to its full power as a result of our many transgressions."[11]

The story has a spatial structure similar to that of the Tale of the Locusts. The fellowship stands outside the city, apparently on one of the mountains around Safed, overlooking the city wall ("And he would always situate himself on a mountain outside the city and from there he could see the entire cemetery of Safed," relates the fourth letter). In other words, the fellowship here fixes the city in its gaze, just as it does in the Tale of the Locusts. Here, too, an axis stretches between heaven and earth, revealed by Luria's declaration that the hour of redemption is this very moment. However, the third axis is different—it stretches between Safed and Jerusalem, the place of the vision of the End of Days. Unlike the vertical axis described by the swarm of locusts, a path of punishment and destruction, here the horizontal axis is one of rebirth and redemption. In both stories the three axes intersect in the fellowship, at a point that is not a geographic location but rather an ontological one. This group of men holds the future redemption in their hands. As in the Tale of the Locusts, the fate of the world depends on a horizontal human axis stretching between the fellowship and the city of Safed. In the Tale of the Locusts the fellowship serves as a moral exemplar for the Safed community, acting as a vanguard. In the messianic story of the frustrated trip to Jerusalem, some members of the fellowship prefer to make their way back to their community—that is, to return to their homes—and thus lose, by their own doing, the special pioneering status of an elect fraternity that stands at the forefront of society.

The concept of the fellowship in this messianic story can be seen also in the change that another ancient motif has undergone: that of "path jumping" (*kefitzat haderekh*), enabling miraculous travel between two distant places. Path jumping, a pervasive Jewish folk motif, is always individual, happening to a saint or a commoner who uses the Tetragrammaton to magically transport himself instantly to another place for some important purpose, for example, to save lives or to prevent the desecration of the Sabbath. That is also the case in a similarly messianic story, the Tale of the Goat, familiar from its modern adaptation by Shmuel Yosef Agnon. There the travel is accomplished by means of underground tunnels through which, according to tradition, the remains of Jews from all over the world will roll to the Holy Land to be resurrected when the Messiah arrives (*gilgiul mekhilot*). But the Safed story is different. Here the actor is not an individual; it is the fellowship. The path can contract only when everyone takes part; when some demure, it does not happen.[12]

In this tale the fellowship's adherence to the horizontal path that leads to the city causes it to lose two other paths that had been open to it: the road to Jerusalem and the conduit connecting it to heaven. In spatial terms the fellowship sinned by preferring the horizontal axis between the fellowship and the city (i.e., the material life, as the people of Safed called everyday activities, the life of their families and community) to the vertical axis connecting the fellowship to the heavenly Jerusalem (i.e., full devotion to holiness and the messianic speculations).

In these two stories the fate of the world lies in the hands of an elect group. Their success sweeps all of Jewish society along in their wake (in the Tale of the Locusts), and their failure constitutes a failure of society as a whole (as in the messianic story). The fellowship stands at the intersection of the axes that define the spatial structure of the Safed legends. They are the center point of the world.

The Galilee as a Semiotic Space

The Tale of the Locusts is also unique in another way. It harks back to ancient Land of Israel traditions that are documented in the Hebrew Bible and expanded on by later homilists, as we have seen. I do not know of any Diaspora narrative tradition that uses locusts as its central motif. We know that locusts ravaged Europe in the Middle Ages and certainly other Middle Eastern countries, but the Jews in these places took little interest in the phenomenon. They were not part of agricultural society in these places and did not, as in most of the Diaspora, make their livelihood directly from the land. As such, locusts, a natural disaster with a specifically agricultural nature, did not number among the major fears and anxieties of Jews outside the land of their ancestors. The appearance of such a story in the Safed narrative tradition is important because it indicates a close connection between, on the one hand, what is well known about the agricultural nature of the Jewish economy in Safed and its environs in the sixteenth century and, on the other hand, the Galilean Jews' direct dependence on the geographic space in which they resided. The reappearance of the Tale of the Locusts and of the anxieties it represents in Jewish consciousness indicates a new encounter between the geographic reality of the Land of Israel and its transformation, once again, into a symbolic space imbued with meaning.

The great openness that Safed culture of the time displayed to the outdoors, the local landscape, and the natural surroundings is evident not just in the city's legends. In his third letter, Shlumil writes:

> Sometimes [Luria] went with the companions to Meron and he would sit them down on the spot where Rashbi [Rabbi Shimon bar Yohai], may peace be with him, revealed to them the *Idra Raba* [one of the sections of the *Zohar*], and he would say, "Here sat Rabbi El'azar, here sat Rabbi Abba, here sat Rabbi Yehuda," and thus with them all. He sat each one down on the place that befit him, in keeping with

his soul . . . and he would prostrate himself on the grave of the *tanna* and knew how to cleave his spirit to the spirit of the deceased. . . . Once, Luria conveyed to our master, our teacher Rabbi Yitzhak Cohen that he should go to the village of Ein Zeitan, to the headstone of Rabbi Yehuda bar Ila'i and convey to him his interpretation of a certain passage in the *Zohar*. . . . And once an incident happened that he conveyed to our teacher Rabbi Hayyim, may the Merciful protect him and give him long life, a mystical formula, to go [with it] to the village of Akhbara where Abaye and Rabba are buried, and to prostrate himself on their [graves], and they would speak with him and tell him. . . . The two of them [Luria and R. Hayyim Vital] went together to Akhbara to study. At the middle of the way there, Luria, may his memory be a blessing, stood and said, "Here is buried Benayhu ben Yehoyada, may peace be with him," and there was no marker there and no sign of a grave . . . and he also revealed the grave of Kruspedai close to here, which had not been known and [no] marker had ever been placed on it, and it is close to the bank of the river. And the same with the grave of Rabbi Pinhas ben Yair, which no man knew, he, peace be on him, revealed, and the same with untold numbers of other *tanna'im* and prophets whose places of burial he revealed.[13]

The cult of holy graves is one of the most notable rituals that connect religious beliefs and practices to a geographic space. It may be one of the reasons that medieval European Jewish culture was almost devoid of such a cult, to the best of our knowledge, whereas devotions at and pilgrimages to sacred tombs were central to folk Christianity of the time. Jews were certainly aware of these practices among their Christian neighbors, but they crafted no parallel rituals of their own. This cannot be attributed to halakhic strictures, given that folk religion frequently disregards such prohibitions and develops customs and rituals it finds meaningful for its society. An example is the cult of holy graves that emerged among North African Jews in the nineteenth and twentieth centuries, in the face of explicit opposition from their religious leaders. In the East, however, the situation was different. Elhanan Reiner and Josef Meri have documented the *ziara* (pilgrimage) customs of Jewish communities in Egypt, Syria, Lebanon, Iraq, and other places as early as the eleventh and twelfth centuries, as well as the development of the custom of making pilgrimages to the graves of saints in the Land of Israel—most (if not all) of them the same graves mentioned in the writings that emerged from Safed in the sixteenth century. These finds, which predate the period under discussion here, bolster my principal claim. Holy graves and *ziara* practices appear only sporadically and haphazardly in contemporary documents, quite different from the pervasiveness of such customs in Christian Europe or the Muslim East. The fact that pilgrimages to the graves of saints, in the Galilee in particular, grew more frequent in the twelfth century shows that it was the encounter with this specific place that set in motion the intensive spread of the phenomenon.[14] Shlumil of Dreznitz's letters and the testimonies of Luria's disciples and other contemporary figures show that the cult of holy graves intensified and grew qualitatively in an unprecedented way in Safed in particular during the second half of the sixteenth century.[15] As the Jewish inhabitants of Safed and its surrounding villages saw it, holy graves were not destinations for a *ziara*, that is, a pilgrimage from a great distance prompted by a vow or a supplicant's wish to beseech a saint to save him from some trouble. Rather, the graves and the holy figures buried in them were a daily and ongoing presence. The living and the dead resided side by side in a way that is possible only when the connection to place is that of the native rather than the tourist.[16]

The cult of holy graves is not immaterial or intangible; it is inseparably connected to a particular place and can occur only there. The cult of holy graves in Safed emerged as the result of a number of factors—for example, the revitalization of Kabbalah, especially under the influence of Lurianic teachings; the development of the concepts of *devekut* (devotion to the divine) and *tikun* (metaphysical repair or rectification in the spiritual sphere); and, as has recently been proposed, the indirect influence of Sufi mysticism.[17] But such spiritual-intangible concepts could emerge anywhere. It seems that only a conjunction of the kind that happened in Safed—the development of an innovative kabbalistic theory along with the mystical atmosphere surrounding charismatic figures and the encounter with the place itself—can explain the crystallization of the cult of holy graves that would have such a decisive impact on Jewish folk religion in the generations that followed.[18]

A number of testimonies indicate that Shlomo Alkabetz and his student and brother-in-law Moshe Cordovero had, before Luria's arrival in Safed, searched for the graves of Jewish saints in the surroundings and worked to establish rituals connected with them. But these two men are principally known for fashioning an important religious ritual known as *gerushin*, meaning "going into exile," in the area around Safed. According to Cordovero:

> He will be exiled from one place to another in the name of heaven, and in doing so he will make a chariot to the exiled *Shekhinah* [divine presence] and will make himself [as if he were in real exile] . . . and subdue his heart in the exile and establish a connection with the Torah, and then the *Shekhinah* is with him *and he will make himself an exile and exile himself* from his home always, just as Rabbi Shimon [bar Yohai] and his companions did and devoted themselves to Torah. And [it is even better] if he walks a long distance to another place without a horse or conveyance.

Cordovero makes another significant remark along these lines in his *Sefer Geirushin*: "And we reached the village of Biria and entered the synagogue and there we devoted ourselves a bit to the matters of *gerushin* and my teacher [Alkabetz] innovated [the idea] that, especially in the days of summer, without a vow, we would go out for a bit barefoot in the secret of the *Shekhinah*" (in his interpretation of Jeremiah 2:25, going barefoot brings the *Shekhinah* closer).[19]

Zvi Werblowsky argues that the *gerushin* has nothing to do "with romantic views of connecting with nature. It is understood as symbolic participation in the *Shekhinah*'s own exile, as taking part in it."[20] The passages of Cordovero's that I have quoted thus stress the ascetic aspect of the ritual—mourning and exile and even the self-affliction of walking barefoot. Luria and Hayyim Vital, who further elaborated the ritual, saw it in the same way.

> Luria, of blessed memory, would always walk in the wildernesses and on the roads and would reveal awe-inspiring secrets to them, and would say that he did so to unite with the exile of the *Shekhinah* and also to vanquish the shells that reside in the wildernesses.[21]

The two reasons for Luria's behavior offered here need to be understood precisely. The exile of the *Shekhinah* is the factor that led Alkabetz and Cordovero to fashion their ritual of *gerushin*, a symbolic departure from the home and place of habitation meant to simulate the state of the *Shekhinah* in exile. The other reason, vanquishing the shells, emerges from Lurianic Kabbalah, which teaches that the shells (evil) that reside in places of demonic character must be defeated before the divine sparks that have been trapped there can be raised up, which is a necessary condition for the final redemption. In other words, both reasons are manifestly conceptual and ostensibly have no connection to the place in which the *gerushin* or war against the shells is carried out. "Ostensibly" because the question is, Why did these customs and beliefs emerge in Safed at the end of the sixteenth century and not in other places and other times? The only possible answer is the renewed encounter with the Galilee. True, there is evidence that Alkabetz began to develop his ideas about going out into the fields as a spiritual act even before his arrival in the Land of Israel. However, his book *Ayelet Ahavim*, which he finished writing in Adrianople in 1535–1536, and even more so at the famous *tikun* on the night of Shavuot that he and Rabbi Joseph Karo conducted there, prove that he saw himself as already residing in the Land of Israel even though he was physically still in the Exile. The tension that Alkabetz felt with the approach of his encounter with the land is sufficient to explain the development of such a view. It is similar to what happened almost 300 years later in the Hibat Zion movement in Eastern Europe—the longing for Zion and songs of Zion first emerged in Europe, and the poets and their readers saw this as a prelude and preparation for the encounter with the land itself. The same can be said about the agricultural training farms at which the young people of the Second and Third Aliyahs prepared themselves for their move to Palestine. No one would argue that this budding of Jewish agriculture was not connected to these people's impending arrival in the Land of Israel.

There is also the matter of proportion. In his book Alkabetz stresses the spiritual advantages of going out into the field, but it is nothing compared to the huge extent, testified to in many sources, of the observance of this custom immediately following Alkabetz's and Luria's encounter with the Galilee. This was not a romantic unification with nature but a reencounter with a sacred topography, the places in which events of the mythic past had occurred.[22]

Walking barefoot was a characteristic practice. It signifies mourning and is ascetic in nature. So why did Jewish ascetics in Europe not think of doing it? And why wait for the summer and not go out barefoot in the chilly Safed winter, so as to magnify the physical pain? The answer may well be that walking barefoot puts the walker in direct contact with the soil, with all it was in the past and all it signifies in the present. This is why Cordovero stresses that they must perform the *gerushin* "just as Rabbi Shimon [bar Yohai] and his companions did." That is, they are to feel with their bare feet the ground on which Rabbi Shimon and his fellowship trod. Luria later seats his own fellowship on the exact same spot where the heroes of the *Zohar* sat. To this may be added important rituals, hugely influential in subsequent generations, that were innovations of the Safed kabbalists, such as *Tikun Khatzot* and ceremonial observance of Tu Bishevat (the fifteenth of the month of Shevat). The crystallization of these customs cannot be understood without reference to the emotional encounter with the Holy Land. The Upper Galilee offered contact with the ancient myths of the *tanna'im* and *amora'im* who, according to the Safed mystics, were the creators of the Kabbalah and the founding fathers of Jewish mystical life.[23] According to Bracha Zak, Rabbi Moshe Cordovero's view was that "the living and the dead in the Land of Israel connect to the *Shekhinah* not *in lieu* of *real* Land of Israel but *through it*."[24] Zak, examining the mystical thinking of one of the founders of Safed culture in the sixteenth century, offers a final proof that only the encounter with the Galilee, rather than any mystical speculations, could explain these rituals and beliefs.

A World Full of Souls

The space between Safed and the higher site outside the city where Luria's fellowship gathered stands at the center of the discussion of two of the stories adduced here. This same space is the subject of a strange depiction that Shlumil of Dreznitz offers in his fourth letter.

> And a disciple of Luria, the sage R. Gedaliya Halevy, told me that, in the days of Luria, the righteous of blessed memory, on each Sabbath eve, when they went outside the city to welcome the Sabbath, the perfect sage, the righteous of blessed memory, would tell his disciples about the awesome and wonderful things he saw each day, time after time, and he would always place himself on a certain mountain that was outside the city, and there he viewed the entire cemetery of Safed and saw hosts of souls rising from their graves into the Garden of Eden above, and also the opposite; he saw myriads who descended against them [to the ground, in the direction of the fellowship], and these were the excess souls that are added to the people of Israel on the Sabbath [according to the Kabbalah, the souls of Jews are enhanced with sanctity on the Sabbath, because of the illumination that descends on the soul]. In the confusion and mixture of souls and hosts there, his eyes dimmed and could not see and he had to close his eyes, and nevertheless saw all the things, with closed eyes.
>
> And once again Luria, the righteous of blessed memory, went to study Torah with his disciples in a field, and he saw that multitudes of souls sat in the trees above them, and also there was a creek close by, and he saw that thousands and myriads of souls were floating and flowing on the surface of the water. Because he saw them, he asked what their nature was, and they responded that they had heard that he and his holiness could repair them and that they were souls who had been thrust outside the *pargod* [the curtain or veil that surrounds the divine presence] for not having performed

repentance, and [they told him also] of the reincarnations they had gone through in this world. And the holy sage promised to do everything possible to raise them up. And afterward the sage related this to his disciples, because they had seen him asking [questions] and responding, but did not know what [it was], and he recounted to them the entire event.[25]

Wandering souls seeking repair play an important role in Lurianic teachings, and that is certainly the principal background for the type of mystical vision described here.[26] But that is not a sufficient or satisfactory explanation; the dozens of Safed stories about souls inhabiting not just the air but also animals, plants, and inanimate objects demonstrate that the motif found its way into almost every aspect of Safed life, as is evident in the following stories.

In the first story, Luria and his disciples are studying one evening when a large billy goat pushes the door open, enters, and approaches Luria (according to some versions of the story, the goat places his two forelegs on the table around which the fellowship is studying), whispers something in the master's ear, and leaves. Luria orders Rabbi Hayyim Vital to buy the goat at any price. Because the goat is not for sale, Vital has to pay a high sum for it. Luria orders one of his students to slaughter the goat, which willingly extends his neck for the purpose. Then Luria orders his disciples to eat the meat while engaging in special *kavanot* (meditations focused on a word or name of God). He explains to them that the soul of a ritual slaughterer had been reincarnated in the goat. The slaughterer had used a faulty knife in his work and had thus caused his fellow Jews to sin by consuming improperly slaughtered and thus forbidden meat. The soul had come to Luria to be repaired by means of slaughter with a lawful blade. That same night the slaughterer appears to Luria in a dream and thanks him for saving him from a harsh judgment.[27]

In another story Luria orders his disciples to prepare for a discussion of a passage from the *Zohar*. They find no difficulty in the passage even after reading it through several times. When they stand before Luria and begin relating the results of their study, "many fowl appeared and crowed so loudly that they could be heard far off, and when the rabbi heard their voices, he laughed and said to his companions, 'Know that these fowl are the souls of righteous people who have come from the heavenly yeshiva to tell you that you are mistaken about this passage.'" When he reveals the real interpretation of the passage, they fall at his feet and say, "Long live the king, may you see offspring and have a long life."

In yet another story Luria and his disciples go to Ein Zeitun to prostrate themselves on the grave of Rabbi Yehudah bar 'Ila'i. "When they reached the olive and fig trees that stood close to this grave marker, a raven came and rested on the branch of a tree facing the rabbi, and called out several times." The rabbi identifies the raven as Shabbetai, the tax collector from Safed, whom everyone knew as an evil man who dealt cruelly with the poor. According to the rabbi, he had been reincarnated as a raven because "he would take their clothing off them and the collateral [they had given] from their hands. He was punished for this suffering by being reincarnated as a raven, and he asked me to pray for him." Luria sends him away.

Similarly, once the fellowship saw "two ravens on a tree, plucked of their feathers. The rabbi said, 'These two ravens are Balaam and Balak, who have been taken from hell to be sent to another, worse hell, and they have come to me to overcome my revulsion of them so that I may pray for them.'" Luria refuses to do so because they had sought to uproot the Children of Israel. He chastises them and sends them away.

Another story has Luria telling his disciples that a certain man who had been a great villain and informer "had, because of his sin, been reincarnated as a mouse." He instructs his students to prepare a mousetrap, and when the mouse is caught in it, Luria tells him:

> "Villain, what did you think when you were in this world informing on poor Jews, that there was no judgment in heaven?" He responded and said, "I have sinned, my lord, forgive me and pray to God to remove me from this trap and I will go to hell and receive punishment there and not here, as I am in great distress." The rabbi said to him, "You are not yet worthy of hell, because you have stolen from the public."

And the rabbi ordered them to open the trap, and the mouse came out and went into his hole.

One of the most fascinating stories on the subject of wandering souls is an incident in which a dybbuk (the spirit of a dead person that has entered and possessed a living person) entered the body of a widow in Safed. Luria warns his student Hayyim Vital, whom he sends to exorcise the spirit, that the spirit intends to harm Vital. When they complete their studies that night, Luria accompanies Vital a long way to his home. After parting from him, "while [Rabbi Hayyim Vital] was still walking down the street, he suddenly saw a large donkey walking toward him, and when it reached him he fell on the ground on his hand in terror and the hand was paralyzed." It also seemed to him as if he had fallen into one of the circles of hell. All that night Rabbi Hayyim could not sleep because of the pain in his hand. When he returns to Luria in the morning, the teacher already knows what has happened with the donkey and explains "that [the donkey] was the spirit that had been in the widow, and he was very angry at you." Luria places his hand on Vital's arm and it is cured, but from that day on Rabbi Hayyim Vital does not go out alone at night, preferring to sleep in Luria's house of study.[28]

The importance of this story is that it bridges daily life and legend. The encounter with the donkey in one of Safed's narrow alleys imbues Luria and his disciple with a clearly mythic dimension. It cannot be just any donkey, and he is not there by chance. Everything is foreseeable and has a purpose. Even Vital's neurotic behavior, familiar to us from his book of dreams, finds expression here. His fear of the dark, his sensitivity to physical pain, and his mental instability transform a routine encounter into a cosmic event. The transition from the real and routine into the visionary and mythic has three sources: (1) the mystical dimension of Lurianic teaching and the belief in reincarnation, (2) the personality and psychology of the protagonist, and (3) the time and place of the event—the streets of Safed on a dark and ominous night. The story is replete with highly significant tension between the concrete and mythic dimensions, which I discuss further in what follows.

The souls that Luria and his disciples meet are also incarnated in plants and inanimate objects. "Once [Luria] went with his disciples to study Torah

"While [Rabbi Hayyim Vital] was still walking down the street, he suddenly saw a large donkey walking toward him, and when it reached him, he fell on the ground . . . as if he had fallen into one of the circles of hell."

in a field, and he alone saw that all the trees were filled with innumerable souls who sat on them. And they filled the surface of the creek where they were, and they covered the water." One day, when the members of the fellowship were studying outside, as they often did, darkness suddenly fell even though it was midday, "and here a very dark cloud passed before them. The rabbi spoke and said, 'God says that there is no peace for the evil, where are you going?' And the cloud answered, 'I am S"M [Samael], the chief of satans.'" He showed Luria an order he had received to bring a plague on Israel, and Luria reprimanded him and commanded him to return to God to have the evil decree revoked, "and it ascended to heaven before their eyes and the land was peaceful during that year." The same thing happened the following year, but this time the cloud refused to accede to Luria's demand because "in this very year a certain man stumbled [and committed the transgression of lying with] the wife of [another] man." The cloud said that the rabbis knew of this but did nothing about it, because the transgressor was one of the great men of the city. The rabbi commanded his disciples to engage in study of the Torah's secrets so as to annul the evil degree. "And once the rabbi passed before the great synagogue in Tiberias and showed the companions a stone built into the wall and said, 'In this stone there is a reincarnated soul and it is telling me to pray for it,' and that is the explanation of 'for a stone will cry out from the wall' [Habakkuk 2:11]."[29]

With regard to the historical development, it is interesting to see the extent to which this view continued among Luria's students and their students. A story was told many years after these portentous events, by Rabbi Hayyim Vital's son Shmuel.

> I remember that on one Rosh Hashanah [the Jewish New Year], when my father, master and teacher, expounded on the water of the day of *tashlikh* [a ceremony in which Jews symbolically rid themselves of sins by casting them into water], we saw a frog come from the creek in his direction, and we began to cast stones on it to send it away, and the eyes of my father and master of blessed memory were closed and explicating the Torah as was his habit, and the sound of the frog's croaking made him open his eyes and he reprimanded us and told us that a certain soul had come to listen to his teaching, and it had come in the guise of this frog, and in its honor he began to preach in the matter of the frog [*tzefardea'*], why it is called a frog, that the word comes from *tzipor* [bird] which has *de'ah* [knowledge].[30]

The recurring element in all these stories, and in many others, is that a group of people is walking in the fields and spaces around Safed, or in the city's streets, when they encounter an animal, plant, or object in which living souls have been reincarnated. These souls speak to the companions and tell them about their past and their hopes for the future. Depictions like those we have seen here, with multitudes of souls in trees, on the surface of the water, and everywhere from the house of study to the stones of a synagogue to a mouse in his hole, present the world as a place packed and replete with souls.

This phenomenon of granting, out of psychoreligious motives, human life and soul to real material objects is what I call neo-animism. Animism,

In Fields and Wilderness • 105

a term coined by the British anthropologist and scholar of religions E. B. Tylor, refers to the belief that spiritual entities reside in all of nature—human beings, animals, plants, and inanimate objects. In his book *Religion in Primitive Culture* (1871), Tylor proposed an evolutionary scheme, based on this concept, of how religions emerged and developed. Tylor's evolutionary theory was sharply criticized by anthropologists who did fieldwork in native societies and by scholars of religion, who saw no evidence of such a developmental scheme. Nevertheless, they agreed that animism indeed represented a religious and psychological way of viewing the world that could be universally applied, both to native societies and to cultures that adopted monotheism on one level or another.[31]

The animistic worldview revealed in the Safed legends is more complex than that of native cultures, because it stands on a foundation of old and new kabbalistic views of the spiritual world, reincarnation (*gilgul*), and *tikun*. Because this book is not a study in comparative religion, I do not intend to contrast these different sorts of animism. Sigmund Freud later offered an original and interesting interpretation of the kind of animism evident in Safed. He proposed a connection between animism, magic, and the "omnipotence of thought."[32] The role of magic in the Safed worldview has long been recognized by scholars, but it still has not been connected to the animistic perspective. The stories under discussion clearly point to such a connection. Studies of magic in native societies have found an unambiguous connection between the nature of the magic that emerged in these groups and the ecology of their area of habitation.[33] The animistic cosmology of the Safed stories adduced here is characterized by a close connection with the natural world in which the Safed community lived. In many societies animism is a product of special intimacy with the natural environment. This dependence brings with it the need to recognize and understand the habits of animals, the predilections of plants, the nature of inanimate objects, and the climactic conditions on which they all depend. The symbolic expression of this dependence imbues all these entities with life, consciousness, and soul.

In the sixteenth century the lives of Safed's inhabitants were no longer utterly dependent on the natural world around them, but another kind of dependence was undeniable and no less critical: sacred dependence.

Because events recorded in Jewish sacred writings occurred in the areas immediately around Safed, the region had a different ontological status than any other. The symbolic consequence of this awareness was that it imbued all of nature with life—stone and cloud, mouse and heifer, trees and creeks. All these things live, speak, hurt, supplicate, and seek repair and repentance. This kind of animism seems to have crystallized in the connection between the Land of Israel and the first generation of Safed mystics during this period, that of Shlomo Alkabetz and Moshe Cordovero. Thus Bracha Zak concludes in her study of their teachings on this subject that Alkabetz and Cordovero "see the Land of Israel as possessing a unique mystical quality that transforms it from a land of inanimate character to one with the attributes of a living creature."[34]

The genre of animal tales is notably rare in medieval Hebrew narrative and is for the most part restricted to a small group of stories found in the *Alphabeth of Ben Sira*, a work of the ninth or tenth century, and Hebrew translations of the *Panchatantra*. Even Berechia ha-Nakdan's thirteenth-century *Mishlei Shu'alim* (Fox Fables), the most comprehensive and original collection of Hebrew works centering on animals, is not really a collection of animal tales but rather a collection of fables. That is, the animals in these stories do not act like animals. Instead, they display and represent human behavior. In contrast, medieval European literature offers a huge panoply of bestiaries—animal story cycles—conveyed orally and set down in prose and verse.[35]

The stories of Safed's late medieval Jewish community stand out against this background. First, they include a relatively large number of stories in which animals, plants, and inanimate objects play central roles. Second, the Safed stories are not fables that offer allegories of the human world. Rather, they are stories that authentically portray the inner lives—the souls—of animal, plants, and objects.

Why did such stories not emerge among Jews during the medieval millennium but appear with such intensity during the flowering of Safed culture, covering just a few decades? The answer can be found, I maintain, in the renewed Jewish physical, religious, and psychological encounter with the Galilean landscape. The Safed inhabitants involved were not astonished by the beauty of nature or the richness of its views; they did not think that there was nothing as lovely as a tree. Instead, they gazed deeply into the landscape with manifestly theological purpose. When Luria and his disciples walk the streets of Tiberias and focus their gaze on a stone in the wall of a synagogue, it is clear that their aim is to identify the soul ensconced in the stone, by way of proving the reincarnation and repair of souls along the path to the cosmic redemption. Yet the theological diagnosis is preceded by an examination of the surrounding world, the wall, the stones composing it, and the uniqueness of one particular stone among all the others. When, before this, have we encountered a Jewish religious leader who attends to a mouse peeking out of its hole in search of food? Luria, according to the story, not only sees the mouse but discerns its human nature. He thus instructs his disciples to capture the mouse so that he can examine it closely and speak with it. The same is true of the trees and bodies of water that every other person passes on a daily basis without paying attention. Luria and his fellowship stop, look, and discern their special nature and construct their mystical cosmology on that foundation. What could be more meaningless than a dark cloud in the afternoon? To see Samael, Satan, in the cloud it needs to be brought closer and looked at so as to fathom its special nature.

One might argue that the same thing could happen anywhere—in Europe and Africa, Yemen and Italy. But in practice it didn't. The pervasiveness of the phenomenon in the Safed stories is so conspicuous, so clear, that it cannot be overlooked. We cannot explain this great openness to nature, or the dozens of stories in which natural objects—animal, vegetable, and mineral—speak and reveal themselves, except by reference to their encounter with the Galilee. They were not tourists or pilgrims to holy graves or holy cities; they were people who lived their day-to-day lives on this soil. They were directly or indirectly dependent on the land, physically, socially, and spiritually. In Safed, as elsewhere, animism emerged in a native society in which the surrounding natural world was both an existential need and an object of longing.

A Mythical Space

O Kitty! How nice it would be if we could only get through into Looking-glass House! I'm sure it's got, oh! such beautiful things in it! Let's pretend there's a way of getting through into it somehow,

> *Kitty. Let's pretend the glass has got soft like gauze, so that we can get through. Why, it's turning into a sort of mist now, I declare! It'll be easy enough to get through.*
>
> —Lewis Carroll, *Through the Looking-Glass*

Hayyim Vital's *Sefer haHezyonot* (Book of Visions) recounts hundreds of the dreams and visions he experienced during his time in Safed, Jerusalem, and Damascus and that others dreamed about him. The work is one of the most fascinating repositories of fantastical narratives written in the early modern age to be found among the Jews and indeed in any other culture. Local and spatial elements are prominent in the work and are critical to understanding the perception of space in the Safed period, which can be done through the creative consciousness of Vital, one of its most intriguing figures.

Some scholars have addressed the issue of the authenticity of Vital's dreams. He relates dreams and visions that he experienced close to the end of his life. Did he write this work over a long period, adding the final dreams during his final years or months? How could he have remembered dreams that he had had fifty years before? Perhaps he recorded each dream the next morning and then redacted these into the notebooks that are together called *Sefer haHezyonot*. His son, Shmuel Vital, offers an interesting perspective.

> Up to this point the Blessed God has helped me complete the books of the great rabbi, my father and master, may his memory be for life in the next world, [such that] nothing is missing from them, from small to large, proofread as if by the hand of the God who is good to me. And afterward I found in my belongings notebooks that my father and master of blessed memory, wrote in his own hand, of things touching on him and the root of his soul. . . . And it seems to me that the rabbi, my father and master of blessed memory, wished to conceal them in his great humility, so as not to proclaim the root of his soul in public, and I in my insufficiency feared, lest this collection be forgotten. I therefore resolved to disobey his wish and, may he of blessed memory forgive

In Fields and Wilderness • 109

me, and I wanted to write them in a book and inscribe them so that they will survive for a long time. . . . These are the things that my teacher [Luria], may his memory be for life in the next world, told me that apply to me and the root of my soul.³⁶

The final sentence in this passage is the beginning of Part IV of *Sefer haHezyonot*, the words of Hayyim Vital himself, copied here by his son. In other words, it seems almost certain that what Shmuel Vital refers to as "notebooks that my father and master of blessed memory wrote in his own hand" is *Sefer haHezyonot* itself. Shmuel's testimony can be understood in two ways. It could be that he found notebooks (meaning, apparently, the four parts of which *Sefer haHezyonot* is composed) written and edited by his father and that all he had to do was have them printed so that they would be preserved for future generations. But another possibility is that he found only the raw material recorded by his father over many years and that Shmuel himself arranged them into the four sections of the book. If so, the work of turning the notes into a book was accomplished by Shmuel Vital a few years after his father's death.

Either way, Shmuel testifies that he found the dreams in his father's handwriting, and we thus have no reason to doubt their authenticity. The fact that Hayyim Vital makes a point of noting the precise day and year of each dream and the fact that he would have considered the fabrication of dates or dreams a sin bolster their authenticity. Of course, this does not mean that he or others dreamed the dreams in exactly the way they are set out. We can presume that when he put them into writing, even if he did so the following morning, he saw, shaped, and interpreted them in accordance with his feelings at that time and as he felt they ought to be. By "authenticity" I mean that the work is not a forgery, a deliberate adaptation or fabrication, but rather a true expression of his thoughts, his self-conception, and especially his profound fears and neuroses.

> [Year 5337 (1576–1577)] I dreamed that I was in the market, at the door of R. Yehuda Unkanina, and I saw a man taller than three [*sic*, should be thirty] cubits lying there along that

"I dreamed that I was in the market . . . and I saw a man taller than thirty cubits lying there along that road, from that door to close to the door of R. Joseph Karo of blessed memory."

road, from that door to close to the door of Rabbi Joseph Karo of blessed memory, and he lay on a bed. And I said to him, "Who are you?" And he said to me, "I am Adam, the first man, your father [because Hayyim Vital considered himself to be the reincarnation of Cain], and I am very ill and am lying here. Therefore I request of you, Hayyim my son, bring me from the doctor's shop good potions and medicines to strengthen my heart, so weak from sickness." I went and brought him and he ate and drank. And I woke up.[37]

The real location of the dream is a street in Safed, stretching from the stores of the marketplace to the door of Rabbi Joseph Karo's home. The street is almost certainly a busy main street well known to everyone in Safed. In the dream this daily reality turns into a surrealistic scene, with a long bed lying the length of the street and on the bed the huge figure of primeval Adam. However, this huge (and perhaps monstrous) figure elicits not terror but compassion, because he is sick and helpless and needs the help of the dreamer, his son, Hayyim Vital, the final reincarnation of Adam's son Cain. The incident is thus manifestly mythical. A motif from the Jewish collective past, inserted into everyday life, inevitably produces a mythic ambience that means that the story cannot be taken at face value.

Vital records the dream as having occurred in 5337, meaning about five years after Luria's death, when the memory of his final days was still vivid in those who were close to him. In many parts of *Sefer haHezyonot* Luria is depicted as Vital's spiritual father. Vital is angry when Luria does not appear to him in a dream or vision over a long period, and he turns to him at times of spiritual and social crisis, seeking reinforcement and support. The figure of the primeval father, a giant who is nevertheless helpless and needs Vital's assistance, parallels the way in which Vital and his fellow disciples viewed Luria. Luria, their mythic leader with God-like powers, spent the last days of his life lying in bed, ill and helpless. His disciples sat with him, came and went. The contrast between the mythic image of the father-leader and his actual weakness is the background to the profound psychological crisis (characteristic of every messianic group when the human weaknesses of their leaders become evident at the time of their death) that finds expression in this dream.

Another look at the landscape in which the dream takes place reveals that Adam's bed stretches from the market to the home of Joseph Karo. If the market symbolizes Safed's material life and Karo's home its spiritual life, then the mythic figure of the first man, extending between these two places, mediates between Safed's two facets. On the one end is its dynamic and prosperous material economy, and on the other is its variegated and rich spiritual life. If I am correct in identifying the huge figure lying on the Safed street as Luria, it means that, in Hayyim Vital's mind, Luria served as the link between Safed's material and spiritual life. Unlike Vital, who was shunned and destitute his entire life, Luria was a well-off merchant who had, as a young man in Egypt, devoted his time to building an international business. Did Luria's material occupation bother Vital? Did he see it as a blemish on his teacher's standing as a holy man? Is that why he lies in the street, between the market and the sage, helpless and in need of a person whose world is (at least in his own perception) purely one of spirit? Perhaps that is the case. Either way, in this dream the street in Safed is clearly a locus of mythic struggle between the material and spiritual worlds, between trade and Torah.

On January 16, 1610, the Friday night of the Sabbath on which the first section of Exodus was read, Vital had a "frightening dream" directly connected to the weekly Torah portion. He saw himself at Safed's Sephardic synagogue, which was led by a figure we are already acquainted with, Rabbi Ya'akov Abulafia. The synagogue was being decorated, as is customary, for the holiday of Simchat Torah (the last of the holidays before the winter, on which the annual cycle of reading the Torah ends and is begun again). In the dream the synagogue had another custom,

> since ancient times, to bring the body of Moses, peace be upon him, to the synagogue. . . . And I looked and here they brought the body of Moses to the synagogue and his length was close to ten cubits. And they prepared a long bench with books on it, and placed Moses's body on it. And I saw that his body was dressed in his garments, and when they laid him down on the table he changed from what he was and turned into an actual Torah scroll, not rolled but spread out to its entire length, like a long letter lying the length of the bench, with all the portions of the Torah written in it from "In the beginning" to "before all Israel" [the initial and final words of the Torah].

The community's sage (Abulafia) took his place by Moses's head and left Hayyim Vital the place by his feet, and it was clear to Vital that Abulafia had done this to humiliate him. Afterward, the sage ordered the community to bring a thin string to tie the mantle covering the scroll (which was Moses's body). Vital mocked him to himself, because Abulafia thought he was being original in doing this, but in fact he was acting according to a well-known custom. The scroll then transformed back into "the actual body of Moses." After this, Vital saw himself on a broad plain outside Safed's walls, with "all the people sitting on the southern side of the plain, and on the north side, right by the wall, was the place of Moses, may peace be on him." It was the time of the afternoon prayer, and Vital felt pained that he could not see

In Fields and Wilderness • 113

"the radiance of the *Shekhinah* that surrounded Moses, may peace be on him, who stood here with us." He saw the sun gradually setting before its time and tried to follow it with his eyes, but the sun disappeared. Afterward he saw himself in the Sephardic synagogue in Damascus at the time of the blowing of the shofar on Rosh Hashanah. But the sage who blew the shofar produced only small and meager sounds, and everyone was surprised, "and all this dream was at the end of the night, and I woke up."[38]

Moses's body, cast before the community on a synagogue bench, is reminiscent of the previous dream's long body of Adam lying on a bed in a Safed street. It may well be that these potent images are influenced by the depictions of Christian saints in churches, showing figures with elongated bodies and limbs laid on benches or beds, with believers surrounding them and viewing them from above. Perhaps the appearance of a Torah scroll as the body of Moses reinforces my claim of the neo-animist consciousness that is so clearly evident in Safed's mentality—a person who gazes at a Torah scroll and sees it transformed before their eyes into the body of Moses is a person of clear animist inclinations. That person sees a living soul in every object, a soul that actualizes its symbolic role in the real world.

The key to understanding this complex dream is a spatial perspective. The dreamer divides the dream space into three parts. The first two parts are in Safed: the first in the Sephardic synagogue there and the second outside the city walls. The third part is in Damascus, at that city's Sephardic synagogue. Destabilizing events take place in all three. The first and most frightening is bringing the body of Moses into the synagogue and the body's transmutation into a Torah scroll and then back into the body of the dead prophet. The second event occurs on a plain outside Safed's eastern wall. The sun disappears behind the mountains to the city's west; Hayyim Vital seeks it with his eyes but cannot find it. The third shock is the weak sound of the shofar, arousing consternation among the worshippers at the synagogue. I would hazard that what we are seeing here is a decline in the potency of the vision, in hopes for a great and promising future. In the first part of the dream, the real world is clearly mythologized; the appearance of Moses's body in a real place in Safed and its transformation into a Torah scroll express the vital and mythic potential of the real world. The full original power of Jewish history is actualized in Safed by the presence of the symbolic figure of Moses. The second episode also takes place in Safed, or rather outside it. The sun conceals itself; Vital seeks its light, which diminishes rapidly, but he cannot find it. The sun seems to function as a metonym for Moses, whose face, so the Torah says, radiated light. In other words, Moses evades the dreamer's sight. Vital had this dream about ten years before his death in Damascus, during a period of bitter disappointment, hopelessness, and social marginalization. In the third episode the fading sound of the shofar expresses this personal disappointment and crisis. The blast of the shofar is meant to herald the redemption, but here it fades and disappoints the worshippers, bringing the vision to an end with the dashing of expectations of the Messiah's arrival. In its fragmentation and its nebulous causal continuity, the dream expresses the sense of crisis, loss, and despair, leading from the wondrous-mythical ambience of Safed at its height to its decline and Vital's own descent from there to Damascus.

In 1570, about a year before Luria arrived in Safed, Hayyim Vital had this dream:

> I was descending from the caravansary of Safed by means of the stone stairway that descends to the market, and at the store of the meat sellers there were two paths, lengthwise and crosswise. And my father and master came toward me on one of the paths, and Rabbi Moshe Cordovero and Rabbi Moshe Sagis came on the second path, on which you ascend from the cemetery to the caravansary.

He joins a procession ascending from the cemetery to the city streets,

> and then we all arrived at the Street of the Jews, and I saw an assembly of all the Israelites gathered together, and at noon the sun set [before its time], and it became dark and murky all over the world and all the Israelites were crying bitterly.

Wondrously, an ascetic and austere figure appears, his hair reaching his ankles, singing a strange song in a loud and pleasant voice, "and there was no one who could understand his words and no one heard his voice except

In Fields and Wilderness • 115

me. And he walked and sang until he arrived at where I was, and the sun went back to shining as before."³⁹

Many years later, in 1609, in Damascus, Vital asked Rabbi Moshe Mitrani, called Hamabit, the "one who sees" demons,

> why my teacher of blessed memory [Luria] has not appeared to me in a dream for a long time, as he used to do. And they [the demons?] also brought to that place an image of my teacher of blessed memory, who was dead and stretched out, and Yosef Hamabit gave me all his signs [described him accurately] even though he had never seen him.

Luria reassured Vital and promised him that the fault was not his, as he had thought. "Here," he added, "all your thoughts go there, to Safed, and because the times are troubled, tarry a bit, and then you must in any case go there."⁴⁰

These two examples, from two central junctures in Hayyim Vital's life, separated by some forty years, demonstrate the centrality of Safed in both his conscious and unconscious mind. This is the actual geography of Safed: the caravansary, one of the city's central landmarks;⁴¹ and the stone steps leading down from it to two other important sites, the cemetery and the Street of the Jews. The practice of the Jews to gather into a single social unit (what the anthropologist Victor Turner calls a communitas) when they emerged from the many synagogues along the street serves in these dreams as an entry point into another, visionary world. The same is true at the end of his life, in Damascus, when Luria's body makes an appearance there. In other words, Vital seeks to recreate Safed in Damascus by means of that which more than anything else symbolizes Safed in its greatness: the figure of his teacher. Luria's body thus joins the two mythological figures we saw in the previous dreams, Adam and Moses, whose bodies also grant a mythic dimension to the real world. The significance of this mythic dimension in the first decade of the seventeenth century in Damascus is that, just as Luria tells Vital, Safed has never been expunged from his consciousness, nor from the unconscious levels of his personality.

The appearance of the mysterious lone figure on Safed's streets, like that of Adam's elongated body in the same place, imbues mundane Safed with

"I was descending the caravansary of Safed by means of the stone stairway that descends to the market."

myth. But this is not the only possible connection between the real and the mythic Safed. Even more interesting is the nature of the *passage* from the first to the second, from the actual to the visionary. Mundane and real Safed is the starting point on a road that reveals the mythic-fantastical space.

> 12 Iyar [5367/1607] Rachel the Ashkenazit [of German origin] dreamed that she was sitting in Safed on the balcony of her upper floor, where I lived, and she saw me flying and descending from the sky and I came down there. I told her the greatest esteem in which I am held there and the great sights I saw there. And while I was there they gave me a key and told me, "Go to a certain treasure room here, which has not been opened since the creation of the world, and open it with this key, because no man has permission to open it except you." I went there with a great angel that they sent with me, who showed me where that room was. There I saw a great sage who has been dead for 500 years and he said to me, "Here, I counsel you not to open it, lest they delay you

In Fields and Wilderness • 117

> here and will not let you go down into the lower world anymore. And out of my love for you I give you this advice." ...
> And I listened to his counsel and descended to this world.⁴²

In this dream Safed itself is not the mythical landscape it was in the previous dreams. Rather, above it and around it there is another magical world for which Safed serves as a grounding point or starting place. This dream, postdating by many years Vital's tenancy in the home of Rachel (the Ashkenazit) Eberlein, opens in a concrete space, the balcony off the upper floor from which she looks out over her yard and the street beyond. It also concludes there—Vital returns from his flight. In other words, the actual place serves as a frame for the mythic or fantastic event.

The character of the fantastical narrative is notably that of myth or fairy tale. It has a flying hero (like Perseus, for example) who receives a magical object, in this case a key (mythological heroes often receive a magic weapon), which he is to use to get into a hidden and closed place. On the way he meets a supernatural helper or a guard, who warns the hero that he will not be able to return from his adventure (as in the case of Orpheus descending into hell). The hero generally disregards this advice and succeeds in his quest (e.g., killing a dragon and saving a princess). But in Rachel's dream the hero takes the advice and does not use the key. In other words, this dream, like the others, uses the materials of myths and fairy tales in a fascinating way.⁴³

If we adhere to classic fairy-tale interpretation, the key (both conceptually and in the dream) to interpreting the dream is sexual. Hayyim Vital, who was still a young man when he lived in Rachel the Ashkenazit's home, is searching for the key to his sexual identity and of course to his sexual fantasies. He knows that the key is in his hands, but he also knows that once he opens the forbidden room (generally a symbol of repressed sexual desires), he will not be able to go back to what he had been before (a young man devoting himself to spiritual matters and asceticism).

That would be a possible interpretation, but it would be wrong to take the dream out of the context of Vital's life and position in Safed at the beginning of the 1570s and thirty-five years later in Damascus, where the dream took place. The first part of the dream belongs to his Damascus period. Vital flies

"Rachel the Ashkenazit dreamed that she was sitting in Safed on the balcony of her upper floor . . . and she saw me flying and descending from the sky."

up to the heavens, where he is treated with the honor he deserves. He is the only one in the world to be given the key to the treasure room, in contrast to his real life in Damascus, where he is scorned and humiliated. Vital is in particular need of such a psychological boost during this harsh period at the end of his life. As a young man in Safed, before Luria's arrival, Vital was on the verge of a promising life and was searching for the right path to take. The key to the forbidden room symbolizes this search. Will he open the treasure room and then be unable to return to his former place, or will he be deterred, because the life he has remains important and precious to him?

Vital's unequivocal choice to return to the Safed of this world and abjure the treasures kept for him in heaven highlights the binary opposition between the two poles that were so salient, as I will show, in the souls and lives of the people of Safed. The starting point is a concrete place—the street, a yard, an upper floor, a balcony—the real Safed as seen by its inhabitants. The protagonists of the legends and visions set out from there into a dream world from which they are in danger of not returning (e.g., the road chosen by the ascetic of the previous dream). But when they face a choice, they choose to return to the concrete, mundane Safed that they know. The dream of the key highlights this dilemma, so characteristic of young people standing at a crossroads in their life. That being the case, the two interpretations of the dream I have offered are actually interwoven; sexual searching and doubt are part and parcel of standing at a juncture where one must choose between the real world and the spiritual existence that mystical lore offered Vital.[44]

On 29 Tammuz 5368 (1608), Rabbi Eliahu Amiel, one of Vital's friends in Damascus, dreamed that the two of them were in Safed. Vital takes him to visit the graves of saints in Safed and its environs. On their way back they encounter Joseph Karo and Shlomo Alkabetz, Moshe Cordovero and Eleazar Azkari, Moshe Galanti and Rabban Yohanan Ben-Zakkai, Rabbi Akiva and Rabbi Meir, the prophet Jonah and Rabbi Judah the Prince (Yehuda ha-Nasi), and others. All of them set out together for the Temple in Jerusalem, actually to a cave under the Temple, where "my Ashkenazi teacher of blessed memory" awaits them. Luria orders them to bring Ya'akov Abulafia, whom they bring "dressed in black garments and he also had a black veil over his head and face and beard." This is in contrast to all the other saints, who are dressed in white. Luria commands that Abulafia be dressed in white as well, but all they give him to wear is "a small white coat that reached only down to his thighs." Luria sends Vital for the prophet Haggai so that Haggai can "write me a document in his hand about all that had happened to him." After Vital undertook to do all he had promised, Amiel woke from his dream. But the dream has an interesting epilogue; a week later, when Abulafia was walking around the synagogue (in Damascus) reciting from the Mishnah, his black garment was mysteriously snatched from him; when he turned around he saw no one. Neither did the worshippers at the synagogue see a thing.[45]

I have already referred to this complex and intriguing dream in Chapter 2, as part of the discussion of the volatile relationship between Vital and Abulafia and the dream's importance for understanding interpersonal dynamics in Safed. But the dream is also noteworthy for its spatial-local dimensions. In Amiel's dream, Vital assumes the role of Virgil in Dante's *Divine Comedy*, serving as guide and companion to the confused Amiel and explaining to him the meaning of the scenes he takes him through. They go from the graves of saints around Safed to the place where Adam, Abraham, Isaac, and Jacob reside, "sleeping, lying in the cave, with a very large torch before Adam alone. And endless flames and candles are included within the great flame of the torch, from top to bottom. And the said R. Eliahu asked me, 'What are these flames?' And I told him, 'These are the souls of the righteous who are included in the soul of Adam.'"[46] They also went to the Temple of Jerusalem and the wondrous cave underneath it, to the cave of the prophet Haggai, and then back to Abulafia's synagogue in Damascus.

In this dream, as in the dream of the key, Hayyim Vital serves as an intermediary between two realms: the real world of Safed and the mythic world that overlays it and extends beyond it. The starting point is a depiction of the terrain in which Safed's Jews live, specifically the saints' graves in and around Safed. The dream describes these in great detail and in close adherence to Vital's own account of the sites Luria and his fellowship visited (as recounted in *Sefer haGilgulim* and Part Four of *Sefer haHezyonot*). The similarity is surprising given that, according to the testimony, it was ostensibly dreamed by Amiel and not Vital himself. When Vital and Amiel return to the city, the story begins to slide into the world of myth and fantasy. They encounter contemporaries of theirs, among them Karo, Alkabetz, and Cordovero, but also *tanna'im*, that is, sages from the Mishnah, such as Rabban Yohanan Ben-Zakkai, Rabbi Akiva, Rabbi Meir, and Rabbi Judah the Prince, as well as figures from the Bible, such as the prophet Jonah, Joseph, Joshua, and Caleb. Later, they enter the cave tomb where Adam, Abraham, Isaac, and Jacob are buried, where they see the bodies of these ancestors enrobed in the halo of light that signifies the souls of the righteous. The transition from the real to the fantastic takes place stepwise, with increasing intensity—from the street to the wondrous cave tomb, and from there a no less wondrous path jumping brings them to a cave underneath the Temple in Jerusalem.

The shift of scene to the Temple constitutes a translation into a different geography but also into a different period; this assembly of saints in the Temple is a messianic event, conducted by the person whom the members of the group take to be the Messiah ben Yosef, that is, Luria. This is no longer a mythic picture copied into the present, as we have seen in previous dreams. Rather, it takes place at the End of Days. In this sense, the concrete Safed, that of the holy graves and biblical caves, serves as a bridge not just into the mythic past but also into the messianic future. The epilogue with which the dream story ends, the mysterious disappearance of Abulafia's black garment, marks a return to the real world, yet without forfeiting the reality of the dream. An element from the dream, Abulafia's black garment, intrudes into and materializes in the real world, blurring the boundary between the two. The dream thus has a strong grip on the waking world, which is not permitted to shake free of the dream. The spatial continuum of the dream is thus no longer only a place in which human beings live and act but rather one in which the stuff of the dreamer's real life blends with the stuff of his dreams and visions.[47]

This grasp of Safed and its environs, as a launching pad from which one can take off into the realm of myth, is conveyed potently and impressively in a dream Vital reports from the month of Tevet in the year 5326 (1566), about four years before Luria's arrival in Safed. The fact that Luria makes no appearance in this long and convoluted dream (as Vital did not know Luria yet) lends credence to its authenticity, in the sense I offered earlier.[48]

The text begins with an introductory event. In other words, long before Freud, Hayyim Vital interpreted his dreams in light of events that took place in his life before he dreamed it. It is nighttime on the eighth day of Tevet, a harsh and cold Safed winter night. After making *kiddush*, Vital sits down to his Sabbath meal,

> and tears flowed from my eyes, I sighed and grew sad, because on the tenth of the previous month of Heshvan [two months earlier], I married my wife, the previously-mentioned Hannah, and they jinxed me with witchcraft [rendering him impotent][49] . . . and I was so apprehensive that I did not eat a thing, and I lay down in my bed on my face weeping, until I fell asleep from so much crying.

The dream begins, then, with severe personal distress. Vital then dreams that an old man, who later turns out to be the prophet Elijah, takes him to accompany the departure of the Sabbath Queen. They walk to the gate in Safed's western wall, which he notes is where the caravansary stands at the time of his writing. There they see a high and steep mountain, which Elijah instantly leaps to. Vital pleads with him, and Elijah then grips his hand and takes him up to the peak. There Vital sees a ladder with its top in heaven, having only three rungs. Elijah refuses to help him climb the ladder and vanishes. Vital again weeps bitterly, until he sees

> an eminent woman, as beautiful as the sun, standing at the top of the ladder, and I thought in my heart that she was my mother, and she said, "Why, my son Hayyim, are you crying here, and I heard your tears and have come to your aid." And she held out her right hand and raised me up to the top of the ladder. And there I saw a large window, with a large flame coming out of it, flashing like lightning, with great intensity and burning everyone who was there. And I knew in my soul that this was the flashing of the ever-turning sword at the entrance to the Garden of Eden. And I called out bitterly to the woman and said to her, "My mother, my mother, save me from this flashing, lest it burn me up." And she said, "No one can save you from this flashing except you yourself. . . . Here, place your hand on your head and you will find there cotton wool as white as snow, and take it and put it in the flashing window and it will be closed and you can pass through quickly."

He does as she tells him and maintains that his hair turned white because he moved from guilt (black) to innocence (white).[50] This way of getting into the world of fantasy, by means of "cotton wool as white as snow," is reminiscent of the way Alice makes her way through the looking glass: "Let's pretend there's a way of getting through into it somehow, Kitty. Let's pretend the glass has got soft like gauze, so that we can get through. Why, it's turning into a sort of mist now, I declare! It'll be easy enough to get through."[51]

Once Vital passes through the entrance to Eden, Elijah appears to him once more, grips his hand, and leads him into a wondrous yard with flowing rivers and fragrant, lush, verdant groves of fruit trees and tall shade trees. Birds of many kinds nest there; they resemble white geese, and as they walk among the trees, "they recited a verse or chapter of the Mishnah and stretched out their necks and ate an apple right from the tree and then drank water from the rivers." Vital understands that these are saints, "masters of the Mishnah," meaning scholars of Halakha. Elijah leads him to a high and marvelous structure. When they enter, he sees "God sitting on a chair alongside the building's southern wall, in the middle, and he has the image of an ancient, old, and with a snow-white beard, glorious without end." God is surrounded by saints, who sit before him on mats and learn Torah from him. Vital understands that these are the saints "who are called *bnei ʿaliyah* [the elite, salt of the earth]," meaning those who study Kabbalah, who in the next world have the form of human beings, as opposed to the halakhic scholars, who have become geese. The *bnei ʿaliyah* are also rewarded with enjoying the divine presence without interruption. Vital falls on his face before God, but God grips his hand, bolsters his soul, and seats him at his right hand (in reference to Psalms 110:1: "A Psalm of David. The Lord says to my Lord: Sit at My right hand until I make your enemies a footstool for your feet"). "Then I said to him, 'How can I sit at your right hand, in this place, when it has been prepared for Rabbi Joseph Karo?' And he said to me, 'So I thought at the start, but after that I gave him a different place and I gave you this place, which I have already prepared for you.'" Vital asks God, "Leave me in this place and do not make me return to the lower world," because he feared sinning and losing his place at God's right hand. But God promises him that he would withstand all his trials and that the place would be kept for him, "and then I descended from there, from the high place I had reached, I alone, and I found myself standing in this lower world in the dream itself, and I did not see anything of all I had seen when I ascended before."

Just as Bernard of Clairvaux leads Dante along the paths of Paradise and just as Vital leads Eliahu Amiel among the graves of the saints and the caves under the Temple in that later dream, so Elijah leads the young Hayyim Vital along the paths of Safed and the Garden of Eden above it. This dream, although an early one, contains most of the characteristics of the dreams so far cited. In fact, they appear here with even greater intensity. The first of these is the liminal zone, intermediary between the real and mythic realms. The elder who invites Vital to accompany him "resembles Rabbi Hayyim HaLevy Ashkenazi, of blessed memory, my neighbor." In other words, it is a real figure, who transforms into Elijah only when he leaps toward the high cliff that is the gate to Eden. The dream's starting place is also real; it begins at the Sabbath afternoon prayer service in the rabbi's house, and from there his neighbor leads him along the street, through Safed to the city wall, past the caravansary and the city gate to the high mountain west of the city. It is only here that the move from the real to the fantastic takes place. The high mountain turns into the gate to Eden, and Vital's elderly neighbor turns into the prophet Elijah. In other words, the mythic space extends *into* the real, actual Safed. The path Vital takes along the street in Safed to the mountain outside the wall is like a runway along which Vital zooms to the top of the mountain and from there to Eden and God's dwelling place.

Another notable feature is the impact of the stress Vital feels, his anxieties and his self-image, on the content and structure of the vision. The beautiful and eminent woman, whom he identifies as his mother, waits for him at the top of the ladder and leads him into paradise. She says that she has appeared because of his weeping and tears. He has ostensibly been weeping because he is unable to climb the steep ladder. But we should keep in mind that Vital fell asleep in tears about the impotence that had afflicted him since his marriage, and also, as noted, the nocturnal emissions that constantly plagued him because of this "knot." His weeping about his misery and incapacity did not, of course, end when he fell asleep. It continued into his sleep, and his mother's appearance is first and foremost a response to this grief and not his sadness at not being able to climb the ladder. The eminent woman, "beautiful as the sun," who is his mother, has come to him because of his mourning over his sexual dysfunction. She resembles in many ways the figure of Mary, mother of Jesus, who during the Middle Ages was depicted both as a mother and as a beloved.[52] It may well be that the dream hints at an oedipal relationship between the young Vital and his strong mother, a relationship that can sometimes have impotence as one of its outcomes. Furthermore, the entryway into Eden that his mother points to and advises him how to penetrate has clear sexual connotations: the cotton-wool through which he penetrates, the fire, the narrow opening. His mother, who brought him into the world through her vagina, now guides him on how to penetrate that orifice that he has been unable to get through.

The connection with the dreamer's personal distress does not end here. In Eden Vital sees two types of saints: those who have turned into white geese, who are the halakhic authorities, and those who have retained human form, who are the masters of Kabbalah, the *bnei 'aliyah*. The geese-halakhists wander the paths of Eden, reciting from the Mishnah, enjoying the fruit of the garden, and from time to time witnessing the glow of the *Shekhinah*. The human-kabbalists are constantly in God's presence and continually hear God teach them Torah. God ejects Rabbi Joseph Karo from the most honored place next to him (in keeping with the verse from Psalms 110:1, "Sit at My right hand while I make your enemies a footstool"). He invites the young Vital to take his place. At the time of the dream Karo was already the acknowledged leader of Safed's sages, the greatest scholar of the second half of the sixteenth century. It took a huge amount of presumption for a young man like Hayyim Vital to put himself in Karo's place next to God—even in a dream!

But the picture gets even more complicated if we turn our attention to the fact that Karo himself, in his mystical journal *Magid Meisharim*, relates what his *magid*—the divine figure or inner voice that revealed secret lore to him, whom Karo saw as a personification of the Mishnah—said. The *magid* informs Karo that, when he reaches paradise, all the saints will gather to receive him with songs and praise, "the *Shekhinah* at their head." They will prepare seven wedding canopies before Karo and seven behind him, and seven rivers of balsam oil to surround him. They will prepare a golden chair inlaid with many pearls and gemstones. They will dress him in magnificent garments, and all the saints will gather around his chair and discuss Torah with him. He will preach Torah before them for 180 days, at the end of which everyone will rise and declare loudly, "Give honor to the holy son of the supreme king and give honor to the image of the king!" Karo seems to have received this revelation during his initial years in the Holy Land, between 1541 and 1547, some twenty years before Vital's dream vision.[53] The Safed community knew about Karo's *magid*, and it seems highly likely that Vital's dream was a response to Karo's vision. Karo had delusions of grandeur, and his younger contemporary, Vital, no less so. But the analogy between Vital's dream and Karo's vision is not just one of personality. There is an ideological factor as well. Whereas Karo presents himself in his vision as the ultimate Torah scholar and halakhic authority, Vital, as Kabbalah's representative in the dream, seeks to shunt Karo and the Halakha he represents to the sidelines and to replace it with the true Torah, the Kabbalah. It is certainly possible, of course, that Karo also meant to say that he would preach the secrets of the Torah before God. The fact that, in Vital's dream, Karo is still numbered among the *bnei 'aliyah*, a kabbalist, rather than standing outside with the halakhists, supports this possibility. However, Karo's standing as the foremost authority on Jewish religious law in his generation (a possible explanation of why God took away from him the favorite seat on his right) would seem to support the former interpretation.

The high literary style in which both visions are presented could not have been maintained had these accounts not been written in fervor and with ideological purpose. Only such a combination of psychology and ideology (along, of course, with the verbal talents of both writers) could produce visions of such poetic force.

But beyond such obvious megalomania (and perhaps a corresponding inferiority complex), Vital is clearly facing a dilemma about the two major paths for spiritual life in Safed. Vital studied Halakha with Rabbi Moshe Alsheikh and Kabbalah from Rabbi Moshe Cordovero. At this point, before Luria's arrival in Safed, Vital had so much inner conflict between the two paths that it found poetic expression in this dream. His request of God—"Leave me in this place and do not make me return to the lower world"—is reminiscent of the dream of the key, in which the wondrous elder tells him not to open the treasure room because he will not be able to return to his place in this world. Vital's desire here, to remain in the company of the *bnei 'aliyah*, is clear and unambiguous. Apparently he reached this decision before Luria's arrival.

Vital's request to remain in Eden and give up the Safed of this world is a manifestly spatial choice. We have already seen that in other dreams he reports that the tension between the realms of the real and the mythical plays a central role. That is no less the case in this dream, where it is expressed in the form of the route that Vital and Elijah take from the city to the mountain and in Vital's passionate desire to overcome all the geographic barriers along the way so as to reach heaven. Yet the final sentence of this dream, which is to the best of my knowledge unique in *Sefer haHezyonot*, indicates something important about his mentality: "And then I descended from [this] high place, I alone, and I found myself standing in this lower world *in the dream itself*, and I did not see anything of all I had seen when I ascended before." In other words, Vital awakes from his vision within the dream itself, not when he wakes from sleep! That is, the tension between the mythic and the real is situated *within* the dream. As in the dream of the key, Vital yearns for the world of mystery but cannot or is not prepared to do without the real world. True, Safed itself was a space imbued with myth, but even Hayyim Vital, and certainly the rest of the city's Jews, did not want to abjure its concrete and local aspects, even to gain a place in the mythical realm that was part of the city's nature.

The Place as an Ideal and a Rupture

Men and women are drawn from the Jaffa Gate and above to the Western Wall . . . "The Place" [God] has brought them to their place and they have not yet found their place.

—S. Y. Agnon, "Tehila"

We have made two essential findings during our examination of Safed's legends and dreams. The first is the importance of the encounter with the land, life, and landscapes of Safed and the Upper Galilee for the understanding of these narratives. The corpus of stories that emerged from Safed and certainly the dreams and visions of Hayyim Vital and his close acquaintances are unique in nearly every aspect that we have examined: subject, genre, worldview, connection to the real world, and the stature of the protagonist, whether an individual or a group. The encounter that Safed's inhabitants of the late sixteenth century had with the Upper Galilean landscape is entirely different from that between Jewish communities and the landscapes they found themselves in during their long years of exile. This is evident in the dozens of foundational legends produced by Jewish communities in the Middle Ages and the early modern period.[54]

In the Safed legends, as we have seen, place shifts from the margins to the center of the narrative structure, granting it uniqueness and meaning. In these stories the urban living space turns into a mythic realm, and the protagonists and narrators see the world around them in a new and inspiring way, which I called neo-animism. Furthermore, the Safed custom of going out "into the fields"—that is, spending time at sites and graves, under trees, in ancient buildings and open fields—had clear theological significance. Although these stories and storytellers benefited from the sanction that their mystical views offered, to leave the house of study and head into the "fields and wildernesses," their source is without a doubt the direct encounter with the local geography through which they walked and to which they felt they belonged. The Safed tales are perhaps one of the only corpuses in the history of Jewish culture in which the place where the stories were crafted, in practice or mentally, has such a central influence on their form and meaning.

However, the picture of the encounter between place and story in Safed is hardly an ideal one. Mordechai Pachter has noted that the connection between Safed's ethicists and the Land of Israel was fraught. On the one hand, there was a sense of holiness, pride, and joy, which grew out of the fact that they lived and worked in a holy place under God's watch. On the other hand, they were anxious about not being able to shoulder the burden of obligations and the grave responsibility imposed by life in a holy realm. This tension nourished Safed's moral literature and the positions taken by moralists over the generations.[55] This tension is clearly exposed in the Tale of the Locusts, examined at the beginning of this chapter. Luria's fellowship sees itself as the vanguard of Safed's Jews. It observes the sins of Safed society and does not satisfy itself only with study or ascetic practices. Rather, the companions seek to mend the society they live in. The huge anxiety about sin that Luria reveals in every location and at every site expresses this sense of tension between the holy soil on which they walk and their society's inability to live up to the high moral demands that such a location makes. The principal tension in the Tale of the Locusts, however, is not moral. As we have seen, it is the tension seen in the story's spatial structure, built as it is on axes running from the real Safed to the worlds above it, which are themselves part of the local ambience.

The contrast between the real place and the mythical-fantastic realm is the source of the major existential tension in the Safed stories. There are almost no Safed legends or dream stories that are only realistic or only fantastical. The fundamental narrative tension in all of them derives from the stress between the real and the mythic realms. The two are connected and derive from each other. The cult of holy graves and the custom of *gerushin* (going into exile in the countryside around Safed) are other facets of the same conflict: They involve a concrete object—a grave, a stone, a site—but see its mythical side, figures from the sacred past. The tension between the here and now and the historical weight of the place is powerfully expressed in Safed culture and is enabled by the encounter with the real Land of Israel. The Holy Land could be encountered in the Exile only on the mythical level, because even the real Holy Land belonged in the Diaspora to the mythical realm. As such, this tension between the real and the visionary barely existed there.

The boundaries between real and mythic places, as I have shown, are never sharp. The protagonists of the stories and dreams move from one realm to the other, and sometimes a real place—Safed's streets, a saint's grave, a lofty mountain—turns into a mythical one when mythic figures appear there. An example is the dream of Adam lying on a bed that stretches the length of a Safed street, from the marketplace—where real life takes place—to the home of Rabbi Joseph Karo—a center of spiritual life. The image expresses the sharp and constant tension between these two poles of Safed life and the need for a mediating space between the two.[56]

Such tension between the two realms could cause acute cognitive dissonance in the soul of any person. Some could overcome the tension and move from daily life into the spiritual and mythic spheres. In Luria's case this happened day by day, smoothly and without causing, as far as we know, a significant crisis. He was a merchant and a mystic, and we have just one piece of evidence that he suffered mental or emotional anguish as a result (see Chapter 7). But for others, the incongruity could be a source of instability, as was the case with Hayyim Vital. Claude Lévi-Strauss notes that the myths told by Native Americans shape the mediating space between the severe binary contradictions that characterize their lives. The role of the mediating space is to bridge the incongruities in their physical or mental lives—that is, to resolve the cognitive dissonance that such tension is liable to produce. It allows people to survive despite the strain that threatens them.[57] Safed's legends perform this task. They shape the mediating space between the physical and the fantastical, managing the tension between them and enabling people to live with it without losing their balance.

The beauty and power of Safed's legends and visions lie not so much in the ideal mythical-spiritual world that they offer but rather in the constant tension that they express between the plane of mystery, in all its many guises, and the weak and drab real world. This tension may have been one of the reasons for the fall of the real Safed. That may have happened when the dissonance between the waking and dream states became unbearable, leading even those who loved it the most, like Vital, to leave. But it might also be that the tension that pervaded Safed was the secret of its potency. Perhaps it is what has made Safed into one of the most vibrant forces in Jewish culture over the last 400 years.

4

And He Woke and It Was a Dream

> Out of the need to survive, a person naturally transforms a life of anxiety into the stuff of legend.
>
> —Mordechai Rotenberg, "If You'll Live"

The Dream and the Fairy Tale

Rabbi Hayyim Vital's *Sefer haHezyonot* (Book of Visions), written in Damascus during the early decades of the seventeenth century, is one of the most fascinating literary-autobiographical Jewish creations to have come down to us. The great importance of this work (if such a compendium of dreams can be termed as such) is that it exposes the nerves of a religious creative process of the most personal and intimate type. Vital can permit himself such exposure—his complicated relations with his wives, his impotence, his deep antipathy for Rabbi Ya'akov Abulafia, his fantasies of greatness—precisely because his foibles are revealed through the medium of the dream. Because dreams are not an intentional or controllable medium but rather, as Vital himself understood them to be, a system of messages from the heavens above, the wishes and fears expressed in his dreams are nothing less than the great truths of divine revelation, over which he has no control at all.[1]

One of the central genres of folk literature, the fairy tale, is based on a similar psychological apparatus. A fairy tale can tell of horrifying acts of cruelty and dismemberment, fathers raping daughters, the neglect of children by their parents, and deviant sexual passions because it is perceived as fiction, not a report of events in the world. It thus provides a way for society—in the form of an individual, family, or community—to unbridle its darkest secrets. Ostensibly, the fairy tale does not inform us about the society that tells it; instead, it tells of anonymous characters in distant and imaginary worlds.[2] Thus it is hardly surprising that, almost from the earliest days of the study of fairy tales in the nineteenth century, scholars have pointed out their close relationship to dreams. They have noted common themes and motifs, including the perception of space and time, as well as the psychological and social roles played by both fairy tales and dreams. The close similarity between the two genres has prompted some to propose that the fairy tale in fact developed out of dreams and hallucinations.[3] Freud viewed the fairy-tale motifs that pervade dreams as the dream's symbolic language. He saw them as "continuous surrogates" for the unresolved elements in dreams.[4]

Such connections between the dream and the fairy tale can be seen in several of the most poetic and interesting of the dreams recorded in *Sefer haHezyonot*. The questions that occupy us in this chapter are, Why are so many of the dreams in *Sefer haHezyonot* shaped by the poetics of the folk fairy tale? What implications does this have for studying the dreams that the book records, and what can we learn from the connection between dreams and fairy tales about the perspectives of Vital and the other characters who appear in his dreams and about the prevailing ambience of Safed? These issues can best be clarified by looking at one of the dreams in particular.

> 11 Av [5369/1609] My son Shmuel dreamed that I sent my daughter to buy me cucumbers, and she immediately returned and said, "Red, greenish, green." I said to her, "Is it that the three kings of demons are coming to my home?" And I saw three demon kings entering through the door of my house, the red and the white and the green. They did not enter standing, but rather seated and drawn on their knees. And their feet entered first and then their bodies, and they sat just inside the door.... Then I asked him [the red king], "Why did you come to me now?" And he said to me, "Here, when you brought down the above-mentioned angel [in the

previous event], since you wanted to know the things that you asked him, but you sinned [because] you did not believe what he said to you, that you must bring the people to repent and you are not doing as he said. Know that all the words of this angel are true, and it is he who sent me to tell these things to you in his name." Then the white king also opened his mouth and said, "I have been silent up until now, but know that everything that that angel tells you is true and firm, and if you do not want to believe what he says, know what will happen to you!" But the green king did not speak at all. And the red king was dressed in a fine red woolen garment, and the white king wore a thin white woolen garment, and the green king wore a green silk garment. And in fact the white king was very short of stature. Afterward the red king went out with Shmuel and went to the neighborhood bakery and said to the owner of the oven, "Give a single loaf of bread to Rabbi Hayyim," and he did not want to. And then he approached him to harm him, and his [the baker's] feet shook and he gave him the bread and he brought it to me. Afterward the white and the green vanished, and only the red remained. And he said to us, "Do you want me to give you a sign that all this is true?" Then he put us into the well in the yard, and at the bottom of the well there was a hole, and he took us from there and brought us into a fine house with fine adornments and many windows, and each window opened out onto a road, on which they go to the place that they wish to go. And he took us out one window and led us to the great sea, and at one position in the sea there was a great darkness, and in the middle of the dark place a tiny hole the size of a pomegranate, and within it was a light like a burning candle. And there was a very great and deep pit without walls around the pit, [to prevent] the water of the sea from coming in, and nonetheless the waters of the sea did not come in. And he said to him [to Vital], "Have you seen this wonder? Know that on this road we ascend from under the earth, because there is our seat. And on this road we ascended to you to tell you at the behest of that angel."[5]

The dream's space is that of a real place: Vital's home, from which his daughter has set out to buy cucumbers. His son Shmuel, the dreamer, sets out with the red demon to the nearby bakery to get bread. When the red demon wants to prove the truth of what he and his companions have said, they enter the well in Vital's yard. However, this everyday reality is challenged by forces that call into question rational validity of the scene. The first of these is the entry of the three demon kings. They are dressed in flagrant colors, they advance as though they are being pulled by their knees, and they are short—dwarfs, in fact. They encroach into the real, bearing messages from the other world. From the well in the yard they lead Hayyim and Shmuel to a mysterious house at a crossroads, and from there, through a small hole, into the great sea, to the gate of the demon world at its bottom. In other words, the most notable phenomenon in the narrative of this dream is the tension between its realistic and fantastic elements, the latter of which come from the world of the fairy tale. Such too is the inexplicable behavior of the creatures that casually appear and disappear and the great distances over when the protagonists leap in an instant. All these arouse contradictory reactions of both attraction and terror.

The fairy-tale elements in the dream narrative can be interpreted psychoanalytically, in the spirit of Freud's symbol-deciphering system. Alongside clearly female symbols such as the home, the oven, the well, the hole, and the sea, there are manifestly phallic symbols, such as cucumbers, the dwarfs and their colors, the loaf of bread, and the men themselves who penetrate the well. This makes the dream that of a youth or a boy (recall that Shmuel is the dreamer), centering on sexual maturation, erotic tension, and repressed sexual hallucinations. We may presume that such phenomena would be common in a conservative religious society like that of the Jews of Safed and Damascus at the beginning of the seventeenth century.

That may well be the picture, but it is certainly not the whole picture or even its most important and most interesting part. The dream as a whole leads in the direction of the message transmitted to Rabbi Hayyim Vital by the demon kings, which they received from the angel who appeared in the previous dream. The deed Vital has been commanded to do is to bring about the repentance of the Damascus Jewish community, but he has failed. His disappointment at this failure appears in dozens of other dreams he dreams himself as well as in the dreams of others in which he appears. Its most common manifestation is the refusal of his teacher and master Rabbi Isaac Luria to meet with him during these visions; Luria is angry at Vital for not accomplishing his mission. The central importance of this subject in the dream is markedly prominent in its last sentence: "And on this road we ascended to you to tell you at the behest of that angel." In other words, in this view the fairy-tale elements—the demon kings, their form, their conduct in the narrative space—are there simply to play the role of messengers, which is central to the dream. One might thus say that the tension revealed to us in the dream's narrative design—between the real and the fantastic—is also present on the conceptual level. The basic tension is that between repressed sexual urges expressed in the dream and the messianic idea that the dream conveys.

Shmuel Vital, Master of Dreams

In his *Sefer haHezyonot* Rabbi Hayyim Vital also records the dreams of others—members of his family and others who were close to him—in which he himself serves as the leading character. The most prominent of these other dreamers is his son and spiritual heir, Shmuel. It was Shmuel who redacted the manuscript of *Sefer haHezyonot*, and as such we can be sure that he endorsed the dreams attributed to him in the book. Among those dreams that have a fairy-tale character—that is, complex, poetic dreams full of details and color—the ones dreamed by Shmuel stand out in both quantity and quality. We have just seen a typical example, the dream of the three demon kings. The others live up to the same standard.

> [On] 7 Heshvan my son Shmuel dreamed that we had gone to bring wheat for *matzot shmurot* [unleavened bread prepared from wheat that has been carefully guarded against moisture] for Pesach, and we were walking in a valley that was full of ascents and descents and there were no seeds there. And from there onward the entire way was full

of brambles. And they said to me, "How can we walk on brambles?" And I said to them, "I will pronounce a name [of God] and you will be able to walk." And my daughter Azmi was walking before me with a juicy fig in her hand. And there was a large river that extended that whole way, on one side, until we reached the source of the waters of that river. And I sat there and took eggshells and walnut shells and wrote a letter on each shell. And all the letters on those shells were these: *alef, dalet, heh, yod, kaf, tet, nun sofit*. And there was a tall ladder of rocks there, with its head in the sky, erect and straight up, not tilted, and no one could ascend it, and I pronounced a name [of God], and we ascended upward, and there was a great roof where there was a house and in it were millstones that had been hidden away from humans. And I ground all I needed, and took one of the shells and ground [it] there. And I took its flour and scattered it on the rest of the shells and they became long stalks, and I went back down and I planted these stalks at the source of the said river, in the soil.

Shmuel dreams that the stalks grew and became very tall; their leaves were red. Then, Rabbi Hayyim Vital instructed his son to hide so that people would not see him. He pronounced a name, and a tree split and he hid within it. After he emerged, Shmuel took grape seeds from a good vine, planted them, and they sprouted into wheat. Then Rabbi Hayyim was angry at him: "Why did you teach my wisdom to these people?" And the father took seeds from a bad vine, threw them on the growing wheat, and the wheat dried out. After they returned to the river's source, Rabbi Hayyim took nutmeal that he had ground above, at the top of the ladder, and cast it at the stalks, after which they produced wheat kernels for Pesach (Passover). When they asked him how he had done it, for real and not as a trick, just as the *tanna'im* had done before him, he said that he had done it in the manner of Rabbi Akiva, who "always adhered to me." After this, the earth opened up alongside the source of the river, and Gehazi, the prophet Elisha's servant, emerged, and it turned out that the red leaves on the stalks were the leprosy with which he was afflicted, and he asked Vital to raise him up from the place where he lay (the netherworld). The rabbi did so, and "then Gehazi went and entered the aforementioned garden and dwelt there." Again the earth opened, and this time Og, the giant king of Bashan, emerged, and he too was enabled to rise from the netherworld, because he had been circumcised by, Og claims, "Abraham, the head of all the circumcised, who was more righteous than all the circumcisers in Israel, and thus I was worthy of rising back to life." He then pleaded with Vital to find him a small plot in the garden, "and I gave him a small plot in that garden, like that I gave to Gehazi, and he entered and dwelt there."[6]

This long and complex dream also blends realistic and imaginary fairy-tale elements. It is anchored in the Jewish calendar (Passover) and the rituals associated with that holiday. It takes place in the familiar Mediterranean countryside—brambly meadows interspersed with farmed plots where typical Mediterranean crops are grown (wheat, figs, walnuts, grapes). But fantastic elements also appear: the magical name that Vital uses to turn the brambles into wheat; the ladder with its top in the sky, leading to a mysterious roof and magical millstones; a tree trunk that splits to hide the dreamer within it; grapes that are in fact magical objects; and a place where the earth opens into the netherworld and produces mythical-biblical figures such as Gehazi and Og, king of Bashan. Beyond all these is the "garden," the place where all the biblical figures who wish to leave the netherworld greatly desire to dwell and where Rabbi Hayyim Vital can take them and find them a place of their own.

This dream also contains many erotic symbols, but again they do not seem to be the most important elements. What stands out is Vital's absolute control over the imaginary-fantastical dreamscape. He turns the brambles into wheat; he raises people up to the top of the heavenly ladder, where he uses mysterious millstones to grind things; he plants the stalks; he determines the fate of biblical figures such as Gehazi and Og; and he controls entry to paradise. Recall that the dream was experienced by Vital's son Shmuel, indicating that it expresses his conscious or unconscious sense that his father controls the world and, in particular, his own fate. The scene that expresses this sense in the most concentrated way is the concealment of Shmuel inside the tree trunk.

And I said to my son, "Go from here and hide, so that these people will not see you." And he entered a garden and pronounced a name and a tree split. And he hid there within. And people went to seek him, and he emerged from the tree and took grapes from a good vine that was there and he sowed them and wheat grew. And I reprimanded him: "Why have you taught my wisdom to these people?" And he took bad grapes from another vine, a bad one, that was there, and took out their seeds and cast them on the growing wheat and it dried out.[7]

Shmuel's father controls his actions and decisions. He tells him to hide, and he sequesters him from the company of other people. Beyond that, when Shmuel seeks to create something of his own—to sprout wheat from grape seeds—his father orders him to destroy his creation, preventing him from having an independent living space. In this sense, Vital appears in his son's dream as a typical castrating father.

However, this episode is even more interesting if we expand its interpretation. In the Freudian scheme a tree is a female symbol. It embodies fertility and rootedness in the soil. A tree that splits in two and allows a young dreamer to vanish within it can hardly be anything other than a patent expression of erotic desires. But the motif of the hero hiding in a tree trunk that has been split with a magical name is taken from a famous legend about the death of the prophet Isaiah. In that story the prophet's pursuers discover him and saw down the tree, killing him. The story first appears in Hebrew sources in the Apocrypha of the Second Temple period, but it was also told by the sages of the Talmud, where Shmuel Vital presumably found it.[8] In any case, these two interpretations are not mutually exclusive; in fact, they complement each other. Repressed sexual tension is part of Shmuel's feeling of being impotent and even castrated—in both a physical and spiritual sense—in the presence of his father's dominant personality. Shmuel sees himself, almost certainly unconsciously, as a kind of Isaiah, persecuted for his beliefs. He must hide his thoughts, and spiritual and sexual independence is denied him.[9]

Two weeks after this dream, on 23 Heshvan (November 2, 1608), Shmuel has another dream that is also recorded by his father.

My son Shmuel dreamed that I and he and my son Yosi and Rabbi Kalev and Musa Najar walked through a planted field until we reached a very large garden, surrounded by a wall made of marble stones, where there was an opening with an old, rotting door, and I wanted to go inside. Rabbi Kalev said to me, "There is a better opening," and we went there and it had a new door of *tidhar* [plane or fir tree] wood that reeked of a wondrous smell. I opened it and we entered through it. And the entire garden was full of all the sorts of fruit trees there are in the world, and high up to the sky and aromatic, something wonderful . . . and we walked more in that garden and I saw a ladder built of stone, immeasurably high, with a railing on each side. The top of the ladder reached an upper door that was closed, and close to that door was a window without a door, but it had a wooden screen. And Rabbi Kalev said to me, "There in that upper chamber sits an old man named Efrayim, and it would not be proper for us to enter until he wakes from his sleep." And my son Shmuel ascended the ladder to its top and grabbed the tangle of high trees and entered through the holes of the screen up to his waist. And the old man grabbed him and helped him all the way in. And he saw the old man standing on fine bedding, with a cap on his head, its color like the heart of celery. And Shmuel went and opened the door from inside, and Rabbi Kalev ascended and then came back down. And he said to me, "The old man is ill and is sleeping." But Shmuel pleaded with the old man to open the window and door entirely and show his face to us, so that it would be seen that he was not sleeping. And then he did as he asked, and we all ascended and sat with him.

After eating from the fruit of the wondrous garden, only the old man and Rabbi Hayyim Vital and Shmuel (the dreamer) remained there, and the first two huddled together and whispered. So that the others would not hear their conversation, Shmuel took them to a different garden, where

"[We] walked through a planted field until we reached a very large garden, surrounded by a wall made of marble stones, where there was an opening with an old, rotting door, and I wanted to go inside."

only grass grew, not wonderful trees as in the old man's garden. "Afterward the old man revealed some of the secrets we spoke of together to Shmuel. And I was sad about that, because I did not want him to reveal to him. And Shmuel woke up and it was a dream."[10]

The main character in the action here is the dreamer himself, Shmuel Vital. He ascends the ladder and enters through the window; the mysterious old man appears only to him, whereas the others see him as "ill and sleeping." It is Shmuel whom the old man commands to bring fruit from the garden, and he decides what to serve the guests. He is also the only one to remain in the room and hear the conversation between the two elder sages, his father and the wondrous old man, and it is Shmuel who takes the rest of the party to a different garden so that they will not overhear the conversation between the two elders. It is to him that the old man reveals the substance of his exchange with Rabbi Hayyim Vital, even though his father is not pleased by this at all.

As in the previous dream, Shmuel engages in several actions that are intended to gain him independence and free him from dependence on his dominant father. He appears here as a dynamic young man of initiative, originality, and discernment who gains the approval of those around him. The climax of his quest for independence comes when the conversation between the old man and his father is conveyed to him by the old man. Why does the old man do this, and why is the father opposed? The answer, it would seem, must be sought only after we identify who the wondrous elder is. There are two possibilities. One is that the old man is a messianic figure (he is named Efrayim, that is, the Messiah son of Efrayim, son of Joseph). This may be an intimation of the messianic figure of Rabbi Shimon bar Yohai, the author and central protagonist of the *Zohar*. The other possibility is that the elder is Isaac Luria, Hayyim Vital's teacher and spiritual father. Whatever the case, the description of him "with a cap on his head, its color like the heart of celery" indicates that this figure is a leader and ruler. (In a famous image, Shabbetai Zvi, who lived not long after the time of the dream and came from the same cultural environment, wears a similar cap as a sign of authority.) In fact, Vital crowns both bar Yohai and Luria as messianic predecessors of himself.[11] Because this is Shmuel's dream, it is clearly an example of wish fulfillment: Hayyim Vital's son seeks to circumvent the authority of his father, who apparently refrained from conveying to him all the secrets of the Kabbalah (perhaps because of his young age). Shmuel seeks the source of the secrets himself, either from bar Yohai or Luria, and receives their lore directly. His vibrant youth enables Shmuel to operate outside his father's authority with dexterity and courage, and the welcome he receives from the masters of secret lore, figures named as messianic, are wishes that are fulfilled in the dream, precisely because they are not answered in reality.

Shmuel's dream is a text, not just because in modern culture every statement, whether verbal, visual, or emotional, is considered a text but because, according to what is conveyed to us here, Shmuel tells his dream to his father, who in turn sets it down on paper. As noted, Shmuel edited *Sefer haHezyonot*, meaning that he approved the text that his father recorded, at least in its general outlines. We must thus address this dream, like the other dreams attributed to Shmuel, not as an unconscious outburst of repressed feelings but rather as a text that was drafted orally and in writing, based on a dream experience but shaped as a manifestly literary text.

Generically, Shmuel Vital's dreams and stories display characteristic fairy-tale elements. Their plots are "defective" in that they are radically unlikely. The characters walk through a field and suddenly encounter a ladder with its top in the sky or a wall made of marble that they had never seen before, even though they are not far from where they live. They reach a millstone floating in the air or a house without any doorway. The stories also jump around in space: from the earth to the stairs in the sky, through a well in the yard that leads to another world, and other such sudden transitions between real places and supernatural ones. In addition, supernatural characters appear and magical events occur in these story-line dreams. There are dwarfs from the netherworld, magic names that are used to ascend the ladder to the sky, ground meal that is turned into wheat, the entire life (or wisdom) of humanity that is contained in a fig. The descriptions are also extreme: wild colors, expensive and eye-catching garments, magnificent gardens with magical fruit, the highest heaven and the lowest depths of the earth, fields full of brambles and splendid gardens with marvelous trees, a parched wilderness full of thorns, and rivers, fountains, and springs.

But the differences between the folk fairy tale and young Shmuel's stories and dreams are also notable. Fairy tales are entirely imaginary. Although there are some realistic elements, their world is an imaginary one. They are disconnected from real time and place and are not meant to be believed by their hearers, because their messages are palpably universal and ahistorical.[12] In contrast, Shmuel Vital's dreams are a tension-charged mixture of the real and the imaginary. There are real characters, such as Rabbi Hayyim Vital, Shmuel himself, his sister and brother, family friends, the baker at the end of the street. The same is true of the landscape in which the story unfolds. We see the home, the street, the well in the yard, and further afield the meadows and orchards, but from there we enter fantastical or mythic spaces—stairways in heaven, the depths of the earth, the realm of the dead, paradise, a secret house.[13] A typical example of this amalgam is Shmuel's penetration of the magical garden, his ascent up the ladder to a house with blocked entrances, and his incursion through a screen that covers a window. A hero who overcomes obstacles that he encounters along the way in order to reach his destination is one of the most common motifs of the fairy-tale genre, and that is what happens in this dream. In the fairy-tale world, the hero who has overcome all the obstacles along his way reaches a golden-haired princess whom many before him have striven to win but have failed. Our hero, young Shmuel, gets a quite different reward. The mysterious old man provides him with secret knowledge, kabbalistic secrets. The story makes fascinating use of narrative elements found in fairy tales, elements that have patently erotic significance, but in relation to a different world of concepts, that of Jewish mysticism. Many scholars of Kabbalah have pointed to the connection between Kabbalah and Eros, a subject to which I will return in Chapter 5. In Shmuel's mind, as expressed in the fashioning of these dreams/fairy tales, the two drives exist side by side, with erotic tension merging with the passion for acquiring mystical knowledge.

If we look at Shmuel Vital's narrative dreams in this way, we can assert that he is the first Jewish fairy-tale writer whom we can identify by name. The authors of previous fairy tales in Hebrew or Yiddish—for example, the thirteenth-century *Sefer haMa'asim* or the fifteenth-century Yiddish *Mayseh Buch*—are unknown. We might possibly point to one such writer, Rabbi Avraham, son of Maimonides, who composed the Hebrew version of "Ma'aseh beYerushalmi" ("Story of a Jerusalemite"), if that identification is correct.[14] In any case, Shmuel Vital stands before us as a consistent narrator with a style that is clearly his own. Although the interests of his father, Rabbi Hayyim Vital, reverberate between the lines of these stories, there are still clear signs that they derive from a single artistic perception. His stories are works of the imagination and personal experience that make artistic use of elements of the folk fairy tale in order to present a world characterized by tension between the real and the imaginary, between the personal and the mystic.

We cannot speak of the composition of fairy tales in the realm of religious literature without mentioning the figure who, more than anyone else in Jewish literary history, is famed for his fairy tales: Rabbi Nachman of Bratslav. Rabbi Nachman also related dreams, but they are of a quite different literary character. His dreams lack the fairy-tale elements that typify Shmuel Vital's dreams, and the fairy tale–like stories of Rabbi Nachman have a clear ideological-allegorical nature. Just to illustrate, I offer here one of his dreams.

> 5665 [1804], the eve of the holy Sabbath after the blessing over the wine. And I saw in a dream that I was in a city and it seemed to me in the dream that the city was very large. And a great saint (*tzadik*), of the saints of old, who was considered a great saint, arrived there, and everyone went to him, and I also went to him. And I saw that everyone was passing by his side and not greeting him. And it looked as if they were doing it on purpose, and I greatly wondered at their having the impudence to do this, without greeting him deliberately, as I said, and the excuse was that he was truly a great saint, but his body was collected from several places, which were considered polluted places, but he himself was a great man and took upon himself to correct that body. And one does not greet a fellow in polluted places, and for that reason they did not greet him.[15]

This dream has been interpreted as giving voice to Rabbi Nachman's anxiety about the passions of the flesh (a body gathered from polluted places) and his attempt, from a young age, to entirely obliterate his sexual urge. Other interpretations are, of course, possible, but they are not of interest to us here. The principal difference between Shmuel Vital and Rabbi Nachman is the artistic use of the materials in these dreams. With Shmuel Vital, the real aspects of the dream are its open, colorful spaces, which are full of light and a variety of characters, perceived as the land of the fairy tale. Rabbi Nachman's dreams are enclosed within an urban or social space, and their template is allegorical, which seems to have been the primary impetus for the dreams. It thus seems more appropriate to compare Shmuel Vital's fairy-tale dreams to Rabbi Nachman's fairy tales rather than to his dreams. A comprehensive study of Rabbi Nachman's dreams, comparing them to dreams of other religious leaders of his type, has yet to be done.

Shmuel Vital preceded Rabbi Nachman by about two centuries, and the dream–fairy tales he told were composed when he was still young. In contrast, Rabbi Nachman told his fairy tales at the end of his career. In any case, the differences between them are numerous and significant. Shmuel's texts are fragmentary and disconnected, making it hard to piece together a continuous narrative. Rabbi Nachman's stories, on the other hand, are well crafted. The plot is developed, and the stories offer a clear narrative conflict with a distinct goal (to bring the princess home, to win a story contest). Their artistic craftsmanship is evident. In this sense, Rabbi Nachman's stories lend support to those scholars who claim that, despite their undeniable link to the unconscious, the fairy tale is, in fact, a deliberate work of art.[16] Shmuel Vital's texts are much closer to reflections of dreams as experienced—fragmentary, fantastic, devoid of conscious regulation and planning. They lack ongoing narrative development; the protagonists skip from place to place without purpose or intention. Why do Hayyim Vital and his companions go out to the fields? Why, when they see a high marble wall, do they seek to find a way to pass through it? Why does he collect seeds from the field, keep them until after he climbs the magical ladder with the help of a holy name, and grind them in the millstones he finds suspended in the heavens? How is it that the members of Hayyim Vital's family receive the three demon kings, with their glowing colors, without any surprise? These texts also lack a clear narrative conflict—Hayyim Vital and Shmuel and the other characters in the accounts face no antagonists. Even when figures such as Gehazi, Og, and the demon kings appear out of the depths of the earth, they do not vie with the dream's protagonist. Rather, they convey messages or make requests.

The other critical difference between the literary design of Shmuel Vital's dreams and that of Rabbi Nachman's fairy tales is the prominence given to description over narrative. In Rabbi Nachman's fairy tales the narrative is long and convoluted. It has narrative logic, and there are movements over large spaces and encounters with many characters. Almost all these elements are lacking in Shmuel's dreams. On the contrary, those dreams are full of rich, colorful description, full of vitality and charisma. There are magical gardens, mysterious houses, vegetation, fruit, springs, exceptional clothing, and glowing colors. Such descriptions are almost entirely absent from Rabbi Nachman's stories, where the plot provides the greater part of the artistic appeal.

But there is one more important difference between these two authors: their connection to the real world. Shmuel Vital's stories are anchored in actual experience. The dreams take place in and around Safed (or Damascus), in a yard or walking distance from a concrete city. The characters are largely members of his family (his father, sister, and brother), friends of the family (his father's students, his own companions), or neighbors and others he knows from the neighborhood (such as the baker). Even the backdrop to the story—the types of trees, varieties of fruit and other crops, the paths, walls, gardens and the houses behind them, stairs, ladders, millstones, foods of all kinds—is firmly part of the real world. Rabbi Nachman, for his part, detaches his stories almost entirely from the real world. They take place in a strange, imaginary realm, as fairy tales typically do. In this sense, Shmuel Vital's fairy-tale dreams resemble surrealistic literature and may very well be one of the first examples of that genre.[17] It is Rabbi Nachman's stories that are shaped like fairy tales, of the artistic variety (*kunstmärchen*) rather than the folk variety.[18] In this sense Shmuel's dreams are closer to Kafka's works than to Rabbi Nachman's stories, as scholars and critics have maintained.[19] But it is not the place here to go into this further.

Hayyim Vital's Nightmarish Dreams

Shmuel Vital's dreams are full of light and color, open spaces, gardens, and the scents of the fields. Far different are two fairy tale–type dreams that his father recorded.

> 5367 [1606], 12 Kislev, the third night whose star is Mars and its angel is Samael. And it was [the week of the] *Vayishlah* [portion of the Torah], which contains Samael's war with Jacob and the matter of the chiefs of Esau, as said our rabbis, may their memory be a blessing, "Captain Magdiel is Rome." Also the reading from the prophets, the Vision of Obadiah.
>
> And I saw in my dream a very great and high mountain, made of flint. And it was carved and straight on all four sides like the sides of a single square wall. And I ascended the eastern face alongside the southeastern corner and asked, "What city is this?" And they said to me, "This is Nineveh." And afterward they said to me, "This is Rome the evil." And the writer, Hayyim, said, "Remember, for you will find this in the handwritten manuscript of the *Book of Zerubavel*."

And I saw that a very long stake was wedged into the inside of the eastern wall and jutted out on the side of the city's buildings, at a height actually about halfway up the wall. And an inverted sword, its point downward, was stuck into the stake. And its handle stood above the top of the wall, because the length of the sword was that of half the wall. And they said to me, "This sword has been stuck into this stake from the creation of the world to this day, and no person has ever touched it." And I looked at it and I saw that it was of incomparable copper [alternatively, "incomparably firm"] and cuts all sorts of iron as if they were dry straw. And it had four edges on its four sides, and the head of the sword, at the end of its point, resembled the mouth of an actual snake, and they said that anyone whom this sword touched could not survive.

And I thought in my heart, perhaps during all that time, from the creation of the world until now, the sword has rusted? And saw that it was really like new. And I took it in my hand. And I said to the emperor of Rome, "Here is that sword which no person has ever touched; it is now in the hand of a Jew." And the king commanded to seek me out and kill me. And while I was still there on the top of the wall, I cast the sword from my hand into the city, and its point pierced the ground in one of the courtyards of the city. And I fled and hid in a cave in Rome in which poor people dwelt, and I hid there until the hour of the afternoon prayer on the Sabbath day. And then I came out and the emperor's men captured me and took me before him. And he commanded, "Take everyone out of my presence!" And I and he remained alone. I said to him, "For what do you seek to kill me? Here, all of you have gone astray in your religion like blind people, for there is no true teaching other than the teaching of Moses alone, and nothing else is truth." And he said to me, "Here, it is because I knew all that that I sent to seek you out, because I knew that there is no one as wise and sage as you in the true wisdom, and I want you to inform me of the secrets of the Torah and some names of the blessed God, your God, because I already know the truth. And therefore do not fear that I have sent after you, because I truly love you." And I then informed him a bit of this wisdom. And I woke.[20]

The scenery here is quite different from what we saw in Shmuel's dreams. Here we have a world of what the poet Nathan Alterman called "long, empty streets of iron." It is an urban world of hard materials: a hard stone wall, a fortress at the top of a high stone mountain, hard iron, menacing houses, a dark cave, a copper sword. Even the context in which the dream takes place—Mars, the war planet, ruled by Samael, and Jacob's war with Samael (Jacob's wrestling with the angel at the ford of Jabbok), or the war with Rome—is one of harsh battles and violence.

The allusions to other texts that can be discerned between the lines of this dream enhance its dark, nightmarish ambience. The most obvious of these is the explicit reference to the *Book of Zerubavel*, whose narrator relates, "A wind lifted me up between heaven and earth and carried me to the great city Nineveh, city of blood." There he encounters "a man [who was] despicable, broken down and in pain. . . . I asked him, 'Sir, what is the name of this place?' He said to me, 'This is mighty Rome, wherein I am imprisoned.'"[21] The identification of Nineveh with Rome and the process of arriving there, over the walls, by means of a wind or some other mysterious way, are quite similar. But Hayyim Vital does not encounter the wretched, repulsive indigent who is the Messiah, because he himself is the Messiah.[22] Nevertheless, the atmosphere of *Sefer Zerubavel*—of the war of the End of Days, the terror, the descriptions of miserable poverty and harsh suffering—pass also into Hayyim Vital's dream and shape its ambience.

On top of this explicit source there seem to be two more that we cannot be entirely certain that Vital knew. The first is the legend of David's general Joab, who conquers the city of Rabat (or Caesarea in other versions). When Joab sees that he cannot take the fortified city by the usual siege, he commands his solders to catapult him over the city wall. He lands in the courtyard of a poor family, where a pregnant young woman tends his wounds and feeds him. When he recovers, he goes to a blacksmith, whom he asks to forge a sword to replace the one broken when he landed. The blacksmith makes Joab a sword, but it breaks from his massive strength when he swings it above his head. A second sword also breaks; only the third sword that the blacksmith forges meets his needs. Joab then sets out on a bloody campaign during which he slaughters thousands of people in the city, including the young woman who succored him and in whose home he hid. In the end he opens the gates of the city and it falls to his forces.[23] The journey over the wall, the mythological sword, and hiding from the king among poor people are all motifs that appear in both the story of Joab and Hayyim Vital's dream. We cannot exclude the possibility that Vital was acquainted with the Joab legend in one of its versions, from the midrash *Yalkut haMakhiri* or some other source.

The second source is even more problematic because, to the best of my knowledge, it is not to be found in Jewish literature. This is the story of the mythological sword stuck in a stone since the days of old, which can be drawn out only by he who is destined to rule over the kingdom and redeem it. This is, of course, the medieval myth of King Arthur and his sword, Excalibur.[24] We do not know by what convoluted path, written or oral, this motif might have made its way to Rabbi Hayyim Vital. Whatever the case, the motif was current in the late Middle Ages, so a path of influence is possible. The significant difference between King Arthur's sword and Vital's is that Arthur's sword was stuck in a stone, whereas Vital's is stuck in a long stake that is itself wedged into a city wall. This is a significant difference, because the stake and the sword stuck into it clearly form the shape of a cross, which Vital ruins when he draws the sword out of the stake. It is almost certainly for this reason that the king chases him.

This depiction of a sword as a cross may have its origin in the legend of San Galgano. The San Galgano monastery lies a little less than 20 miles south of Siena in Tuscany and is named after a saint entombed there. San Galgano was a knight who decided to abjure the life of war and wantonness and become a monk. The symbol of his decision was his act of plunging his sword into a boulder, turning it from a bloody instrument into a holy cross. He became a monk at that same site, and it was there in 1185 that the monastery named after him was built. The ruins of the monastery remain there today; at their center is the holy sword, still jutting out of the stone. It is a major tourist attraction. Recall that Rabbi Hayyim Vital's family came from Italy. It may be that he heard about or even saw the miraculous sword in the stone, shaped like a cross.[25]

Here is where the messianic nature of the dream comes out. Breaking the power of the cross precedes the redemption, which ends with the acceptance of the authority of the Jewish messiah by the king of Rome (meaning, apparently, the pope).[26] What is interesting and innovative in the messianic nature of this dream is its placatory resolution, which is different from the ending in the *Book of Zerubavel* (which largely involves horrible war and bloodshed) and the ending to the legend of Joab (Joab conquers the city after a bloody rampage through its streets). Hayyim Vital casts the sword away and does not fight with it. He captures the heart of Rome using the Torah teachings he imparts to the king. I know of no other appearance of this peaceful resolution to an eschatological conflict, coming in place of the terrible war of the End of Days, in contemporary literature.[27]

The second fairy tale–type dream that Hayyim Vital recorded is the following.

> 16 Tevet 5368 [1607] I dreamed a great dream and forgot it. I will write what I remember of it.
>
> I and my son Shmuel were sitting on the banks of the Great [Mediterranean] Sea and I touched the water to see if it was cold or warm, and I saw that it was warm. And I ascended from there to a very high mountain on the edge of that sea, and alongside the mountain that was beside the waters of the sea was a wall built of stones, and there was no slope to the mountain there and there was an open road between the wall and the sea. And I extracted a stone from the top of the wall and cast it onto that road. And after I cast it down I watched that stone, and it changed into a large bone the size of a human skull to the throat, and at one end it was cut, as if it had been cut from its joint, but it had no visible image on it. And it gradually took on the image of a human

head. And then its eyes opened, and they gazed and looked at me with great anger, and I saw it and grew frightened at seeing all this. And the skull opened its mouth and said to me, "Do I not know that you are he who took me from the wall and cast me down? And here I am a *telfas*,[28] one made of sorcery. And it placed me on the top of the wall to hold Israel enslaved under the hand of the nations so long as I am there. And now that you have taken me and cast me here, my power from those enchantments has been removed, and Israel will leave slavery. And you caused all that and therefore I am angry with you."

And I watched and all the parts of his body were completed, with the face of a tall hero, stocky, of reddish flesh, and he ascended to me to the top of that mountain to fight there. And I saw that I had two knives, one large with a cropped iron blade and the second smaller, with a whole iron blade, but its hilt and handle were of wood, and the upper half of it, close to the blade, did not have anything on either side. And I took them, and I fought stalwartly with him, and I struck him and wounded him and dealt him huge blows on his neck and his two shoulders down to the chest, and a stunning amount of blood flowed from him. And then his friend came to help him and I did not know where he came from and he was a black man of small stature, weaker than him and weaker and of worse quality, and he came to help him. And I struck him as well just as I had before.

And I feared that the lord of the city would capture me, because I had shed their blood, and I recanted and fell back. Then the first one came and took one knife from me and I was scared that he would overcome me. And I began to excommunicate him, and said to him, "You will be excommunicated and banned by the Holy One, Blessed Be He, in two worlds, if you harm me." Then we began to argue in the manner of an apology [or polemic]. And then I realized that I knew who he was. And I woke up.[29]

A grim medieval atmosphere prevails here as well, but it is even more powerful. There is a narrow road alongside a stone wall that runs along the sea (reminiscent of the Crusader walls of Acre, which were familiar to Hayyim Vital from his period in Safed). There are human body parts, such as a skull, scattered on the street, knife battles, deformed figures—the red-haired giant and the dwarf who appears out of nowhere—that fight with Vital until bloody. Above all is the transformation of a stone from the wall, first into a skull and then into a giant, that had previously been a magic charm that constituted the obstacle to the redemption of the Jews. The dream's nightmare atmosphere is replete with typical apocalyptic motifs: flowing blood, terrifying supernatural events that take place before our eyes, bloody clashes between huge and powerful figures, and freakish figures—giants, dwarfs, monstrous faces. These images are taken from the apocalyptic visions found in the apocalyptic midrashim, in particular the *Book* (or *Apocalypse*) *of Zerubavel*, which Vital cited in the previous dream. The messianic nature of the dream is also demonstrated by its similarity to a messianic event involving David Reubeni that took place at the Western Wall. Reubeni, a sixteenth-century Jewish adventurer and mystic, extracted a stone from the wall, alleged to have been an enchanted stone, "and as long as it was in the wall Israel could not leave the Exile."[30]

In the penultimate sentence of his dream account, Vital writes, "And then I realized that I knew who he was." Clearly, he means Armilus, the infamous anti-Messiah, who blocks the redemption of the world. In medieval Jewish eschatology Armilus must be defeated in the wars of the End of Days to enable the redemption to proceed. Vital's dream does not end with victory over Armilus and the arrival of the redemption, but it is clear that the deed can be done by only one man: Rabbi Hayyim Vital, the dreamer. It may well be that Armilus the anti-Messiah is here melded with Vital's personal Armilus, Rabbi Ya'akov Abulafia; Abulafia's envy of Vital, so Vital believes, prevents the Jewish people from repenting, a precondition for enabling Vital himself to bring the redemption. Abulafia has already appeared explicitly in the role of the anti-Messiah in some of Vital's other dreams, as we have seen.[31]

The quite meaningful differences between the dreams of Hayyim and Shmuel Vital are evident at even a quick glance. Shmuel's dreams are painted in strong colors; they are set in open spaces like fields, gardens, springs, and the heavens. Shmuel's dreams also have a plethora of characters—groups of people walk through fields, enter a wondrous garden, and proceed to another garden or climb a stairway to heaven. His father's dreams are, in contrast, dark, black-and-white, and take place in a cramped urban space of narrow alleys or murky caves. These spaces are also empty of people; other than Hayyim Vital and his son, no other characters appear, with the exception of the antagonist, Armilus. In the dream just described, even Shmuel vanishes early on, and the hero, Rabbi Hayyim Vital, acts alone. The father's dreams are also rife with violence—battles, bloodshed, weapons, deadly danger. Shmuel's dreams hew closely to the world of the fairy tale (including its sexual aspects), whereas Hayyim Vital's dreams bear a resemblance to the medieval romance, with its cold, cruel backdrops, its connection to religious myth, and its placement of the hero at the center of the narrative.[32] Thematically, however, the real and direct context of Hayyim Vital's dreams is, as I have shown, the apocalyptic-medieval midrashim and their national-messianic symbols and goals.

THE ENCHANTED GARDEN

In a previous dream, Gehazi and Og, king of Bashan, ask Hayyim Vital to allow them to leave their places in the depths of the earth and dwell in his garden. In another dream we see Hayyim Vital and his band arrive at a marble wall, and after they discover an opening in it, they enter a magical garden where fruit trees of all kinds grow. In the dream I adduced in Chapter 3, Vital ascends a heavenly ladder until he reaches a narrow opening through which he enters such a garden. There he encounters Elijah, who takes his hand and leads him to a wondrous yard through which rivers flow. There are flourishing and robust fruit trees, wonderful aromas, and tall shade trees. Many fowl, resembling white geese, nest there. "They recited a verse or chapter of the Mishnah and stretched out their necks and ate an apple right from the tree and then drank water from the rivers." Nisim Cohen, one of Vital's companions, dreamed that on the way to Jerusalem he and a friend were washed up on a lonely island in the middle of the river, an island encircled by a wooden wall, within which was a "perfectly beautiful garden." He is told that the garden belongs to Rabbi Hayyim. When they reach the center of the island, they find Vital at the head of a group of sages; the two new arrivals complete a *minyan*, a prayer quorum. The wife of Rabbi Shmuel Hayati dreamed that she went into the field and saw an opening and entered it. She finds herself in a large garden with trees that smell like "myrrh and aloes." There is a marvelous pool and fountain, but she does not see any human figure. She hears a voice declaring that it is the place of Hayyim, the kabbalist.[33]

In these dreams the garden's meaning can be assumed, but in an earlier dream from 1590 the different motifs of the wondrous garden are fully fleshed out and precise.

> In the same year my wife Hannah became very ill, and one Sabbath she was dying and insensible. On the night after the Sabbath we approached her to see her soul leave her. And suddenly she opened her mouth and closed eyes and made the blessing over fragrant trees [one of the blessings recited in the Havdalah ceremony at the end of the Sabbath]. And we asked her what this was. And she answered in a low voice, "Your voice will come ghostlike from the earth" (Isaiah 29:4), and said, "Know that that they now led my soul to the netherworld and I saw that they were stoking the fire that went out on the Sabbath, and I smelled much fire and sulfur. And then they led my soul and other souls to a field before the opening to the Garden of Eden, where there were myrtle bushes, so that we could smell a good scent to overcome the smell of the sulfur of the netherworld, and then I made the blessing on fragrant trees. Then I entreated them to take me into the Garden of Eden to see the place of my husband, Rabbi Hayyim. And they led me to the Garden of Eden and brought me into a large courtyard, all of it planted with fragrant trees and good fruit, and in the middle a high jet of water from which the water spurts from below to above into the air, and then falls back down and fills the pool. And in the jet of water were vessels like glass, of gold and silver, rising and falling in that water. And I said to them, 'What are these?' And they said

to her, 'These bottles are the souls of your children who died young and remain always in the waters of their father's pool in the Garden of Eden.' After that I saw on one side of the yard a very high ladder, on which one could ascend to a high platform above on that side, and it was like a gallery with a roof and three walls, and the fourth wall, on the side of the yard, there was empty, so that it was possible to see from there the pleasures of the trees in the yard. And many sages sat on this balcony, studying with my husband. And I saw one sage wrapped in a *tallit* sitting there. And I asked about him. And they said to me, 'That is Rabbi Ashkenazi [Luria], your husband's master.' And I said to them, 'And how is it that he does not have his own yeshiva?' And they told me that there in the Garden of Eden he always sits with my husband. And I wanted to climb the ladder to see the place where my husband sits, but they would not allow me. And they said to me, 'You are not allowed to enter any of the houses on the yard and all the more so this gallery because they are all your husband's portion in the Garden of Eden. And had you not had the merit of being his wife, they would not even allow you to enter the yard itself. And that should be sufficient for you.'

"And here was Rabbi Gedaliah Levi, the husband of my husband's sister, ascending the ladder. And my husband was angry and rebuked him and said, 'Go down quickly because you do not have permission to ascend here.' And he went."

And when she finished speaking, she became mute as she had been, until morning. And then she opened her eyes and returned to her senses. And we asked her if she remembered the things she had said on the night after the Sabbath. And she said that she did not remember anything at all. And it seems in my humble opinion that it was for Rabbi Gedaliah, because at that time I was angry with him.[34]

This text is not a standard dream; it is a classic example of a return from the dead or a near-death experience. The narrator dies and crosses the

"A perfectly beautiful garden."

boundary into the world of the dead but returns miraculously to report what she saw there. Many intriguing accounts of this sort have come down to us from the Middle Ages and from the modern era. Scholars of the phenomenon, be they psychologists or folklorists, agree that it reflects the need to reinforce the cultural values in the world of the person who has this experience, in particular, values that are in doubt or dispute.[35] Hayyim Vital himself seems to have been aware of this aspect of the phenomenon, as he states that the secondary episode in which his brother-in-law is mentioned is simply a reflection of a quarrel they were in fact having. In other words, in this dream, according to his view, there is a direct correspondence with the real world. To take the analogy further, Vital's wife believes that he is the central and leading sage in this world and the next and is deserving of honor that no other sage, not even the master, Luria himself, is given.

That is not what we know about Vital and Luria's students at the time. The year 1590 was seventeen years after the death of their leader and fifteen years after his students signed the famous document in which they recognized Hayyim Vital's custodianship of Luria's teachings and the leadership he was supposed to provide.[36] After that document was signed, Vital's position as

Luria's primary student began to erode, to the point that he was compelled to leave Safed, apparently humiliated and bitterly disappointed, first to Jerusalem (in 1578) and then to Damascus.[37] The vision and testimony that Vital's wife offers regarding her husband's status in the next world, above that of Luria himself, is diametrically opposed to her husband's status in this world. Thus, although Vital, in commenting on his brother-in-law's appearance in the dream, sought to make a direct connection between the vision and the real world, one that would instill confidence, we know that the correlation is an inverse one. That the magical garden is, as was presumed thus far, the Garden of Eden is obvious.[38] But more than that, it is a wish fulfillment, metaphorical compensation for the real world's failure to fulfill Rabbi Hayyim Vital's personal vision.

Turning Distress into Legend

The wondrous gardens described in great detail in the visions involving Rabbi Hayyim Vital are similar to those of Oriental gardens of the type that appear frequently in *The Arabian Nights*. Among the common elements are encircling walls, trees with colorful fruit, wonderful aromas, pools of water, spurting fountains, and sumptuous dwellings scattered among the foliage. The Oriental imagination that operates here in full force is much like that which shapes the fantastical world of the fairy tale. Why were so many of the visions of Hayyim and Shmuel Vital imprinted with the fairy-tale template? One explanation, already mentioned, is the similarity and perhaps even causal relationship between dreams and fairy tales. But an even more important explanation links the private or social life of the narrator to the contents of the story.

Students of the fairy tale have pointed out that the fantasy played out in the plot of a fairy tale can be seen as a desperate attempt to make order out of a difficult, chaotic, and disappointing reality. The fairy tale places details and events in their "correct" places. It says, If the world operated as it should, this is how it would look. The supernatural events of the fairy tale give expression to the narrator's and auditors' internal confidence that the injustice of a harsh reality has come to an end, making way for repair and reparation.[39] In a passage that might have been written precisely for the interpretation of fairy-tale visions, psychologist and philosopher Mordechai

Rotenberg says, "The reason that the psychological narrative explicitly assumes that only a subjective autobiographical interpretation shapes personal truth is that it alone creates a continuous identity that enables the individual to survive." Furthermore, "The psychological narrative . . . is subjective, because its aim is to turn difficult life events into a personal 'myth' that can be lived with. . . . Out of the need to survive, a person naturally transforms a life of anxiety into the stuff of legend."[40]

Damascus in the first two decades of the seventeenth century was in every sense the end of the road for Rabbi Hayyim Vital. He was already elderly and ill (and apparently nearly blind). He was far away from Safed, where he had reached the acme of his life. He was a social and religious outcast, not accepted by the city's Jewish community leadership; he was even ejected from his pulpit in the Sicilian synagogue. This seems to have deprived him of his livelihood and plunged him into abject poverty. Although he saw himself as the designated heir of his great teacher, Rabbi Isaac Luria, who, he believed, had called him to a messianic destiny, he had to come to terms with a difficult actuality in which he was denied any position of authority or honor. On top of all that, there was his short stature, threadbare clothing, debilitated appearance, white hair, and blindness, all of which no doubt added to his wretchedness and sense of having been wronged. If we were to seek a model for a person who needed to wage an all-out war, both within himself and outside, to survive in a chaotic world, we could do no better than Rabbi Hayyim Vital.

What is fascinating here from a literary or cultural point of view is the Vital's choice—conscious or unconscious—of the fairy tale as the means for maintaining his personal identity and ensuring his mental survival. What makes *Sefer haHezyonot* unique is the creative consciousness of one of the most tragic and fascinating figures in Jewish culture of the early modern or any other period. The work uses fantasy, both colorful, open, flowing into open spaces, and illuminated images and horrifying nightmares that well up from the unconscious. These elements are not just expressions of anxieties, disappointments, or secret wishes but ways of enabling a tragic figure like Hayyim Vital to maintain his identity as a writer and a human being in the midst of the chaos in which he lived.

5

Sin Crouches at the Door

A certain old man [Elijah] came up to him and taught him: The greater the man, the greater his Evil Inclination. R. Isaac stated: The [Evil] Inclination of a man grows stronger within him from day to day.

—Babylonian Talmud, *Sukah* 52a

From Birth to Death

ONE OF THE MOST beloved themes of Jewish legends over the generations consists of stories on the foundation of centers of Torah study. Such stories were told about the great yeshivas (seminaries) of Babylonia, Egypt, Kairouan, Provence and Spain, the Rhineland, and Poland.[1] One of the foundation myths of Safed as a center of Kabbalistic study appears in the following legend:

> When the great and wondrous pious sage, our honored teacher Rabbi Moshe Cordovero, may the memory of the righteous be a blessing, died, Rabbi Yitzhak Luria, may the memory of the righteous be a blessing, began to call out and said, "Who sees what I see?" And no one answered him. And a 13-year-old boy began to say, "I see!" And the sage called out and said, "What do you see, my son?" He said to him, "I see a pillar of fire going before the bier of the sage who died." He said to him, "Here is proof that you

have never had a seminal emission. I hereby give you my daughter for a wife and you are worthy of being given all the secrets of the Torah." And he went with him to his home and his daughter and took him as a real son. After half a year had gone by, the boy had a seminal emission before the wedding. The sage immediately knew this and expelled him from his house, saying, "The virtue you had you have lost, and if so, what makes you better than other men?"[2]

Luria's choice of a 13-year-old to be his son-in-law and successor is diametrically opposed to the assertion that appears in a range of versions in *Shivkhei ha-'Ari* that he came from Egypt to Safed for a single purpose: to meet Rabbi Hayyim Vital and convey to him his secret teachings. Here, in contrast, Luria seeks to pass his teachings on to a boy whom he found worthy to receive them and, on top of that, to make the boy part of his family. But when the boy ceased to meet the severe moral standard Luria insisted on, he sent the boy away.

The pillar of fire is a familiar kabbalistic symbol, expressing the connection between the human and divine worlds; it crosses the *sefirot* (spheres, the mystical topography of the divine realm) and serves as a conduit for the flow between the two worlds. A pillar of fire proceeding before Cordovero's bier symbolizes the dead man's leadership and his status as a sage who served as a link between the two worlds. It also imbues him with the same sacredness as the Ark of the Covenant, before which a pillar of fire proceeded in the wilderness. After his death, the person whose eyes could see the pillar of fire was the person who would become his heir. The young boy who saw the pillar was designated to succeed Rabbi Isaac Luria, who himself succeeded Cordovero. The story's theme is the transfer of wisdom (*translation studii*) from a sage to his successor and from one generation to the next. The moment that the most important mystic of the previous generation dies and the pillar of fire passes on to Luria (he is the only one to see it) is the moment of the establishment of Luria's school of Kabbalah in Safed.[3]

What makes this foundation story so unique is its connection to an explicitly sexual sin. The 13-year-old boy has the merit of seeing the pillar

"When the great and wondrous pious sage, our honored teacher Rabbi Moshe Cordovero, died . . . the sage called out and said, 'What do you see, my son?' He said to him, 'I see a pillar of fire going before the bier of the sage who died.'"

of fire in front of Cordovero's bier because he is pure—that is, he has never had a (nocturnal) seminal emission. Because Luria also saw the pillar of fire, we can presume that he never had one either—indeed, his purity is stressed again and again in all the legends of praise about him. In this legend sexual purity is the determinant of a sage's virtue and his mastery of the secrets of the Torah.[4] Shlumil of Dreznitz, from whose fourth letter I have quoted this foundation myth, marvels there at Safed's unique burial customs.

> And they make seven circles around every dead male, that is, they place the body in the grave and ten sages or ten elders come and circuit the body seven times, and each time they read the Song of Misfortune [Psalm 91] in its entirety and in the end they recite the verse "But to Abraham's sons by the concubines" [Genesis 25:6] to the end and that is efficacious for driving away from above the body all the evil spirits that are called the Afflictions of the Sons of Adam

Sin Crouches at the Door • 163

which were made by drops of semen that were emitted futilely [other than in lawful sexual intercourse]. And it is a long-established practice among them.[5]

Both the legend and the local burial ceremony make sexual sin their alpha and omega. It is what determines a man's place in this world and the next. Both are classic expressions of Safed's folk culture. The legend was told by an entire generation following Luria's death, from which Shlumil heard and recorded it (more than thirty years after Luria's death). The local funeral ritual had no halakhic source, nor was it followed by the entire Jewish people, but it had long been accepted practice in Safed. These manifestations of folk religion highlight the difference between the attitude toward sex in Kabbalah and how it was seen in folk culture.

Few aspects of the study of Kabbalah have received as much attention in recent years as its erotic and feminist symbols. Scholars have written comprehensive books that survey and interpret the eroticism—which sometimes approaches the pornographic—of kabbalistic language and symbols. The apparent contradiction between kabbalistic mysticism, which centers on divine secrets and higher worlds, and the sensual world of the body and the sexual act has been one reason for the great interest in the subject.[6] Another reason is the unavoidable fact that the Kabbalah, from its origins in Spain and Provence in the twelfth century through and beyond the school of Safed, has been replete with symbols of a sometimes overtly sexual nature. Principal kabbalistic concepts such as *devekut* (adherence to God), *mayin nokvin* (feminine water), *zeir anpin* (lesser countenance), *ibur* (pregnancy), and *keter* and *ateret malkhut* (crowns), to name just a few, draw their symbolic language and rich images from the human body, in particular the genitals and their sexual activity. These descriptions and processes were used by mystics, acting alone or in small groups, who viewed the writings and certainly those containing erotic passages as "secrets" that were accessible only to a select elite like themselves.

The question of whether and how the Kabbalah's erotic symbolism is reflected in the legends told in Safed circa 1600 is of vital importance, because it involves an examination of a corpus of sources that has not thus far been used for this purpose. For example, scholars accept that early

Kabbalah's concept of sexuality was not identical to that of the Safed kabbalists. Safed Kabbalah was much more ecstatic than what had preceded it. Whereas earlier Kabbalah stressed the legitimacy of sex between husband and wife and the connection between it and cosmic events, the Kabbalah of Safed leaned toward strictures: It was forbidden to have sexual relations during the week, only on the Sabbath, and, most important, enjoyment of the sexual act was proscribed and seen as a violation of the kabbalist's purity and his ability to live a fully contemplative life.[7] Can such ideas be found in the tales produced in Safed during this period?

The tale of the pillar of fire at Cordovero's funeral presents the full complexity of this picture. Jews were anxious about nocturnal emissions long before the advent of the Kabbalah. The Midrash warns that such emissions, outside permitted sexual relations, are forbidden because they can produce demons and spirits, whereas the Kabbalah claims that they interfere with the transmission of divine abundance. An echo of this kabbalistic view can indeed be seen in the tale, with its linking of the pillar of fire to futile seminal emission. But the tale does not explain what the nature of the connection is. It views the real world in fairy-tale terms: The pillar of fire, like a king's crown, symbolizes the kingship of Luria, who received it from Cordovero, the previous "king." Luria himself chooses a successor, intending for him to marry the "princess," that is, his daughter. But the designated bridegroom does not accomplish the task assigned to him: to remain sexually pure. He is thus ejected from the royal court, to be replaced by another: Hayyim Vital. The power network active in this tale is not one of ideas but rather of narrative. It draws on a prevailing Jewish and general literary tradition, the model of the ancient story, but grants it new meaning; the condition for the transfer of kabbalistic authority to Luria, leading to the establishment of a new center of Kabbalah, is conditioned on the severe sexual prohibitions imposed on its protagonists. The victory over the dragon to win the princess and the kingdom is replaced in this story by a victory over the sexual urge in order to gain the spiritual inheritance of the Kabbalah, which is the most desirable kingdom of all.

A speculative passage from the *Sha'ar Ruach haKodesh* (Gate of the Holy Spirit) section of Vital's book *Etz Hayyim* (Tree of Life) is helpful in understanding this idea.

> I also found written by Rabbi Moshe Yonah in this language, that my teacher [Luria], may his memory be a blessing, [prescribed] a correction for the transgression of futile emission of semen. And this transgression has several types: there is he who sins by thought, who thinks of an offense and his [evil] urge attacks him and he sees his semen [emerge] on its own without any act at all. And there is he who touches with his hand and brings out his semen. And there is he who thinks of a woman and commits adultery with his hand and brings out his semen. And there is he who thinks of a male and brings out his semen. And there is he who touches with saliva from his mouth and brings out his semen. And there is he who, when he commits adultery, covers the crown [of his penis] with the skin of the organ that continues from it below, and this is called pulling his foreskin.[8]

Ostensibly there is a need for such detail about the different ways of bringing on a futile seminal emission. Each technique requires its own penance. But the explicit verbal description of the act cannot but stimulate the imagination and boost the sexual tension that already exists in a company of men who spend long hours alone together each day. As opposed to the narrative account, which is emotional and suspenseful in its identification of the heir to Safed's school of Kabbalah, the description here is deliberately dry and neutral. Yet the emotional effects are diametrically opposed. Although the tale cautions against such deeds, which might exclude a man from his proper place in the world, the ostensibly technical and legalistic description in *Sha'ar Ruach haKodesh* offers a how-to manual of masturbation. It is more likely than the tale to awaken sexual desire and fantasies.[9]

Another tale, which does not require much interpretation, points unambiguously to the connection between extreme sexual asceticism and sexual temptation.

> A tale of a [pregnant] woman who was having difficulty bearing her child, and who was in danger, and her relations came to the home of the Rabbi [Luria] to do a rectification

[*tikun*, penance] for her and to save her. And the rabbi replied, "It is true that she is in danger, and she has two sons in her womb, and there is a rectification, if it can be found." They said to him, "Tell us, master." He said to them, "The rectification is that a man who has never seen a drop of semen in his life will come, and he will put his covenant [penis] into her mouth, and she will immediately give birth and be saved." They said to him, "Who is this person? We will go to him." He said to them, "I know, but I am not permitted to reveal him so as not to slander others. But do this, put out a notice all over town: Whoever is the man who knows of himself that he has never seen a drop of semen in his life, he should come and save three souls of Israel." And so they did. And when the great man, our teacher and master, the elderly Rabbi Moshe Galanti heard this, he immediately got up and came with them and put his covenant in her mouth and she immediately gave birth.[10]

One could, of course, read the story in the innocent way in which it is told, as a testimony to Luria's wondrous knowledge. The act itself is done solely to save the lives of Jews, and the Halakha itself rules that prohibited acts are permitted when they are the only way to save Jewish lives. The fact that the elderly Rabbi Moshe Galanti never woke up to discover that he had had a nocturnal seminal emission proves that he did not act under the influence of the evil sexual impulse. Therefore his act of putting "his covenant in her mouth" was not a sexual act but a manifestly magical one (the foreskin is a magical artifact in ancient Oriental folklore, for example, in the story of Moses and Tziporah [Genesis 4:24–26], linked also to sexuality and birth). Furthermore, the advanced age of Galanti is stressed, and the common wisdom is that elderly men no longer experience sexual desire, itself evidence in favor of a surface reading of the story.[11] Nevertheless, any other reading, whether critical or gendered, can hardly overlook the uneasiness we feel about the exploitation of magical arts and stressful states to carry out sexual fantasies that are by their very nature not entirely pure. The connection between placing a penis in a woman's mouth and the opening of her vagina for birth cannot be understood only by means of the guileless description of the event that I offered. Such a story, one that was widespread in Safed's folklore, constitutes appropriate raw material—certainly not the only such—for the erotic fantasies that were commonplace among the fellowships of students there.

Such was the case regarding another speculative passage from Hayyim Vital's *Sha'ar Ruach haKodesh*.

> *Yikhud* [kabbalistic invocation] no. 11. It is correct to do it at any time you wish, or if you wish to do it before you sleep or after you sleep, when you get up after midnight. And here, if you do it before you sleep, do so in this manner: First, recite the order of the recitation of the Shema and the rest of the order [recited] before lying down, as we have explained [earlier]. And afterward say this verse, "Let me take hold of its branches; let your breasts be [like clusters of grapes]" (Song of Songs 7:9), and begin from "take hold," which is one very holy name [of God] . . . and direct [your concentration] at this name being the secret of the upper breasts, which are called branches. And direct [your concentration] at taking hold of them and suckling and receiving a great light from them, and that is take hold of its branches. And direct [your concentration] at these breasts as being the AHB"A [literally, "love" and an anagram for "the light of the Holy One, Blessed be He"] sanctuary of Creation that is mentioned in the *Pekudei* portion of the *Zohar* . . . then recite the verse "Great is our Lord and full of power" [Psalms 147:5], which is in *gematriya* [the numerical value of its letters] "its branches," as mentioned above, in its vocalization and full of power and in the *gematriya*. And direct [your concentration] on the secret of the said breasts and direct that they are the secret of Eldad and Medad in this way: because two times D and D are the two breasts [*dadim*] themselves, one DD on the right and the other DD on the left. And therefore the name E"L, which is lovingkindness, is hinted at in

the first breast on the right . . . and is hinted at in the second breast on the left. And these are the four letters EL-YM in the name *Elohi"m*. And direct [your concentration] that they are the H that remains from the name *Elohi"m*, which is in the middle of the two breasts. And if you want to do this *yikhud* when you get up from sleep after midnight, do everything mentioned above, but precede the verse "Great is our Lord" with the verse "take hold of its branches."[12]

This *yikhud* gives powerful expression to a kabbalistic ritual. But imagine a mystic who carries it out during those most sensitive hours of the night, after midnight, when he directs his concentration on those "upper breasts," taking hold of and suckling from them, focusing first on the right breast and then on the left, and in the end fixing his attention on the letter H in the word *Elohim*, which lies in the space between those two sublime breasts. We again see how sexual energy is distilled in this speculative passage, in a way far more powerful than in any narrative. The tales stress prohibitions, sinners, and their punishments, whereas nonnarrative, speculative texts express the huge erotic potential and sexual energy inherent in mystical contemplation and the social context from which it emerges: fellowships of young men acting in a closed and insular space.

Nothing Is Hidden from His Eyes

All the tales about Luria known to us from Shlumil of Dreznitz's letters and from other contemporary sources belong to the genre of saints' legends. In other words, their overt goal is to acclaim their protagonist and to add merits to his greatness and uniqueness. That being the case, Lurianic legends that relate to sex and sexuality offer unwitting testimony about these subjects. The goal of these tales is not to talk about sexuality; rather, sex is used as a secondary means that serves the principal purpose of portraying Luria. As such, when they relate to these issues, they should be taken as sincere and credible. By that I do not mean that the events described in the tales actually took place, but rather that the way they reflect the view of sex and sexuality in Safed around 1600 is grounded in social reality, not just the sexual fantasies of individuals. Let's take a look at a typical story of this sort.

A tale of when the Sages of Safed, may it be built and established quickly in our days, appointed ten supervisors to oversee the transgressions, and all of them were knowledgeable and wise, and among them they appointed Rabbi Yitzhak Luria, may his memory be a blessing. And one day, on Monday, one of the overseers woke early in his garret to study, as was his custom. And he opened his window to see if there was light in the east so that he could go to the synagogue and be one of the first ten, as was his custom, and he saw a [beautiful] woman dressed in Sabbath clothes leaving her yard. This sage said to himself, "I will go and see where this woman is going at such an hour." And he walked after her, and saw that she entered a yard where there was a man who was suspected of [sinning] in the matter of another man's wife. And when he saw this, he said, "It is indeed known that this woman went there for the purpose of harlotry with this man." And he appointed there people to guard them against transgression. And the overseer went to the synagogue and told the beadle to gather all the overseers after the service. He did so and they all convened. And the overseer rose and testified about what he had seen that morning. And before he opened his mouth, the Rabbi [Luria] preceded him and said to him, "Shut your mouth and do not speak ill of the worthy daughters of Israel, for the woman you saw is innocent of all sin and she thus went at an early hour so that people would not see her. And the reason she went was that a man from the west has come to that yard and has brought her a letter and pledge from her husband, and she went to him and said that he should send her the pledge she had given. And he sent her after her husband conveyed to him a secret that he should say to her, things that one does not say [usually] to an emissary, and therefore she went." And when the overseer heard this, he closed his mouth and went to investigate the matter, and found that what the Rabbi had said was true. And he came before him and said, "I have done as you say, forgive me." And the Rabbi replied, "What have you done to me? Go to the woman and ask her for forgiveness for you having suspected her," and so he did. And then they took him to be a prophet.[13]

The overt purpose of this tale is clear. It aims to bolster Luria's standing as a man of supernatural powers and knowledge beyond that which is evident in the world, just as the conclusion of the story states: "And then they took him to be a prophet." The question of sexual morality and normative moral rules in Safed in this period is secondary in this context and thus can be taken as more reliable: Because they were not the focus of the tale, details regarding sex in the story were told as they really were, or were expected to be, and thus we should accept them as more reliable. We do not know whether an association of "overseers of transgressions" was in fact established in Safed, and if it was, whether Luria—a merchant and Torah scholar who had just recently arrived in the city—was appointed a member. What is important is that the legend reflects the atmosphere in Safed, which promoted the establishment of such a "vice squad" and which saw public scrutiny of the private lives of Jews, and investigations and intervention in their daily actions, in a positive light, aimed as they were at guarding them against transgression. Luria, who might seem in this story to be more "liberal" than the others, is not so in fact. He does not protest inquisitorial stalking of private individuals or violation of their privacy. He simply claims that an error was made in this particular case. Had he opposed the system itself, he would not have consented to be member of a body that was set up for that purpose.[14]

As we will see, Luria was in fact quick to point to such sexual transgressions, reveal them publicly, and publicly humiliate their alleged perpetrators. Again, it must be stressed that we have no way of knowing whether Luria actually acted in this way or whether such cases of sexual transgression in fact took place. The legend as a literary genre reflects the way that the society telling the tale views itself, its relationship to the reality shaped by the tale, and the way society copes with it. The tale of the overseers of transgressions reflects the tense moral atmosphere in Safed at the time the tale was told. The fact was that any person, even an innocent woman acting at her husband's behest, could be suspected of an act of adultery and harlotry. The sin in this story is not that the woman was spied on but rather the mistake in understanding what she was doing. Although this woman was not cheating on her husband, certainly other women were doing so. The establishment of a board of overseers of transgressions was indeed necessary, and every person was a suspect because, as God tells Cain, sin always crouches at the door (Genesis 4:7).

But whereas the sin overseers and other moral proctors in Safed needed to investigate the private lives of men and women, Luria knew of their lives without having to inquire. One example involves a wealthy Jew from Constantinople who made a pilgrimage to see Luria. Even before the man arrived, Luria knew that the pilgrim had lain with other women and that he had committed other severe sexual sins as well, including homosexual acts. In another case, a young man left Palestine and married a beautiful woman. She died a short time after their wedding, leaving him all her property. Luria knew that the beautiful women had been, in her previous incarnation, a man who owed the young husband a large sum of money. Her death effected repayment of that debt. Another example: A rich man confessed all his sins to Luria, but the rabbi knew that there was another sin that the man had not confessed—he had had sexual relations with his non-Jewish serving woman, who had since been attached to him like a dog.[15]

The genealogy of the story about a suspected adulteress in another context is quite interesting. In this version a man passes by Luria and, by chance, brushes the edge of his garment. Luria immediately knows that the man has engaged in unnatural sexual acts with his wife. This story also has a nonnarrative expression in his students' writings. Hayyim Vital relates an incident he says he heard from Luria.

> Another time he also saw on the forehead of a man that it was written there that his wife had made a demand of him with regard to a commandment [i.e., demanded that he have sexual relations with her], but he did not want to because it was a weekday. I asked my teacher, may his memory be a blessing, what he had seen in him, and he said to me that he saw an upside-down *gimmel* on his forehead . . . and the

matter is that the letter *gimmel* is the *sefirah* of *yesod* . . . and the significance of it being upside-down is that it indicates the female secret [or essence], from which he thwarted benevolence. Because every upside-down letter indicates the female, when the letter upside-down, from below to above in all the rest of the letters. And there is a letter that by being upside down regards a man who penetrated his wife unnaturally.[16]

The principal subject of this passage is Luria's claim that a man is not obligated to have sexual relations with his wife except on the Sabbath; during the week he is exempt from the obligation. Therefore a man who rejects his wife's demand that he have relations with her during the week has not sinned. Luria knew this by means of his "lore of [Divine] Visages" (*Torat haPartzufim*), by which he saw a person's deeds by means of various signs on his face.[17] Here Vital explains how it is possible to know that a man has had unnatural relations with his wife: A certain letter appears upside-down on his forehead (he does not say which letter).

About twenty-five years before Luria's time in Safed, an incident occurred that is reported by one of his most senior students, Rabbi Eleazar Azkari, in his influential ethical work *Sefer Kharedim*.

> It so happened here in Safed in the year 5308 [1548] since creation, before the great rabbis our teacher and rabbi Yosef Karo and our teacher and Rabbi Yitzhak Mas'ud and our teacher and Rabbi Avraham Shalom and my teacher the pious Rabbi Yosef Sagis and several other rabbis, a woman came and said that her husband had had unnatural relations with her. And they excommunicated him and condemned him and said he should be burned in fire, and in the end they banished him from the Land of Israel. May God save the remnant of Israel from iniquity and guilt, amen.[18]

This story appears at the end of a lengthy discussion of the subject of unnatural relations in all its aspects. It defines precisely what the phrase "sexual intercourse in an unnatural way" is, what the opinions of the sages dating back to the rabbinic period were, and why they considered this such a severe sin—because it is an indirect way of spilling one's semen futilely (i.e., not for the purpose of conception), which endangers the ongoing existence of the world. The passage raises some interesting historical questions that arise from this testimony, such as the existence of a high rabbinic court in Safed as early as the 1540s and the connection between the members of the court and Rabbi Ya'akov Beirav and his initiative to reestablish official rabbinic ordination and the Sanhedrin in Safed. But these are not the questions that interest us here. We need to look instead at two ostensibly marginal issues that also appear in the text. First, can we discern fully the sort of distress the woman was in, and what level of despair and misery led her to resolve to appear before a group of strict men and offer a detailed description (clearly, the rabbis would not have accepted anything less before issuing a ruling) of what her husband did to her on many occasions? Did they offer any empathy for her suffering and degradation? They almost certainly did not. According to Azkari's analysis in the discussion that precedes this story, the sin in question is a terrible one, not because it harms the woman who is its victim but because the man who perpetrates it spills his semen futilely and in doing so disregards the sages' injunction against this. The second interesting subject the testimony broaches is that the great rabbis of the generation who were members of this panel of judges did not know and could not know anything about what had happened to this woman until she came before them and testified. In contrast, twenty-five years later Rabbi Luria needs no testimony from the parties to the act to know what has occurred. He knows immediately, on the basis of signs that only he can see and decipher, who has engaged in unnatural sexual relations with his wife and who has committed other sexual sins.

This is a small-scale example of the huge revolution that Luria and his disciples brought about to Jewish folk religion. In the development of the tale from Azkari to Hayyim Vital, the halakhic court before which plaintiffs appear, witnesses testify, and evidence is produced is replaced by intuitive and emotional mystic contemplation. Legal logic finds itself bankrupt when faced with mystic ritual. That is one reason that I included in Chapter 1 a number of stories in which Rabbi Joseph Karo, Moshe Alsheikh, and other great halakhic authorities submit themselves to Luria and plead with him to teach them Kabbalah. In each case, Luria turns them away, telling them that they are unworthy. The fact that not a few mystical considerations appear in the halakhic literature of that period is further proof that the center of gravity shifted from halakhic-rationalist discussion to mystical contemplation and the practical conclusions that derive from it.

REALITY IS UNINTELLIGIBLE, BUT ITS SIGNS ARE OPEN

As a result of the activity of Luria and his disciples (as reflected in these legends; we do not know whether they happened also in real life), the sex life of Safed's Jewish community metamorphosed from a matter that was sometimes brought before a rabbinic court, as it had always been everywhere, into a matter of constant surveillance to seek out signs that indicate the transgression of sexual prohibitions.

> There was a pious man named Rabbi Avraham Puah, may his memory be a blessing. He was a very wealthy man who was very generous with the poor and unfortunate. And he had a neighbor who dealt in merchandise, negotiating with the wife of the above-mentioned Rabbi Avraham, because his wife was gifted at [commercial] negotiation. And suddenly this neighbor fell ill and became bedridden for many days, until his flesh began to rot and his sexual organ putrefied, and pieces of [his flesh] began to fall off. And he [the neighbor] expended much money on doctors and found no remedy for his ailment. And he would cry out constantly in his agony, [so loudly that] his voice could be heard ten streets away. And this neighbor died in great, horrible, and bitter agony. And for a few years after his death, an extremely ugly black dog could be seen roaming close to the home of the above-mentioned Rabbi Avraham. And when people saw it, they were horribly frightened as if he were a demon, God save us, and he was famished and always found ways to get himself into the house, and they would drive him out of the house with sticks. And always, when R. Avraham arose

in his home to go out his door to the synagogue, he would find this black dog going after him. And when R. Avraham returned in the morning from synagogue, he would find the dog clawing and pushing at the door to try to open it, and he would chase it away. And once it happened that Rabbi Avraham left his home in the morning and forgot to lock the door of the house and of the outer room [*heder hitzon*] of the house. And the dog immediately leapt into the house and entered the winter house [inner room] and from the winter house to a room the door to which was also open, and entered there to the place where Rabbi Avraham's wife was lying on her bed. And [the dog] found her sleeping and jumped on her and bit her many times, causing wounds and bruises and [then it] fled. And they went to tell this to the holy Luria, may his memory be a blessing. And he said that this woman had, forgive our many transgressions, become the woman of the neighbor [had sexual relations with him], and he was the dog, into whom his soul had gone, and she had seduced him to have relations with her using words and by doing things close to this sin, and for this reason he took revenge on her. And he [Luria] had the woman take an oath to tell the truth, and she confessed that this indeed had been, and having marital relations with the neighbor, and for this reason his sexual organ had putrefied and his soul had gone into the dog.[19]

This story is of great interest both in its own right and because earlier versions of it show how it developed and spread. A version related by Moshe Cordovero in a chapter of his book *She'ur Komah* addresses reincarnation.

> And sometimes he will transmigrate to bring into the world a soul that he killed, and as he took him out of the world, so he brings him into the world, or he will bring his father into the world just as [his father] brought him. . . . And a human being does not know of this; he only knows that all

the hidden things that transmigrate in this matter, or brings his daughter to him, or grants him his assets and so on in the laws of God and under his direction is unintelligible and the door is locked before human beings. And we have already found in our time and seen it with our own eyes, not those [of an unreliable] stranger. An adulterer who has died took on the form of a dog and killed the adulteress, and the son of the adulteress killed the dog, and afterward the son of the adulteress died in accordance with God's laws to kill bastards in secret, and people wondered at the deed, and the entire event was not revealed but to a very few. And without a doubt it was astonishing to those who saw it, because it was terrifying, and this we have seen with our eyes.[20]

Cordovero's student, Rabbi Avraham Galanti, offers the following version.

And there was also a great deed in our time concerning an adulterer who died and was reincarnated as a dog. And he entered the house of the adulteress who had lusted for him and bit her in that place and fled, and returned a second time and bit her in the same place and fled. And they pursued him and they were unable to catch him, until the son of the adulteress, whom she had from her husband, chased him. And when he saw him, he allowed himself to be tied to a rope and killed him [the dog]. [This is a proof that the adulterer] knows his reincarnation and his punishment and his sorrow.[21]

In addition to the three versions quoted here, other versions are included in *Hemdat Yamim* and *Kav haYashar* from the beginning of the eighteenth century. They display interesting narrative development over time. Cordovero's version is in fact a rumor related in the first person by a person who was present at the event or who knew its participants ("We have seen with our eyes," meaning that it is a memorat). Galanti, for his part, does not claim to have been an eyewitness; he says it was an incident that happened "in our time," that is, he heard about it from others who were present at the event or who knew its protagonists. The later versions, those found in *Hemdat Yamim* and *Kav haYashar*, are related as fully developed folktales, no longer dependent on direct or indirect testimony of any kind.

One of the most interesting literary phenomena in these renderings is that they are not dependent on each other. Cordovero's version speaks of the death of the adulteress, her son, and the dog. Galanti's version tells only of the dog's death but specifies exactly where the dog bit the woman, who caught him, and how. Whereas Cordovero's version claims that the son who killed the dog (meaning the reincarnation of his father) was a bastard born out of the act of adultery and that he died after killing the dog (killing his father, as punishment for his birth), Galanti stresses that he was the son of the woman from her legal husband. Nevertheless, the overt purpose of both versions is to reveal the motif of reincarnation, which had already come to assume an important place in the folk religion of pre-Lurianic Safed. But the two sages do so in different ways. Galanti stresses the sorrow involved in such a reincarnation—he stresses the theme of reward and punishment—whereas Cordovero focuses on the mystery of the incident, the profound meaning of which is revealed only to a few. This approach, which views external events as signs of a hidden reality that only a few can comprehend, was developed considerably by Luria, as we will see.

The most interesting and fleshed-out version of the story is that recorded in more widely circulated and later sources such as *Kav haYashar*, *Hemdat Yamim*, and *Shivkhei ha-'Ari*. The importance of these versions is not that they are rare or original but rather that they are widespread. This is the version that passed on to later generations and that influenced the way they viewed the Safed period. The story is based around three exceptional events, the meanings of which remain invisible to those with an outside vantage point: (1) the business relations between Rabbi Avraham Puah's wife and his neighbor, (2) the mysterious and awful disease that afflicts the neighbor, and (3) the strange behavior of the dog, which ends with its attack on Avraham's wife. Each of these three components of the story has its origin in a widespread folk belief: A woman who spends lengthy time with a man or men, even if on business matters or other "legitimate" affairs, will in the end commit adultery; a mysterious and harsh disease should be a punishment for a sin that the sinner has succeeded in concealing; the dog, a black dog in particular, is not just an animal but rather a demonic being sent to cause damage, or to punish, for which reason he is dangerous. These are not elements of any mystical system; even if they are intimated in mystical theory, their vitality lies in the folk beliefs of society at large, not in one or another tiny brotherhood of kabbalists.

When the matter is brought before Luria (in some versions he hears the cries of the woman when the dog attacks her), he deciphers the signs and resolves the three parts of the puzzle. His solution is based on discerning that these are not three separate events. Their meaning grows out of the connection between them: When a man and woman spend time together, it inevitably ends in immorality. The adultery brings on the horrible punishment, and it is the punishment that causes the dog's peculiar behavior. In other words, the purpose of this version of the story, the most developed and narrative of the versions that are known to us, is not to provide evidence of the doctrine of reincarnation, as is the case in the versions related by Cordovero and Galanti. Rather, it is one more entry in the praises of Isaac Luria and the magnification of his name. Luria's dominant presence in the last part of the story (compared to the earlier versions adduced here, where there is no involvement of any outside figure, just an account of the incident), along with his wondrous elucidation of an event that must certainly have kept many people in Safed up at night, reinforces this impression.

But it would seem that the praises of this holy man are but the story's overt exterior. Luria's principal contribution here (the beginnings of which we saw in Cordovero's version) is to prove that outward events are not what they seem to be to the untrained eye. Rather, they are momentous signs of profound and hidden events. They are the tip of the iceberg. They are not evident to the untutored viewer. This would seem to be the greatest contribution made by Luria (or by the views attributed to him) to the nature of popular faith and belief in the Safed era and thereafter: Exceptional events in the world are to be seen not as natural occurrences but rather as signs that need to be read and through which a complex and important hidden reality can be understood. The keys to understanding these signs, the code for deciphering them, are to be found in the kabbalistic theory Luria fashioned and in the works of his disciples, which put that theory into writing.

Thus in Safed culture folk beliefs and folk customs are connected to elitist mysticism, and together they formed a single view of the world that wielded huge influence on the Judaism of the generations that followed.

From the Erotic to the Demonic

The connection between sexual transgression and the demonic sphere, which lay at the center of the story about Rabbi Avraham Puah's wife, is an ancient one. Its roots lie in the Bible and even earlier. The connection between prostitution and enchantment, adultery and the world of evil spirits, sexual orgies and pagan rites, is one of the best-known and most common in the literature of religion and folklore.[22] The principal difference between these ancient traditions and the legends of Safed is not the mere connection between sexual transgression and the spiritual and mystical spheres, as that is not new. The innovation is the proliferation of such stories in a relatively short period, their concentration in a single geographic area, and their status as part of a community's theological and folk worldview. This spiritual reality of hovering spirits, of dead people making repeated appearances in the world of the living, of omnipresent reincarnated souls and evil spirits, reserves a special place for the connection between sex and the demonic world.

> And so at one watch [of the night], [Luria] sat in his home and said to his students, "I now see two female demons dressed in garments of red silk, adorned with gold jewelry and precious stones on their heads and gold necklaces on their necks, and they are entering a certain room to defile two youngsters." And as he divined it for them, so it was.[23]

Late at night, while the people of Safed slept and Luria and his students were studying the higher worlds, the master interrupted his sacred teaching to direct his disciples' attention to a sexual orgy taking place not far away. How did Luria know what was going on elsewhere? We have already seen that there could be any number of explanations. In this case, even though it is hard to imagine that his students doubted his word, an examination was made and the master's words were found to be precisely true. Of special interest is the crossing of boundaries between the sacred and the profane in Safed's consciousness, as expressed in its legends, and the unique blend of the human and the demonic. This can also be seen in the story mentioned earlier about the overseers of transgressions and the God-fearing man who opened the windows of the synagogue in the early morning and saw a beautiful and bejeweled woman about to have relations with a man in an alley. It can also be seen in the story of the man who had unnatural relations with his wife and whose impure garment brushed against Luria's holy body. In all these tales, defilement and sanctity converge.

This association between the sexual and demonic characteristic of women finds expression in the identification of the two women who join the orgy as demonesses—after all, it would be unthinkable that flesh-and-blood women would do such a thing. But in the folk culture that developed in Safed, even this familiar and common equivalence, as old as the ancient myth of Lilith, finds an exceptional literary expression.[24]

> Also, it once happened that several young men went walking in the field and they saw a finger that was going in and out of the ground. And these young men said in jest to each other, "Who of you will place a golden wedding ring on this finger?" One of the young men jumped up and placed a ring on the finger and said, "You are hereby betrothed to me." And when he had finished speaking, the finger disappeared, and the young men were very fearful and returned to the city.

Years later, on the night of this young man's wedding, "the same demoness appeared in the form of a woman whose beauty was unparalleled in this world." She displayed the ring to everyone there and claimed that she was his lawful wife. The wedding celebration turned into sorrow, and when Luria was told what had happened and the bridegroom said that he did not want to marry a fiend, the rabbi summoned the demoness, "and here that woman descended, wrapped in her sheets in accordance with the custom of Safed, may it be built and established quickly in our days, and her serving woman after her, and the young man after them." Luria and the demoness conducted a learned debate, and Luria proved to her that the betrothal was an error, as he did not see your face and he just put a ring on your finger, and had he known that it was the finger of a demoness, he would not have betrothed you. And she responded to each question that the master put to her. Until the master reprimanded her and said, "Even though there is no legal need to grant you a bill of divorce, just so that there will be an appearance [of justice being done to you], I will order him to grant you a divorce." . . . And when the demoness heard this, she accepted the divorce. And the master swore her not to ever appear in the home of this young man, not to do him or any other member of his family, nor to his home, also not any member of her [the demoness's] family, and she took upon herself this obligation and left. And then the young man went back and married his wife and she became his wife.[25]

This story, known as "The Marriage of a Man and a Demoness," has a long genealogy in Hebrew and Yiddish literature. Its many variants divide into two major branches: a Hebrew tradition called "Tale of the Jerusalemite" and a Yiddish one called "Tale of a Man from Worms." The Safed story shares its narrative template with the Jerusalemite version, which is known from as far back as the Middle Ages. In both versions a young Jew is married, by compulsion or by mistake, to a demoness, and she demands that he give up his human wife on the grounds that she, the demoness, is his legal wife. But the rabbi before whom the demoness presents her claim rules against her. However, the Safed story shares with the Yiddish version, which is known from the beginning of the sixteenth century, a preliminary scene outside the city, in a forest. In this version, a group of boys goes out to play hide-and-seek among the trees close to the city of Worms, on the Rhine. When one of the boys sees a finger protruding from one of the trees, he thinks it belongs to one of his friends, and, in jest, he places on it an expensive ring he received from his parents. Years later he marries, but when the newlyweds lie in their bridal bed, a beautiful and finely dressed woman appears. She displays the ring and demands that the bride depart and leave her with her legal husband. When the bride refuses, the demoness strangles her. The young man marries again and the same thing happens. When he marries a third time, to a poor girl who agrees to sacrifice her life for her family's welfare, the bride does not refuse to get out of the bridal bed, leaving her husband to the demoness, and thus saves her own life. In the end, she brings about the demoness's death and goes on to have a full family life with her husband. I would add only that the impressive opening episode—the sin—in which a ring is placed on a demoness's finger, appears also in Christian tales of the medieval period. In these versions a young Roman who has just married goes out to sport with his friends in the forest. He places a wedding ring on a statue of Venus that happens to be nearby; when the game is over, he no longer finds the ring there. That night, when he goes to lie with his wife, the figure of Venus appears between them and claims that she is his wife. This happens every night, until the young man is saved by a powerful magician.[26]

The Safed version of this long narrative tradition borrows motifs and narrative structures from both the Hebrew and Yiddish traditions. "The Jerusalemite" version of the tale was well known and familiar in the medieval and early modern periods, appearing in many oral and written versions, both in Europe and in Jewish communities in the East. The Worms version, according to its principal researcher, Sara Zfatman, originated in northern Italy at the beginning of the sixteenth century, which makes it hardly surprising that it was known in Safed around 1600, whether in a Yiddish-language version or through oral transmission from Jewish immigrants to the city from Italy. The seminal contribution of the Safed version to these narrative traditions is that it makes Luria its central protagonist. In the medieval Jerusalemite versions of the story, the young Jew and the demoness also appear before a local rabbi so that he can rule which marriage is valid: that with the demoness or that with the human wife. But in the Safed version the narrative scene is more complicated. The rabbi is essential not only because he rules on the conflict but also because he discovers it. It is he who explains the enigmatic event that the members of the community witnessed and were frightened by. The reason the story changes in this way is because here it becomes a saints' legend of Luria, and his role in that context is obvious and clear.

A variety of interpretations have been offered for the Yiddish story from the beginning of the sixteenth century—historical-philological, feminist, social, and economic—but these are not of much interest in the Safed context. Nevertheless, the episode of the finger in the forest, which is the principal element it shares with the Safed story, remains an unresolved riddle. Although the placing of a ring is a widespread motif found in medieval Christian traditions and Yiddish versions of this tale type, I propose to read the story from the vantage point of a specific time and place: Safed circa 1600.

If the finger belongs to the demoness, whose purpose is to trap a Jewish boy—which is how the storytellers and listeners in Safed of that period might well have understood it—then things would be simpler. But the language of signs, not necessarily Lurianic ones but semiotic ones, turns that analogy on its head. In other words, it is not that the figure who looks like a bejeweled and seductive is a demoness; rather, the demoness is simply a woman. That offers an entirely different reading. Furthermore, we cannot disregard the erotic, even pornographic nature of a sentence like "and they saw a finger emerging and going back into the ground." That depiction appears only in the Safed tale. The form and action of the finger is too close to that of the male member during the sexual act to be ignored. I have no doubt that the image was quite transparent to many storytellers and listeners of the story at the time.

What do we get from these two insights taken together? That a group of adolescent Jews from Safed went out to have fun in a way that was accepted practice in the Ottoman Empire at the time—with a prostitute, or perhaps to play sexual games with each other, whether homosexual acts or some other sexual pastime. The large length of time that passed, for social and economic reasons, between sexual maturity and marriage created a situation in which such phenomena were common and even accepted as normative.[27] One of the boys, either lacking money to pay the prostitute (as in the biblical story of Judah and Tamar) or as a practical joke, placed a ring on her finger, promising to return to pay her fee. Or perhaps he made a more serious commitment in the heat of the moment. In any case, he forgot all about it. She then came to demand her fee and protest the insult. When Luria asked the young man whether he wanted to marry her, "the young man responded, 'What fool would want to marry a fiend?'" Only one word changes from what was presumably his actual response, "Who is the fool who would want to marry a prostitute?" In other words, should a young man be punished for youthful sins?

This fascinating story teaches us not just about the place that Luria occupied in everyday Safed's popular consciousness but also, especially, about the language with which that culture expressed its tensions and anxieties. In Safed's almost messianic ambience, everything was directed at and ready for the coming redemption. The redemption was eminent because the place was sacred and the people living in it were holy, and the way of achieving the redemption was known and recorded; all that was lacking was a life free of sin and defilement. These legends, in which the defiler is not a person but an evil spirit, were meant to replace, in the consciousness of the members of that society, the reality that was so different from the messianic ideal that was at hand. Defilement was a blemish and delayed the realization of the messianic ideal. Its main source was sexual transgressions. Everything was full of pollution that tarnished the ideal that Safed was closer to than any other place since the destruction of Jerusalem. The perpetrators of that pollution were not human. They were demons (or, more precisely, demonesses) who lay in wait for a moment of weakness to keep believers distant from the messianic age. The transformation of actual events into the language of demonology is common to all the stories we have seen thus far and is one of the important salient characteristics of Safed's folk culture circa 1600.

A Spirit Entered Her

The most powerful demonic manifestation that emerged in the culture of Safed and its environs circa 1600 cannot be found in the Lurianic legends, however. It comes from the narrative theme about possession by an evil spirit, or dybbuk (wandering soul of a dead man). The Tale of the Spirit in Safed is one of the most interesting and detailed testimonies that have come down to us from that time regarding such an incident. The entire testimony is found in the 1629 *Sefer Ta'alumot Khokhma*, by Rabbi Joseph Solomon Delmedigo (Yosef of Kandia). This book is also the first work to include the letters of Shlumil of Dreznitz. It is, of course, of special interest that the possession story immediately follows the letters. It does not state its source, but it is certainly not Shlumil, because had the story been his, the publisher would have provided an attribution, as he did with the letters. However, there can be no doubt that they both the letters and the tale originate in Safed.

During Luria's time in Safed, an evil spirit possessed a widow. Experts tried to exorcise the spirit but to no avail. They turned to Luria, "and as the master, may his righteous memory be a blessing, did not have time to go with them, he sent his disciple, our teacher Rabbi Hayyim Kalibres [Vital] of righteous memory, and lay his hands on him and conveyed to him devotions of names [of God] and also ordered him to condemn the spirit to excommunication and banishment and to exorcise the spirit against its will." Following an exchange, the spirit agreed to respond to Vital's questions. "The rabbi said to him, 'Tell me what your sin and crime was, that they meted out such a heavy punishment?' The spirit responded and said, 'I sinned with a man's wife and sired bastards and now for twenty-five years I have wandered the earth and have not had even an hour and a moment of rest.'" The dead spirit began to tell those present of his long travail of wanderings and agonies, lasting from the minute of his death to the time he entered the body of the widow from Safed.[28]

The account is of great interest in terms of its literary structure and the religious worldview that it reflects, but that is not our main interest here. The last stage in the spirit's wanderings is of much significance.

> The Rabbi, may his memory be a blessing, said, "How long will you have this sorrow, and do you have no restitution forever?" The spirit responded, "Until all the bastards I sired die, because as long as they live and thrive I have no restitution." And then all the people who were there, a very large crowd, wept a great deal because the fear of judgment fell on them, and there was a great [moral] awakening in that country from that affair. Then the rabbi asked him, "Who gave you permission to enter the body of this woman?" The spirit went on to say, "I slept one evening in her house, and at morning this woman rose from her bed and wanted to produce fire from the stone and iron and the burnt rag did not take her sparks, and the woman pled a great deal but did not succeed. Then she was very angry and cast the stone and the iron and the

burnt rag, everything from her hand, and said in great anger, 'May it be for the Satan!' And immediately I was given sanction to enter her body." The rabbi, may his memory be for a blessing, asked him, "And for such a minor transgression they gave you permission to enter her body?" And the spirit responded, "Know, my wise sir, that this women's interior is not like her exterior, because she does not believe in the miracles that God made for Israel, the Exodus from Egypt in particular. And on every Passover night, when all the Jews are joyous and of good heart and recite the great *Halel* [psalms of praise] and tell the story of the Exodus from Egypt, for her it is all a joke and jest and she thinks in her heart that there never was such a miracle." The Rabbi immediately said to this woman, "Do you believe in perfect faith that the Holy One, blessed be He, is one and only and that he created the heavens and the earth and that he has the power and ability to do whatever he wishes and no one can tell him what to do?" And the woman responded, "Yes, I believe it all with perfect faith." And the Rabbi, may his memory be for a blessing, further said to her, "Do you believe with perfect faith that the Holy One, blessed be He, took us out of Egypt, from the house of bondage, and split the sea and did many miracles for us?" The woman responded, "You are a wise man, I believe everything in perfect faith, and if I at times thought otherwise, I regret it." And the woman began to weep, and immediately the rabbi ruled that the spirit must leave her.[29]

From beginning to end, sexual motifs, some more overt and some less, are woven throughout the story. The dead man's sins are all sexual: "I sinned with a man's wife and sired bastards." As long as the bastards still live, he has no restitution and his agonies will continue. The spirit explains, "And so I wandered the land to the city of Hormuz, which is a large city close to the land of India . . . and when I arrived in that city I saw that the Jews were most evil and sinful against God, having sexual relations with Gentile women and all other sins. I could not enter the body of one of them because of the great forces of pollution that reside in them and in their surroundings."[30] In other words, these sexual sins are rife not just in the Jewish community of Egypt, the place from which he came, but had reached Jewish communities at the ends of the earth. The spirit had found refuge in the body of a pregnant doe; he suffered greatly there because he had to share room with the fetus—another description with clearly sexual connotations. A male's penetration of a female body—all the more so that of a widow, whose husband can no longer satisfy her sexual needs—is a sexual act, as anthropological and psychological studies of demonic possession have found. This understanding is reinforced by the description of how the spirit exited the widow's body. In the version I have quoted here, the spirit leaves, at Vital's express command, "via the small toe on the left foot," so that he will not leave any other way. In other dybbuk stories the spirit enters and also asks to exit through the woman's vagina, and in some cases bloodstains appear between her legs as evidence of this.

Of particular interest are the reasons why the spirit entered the body of this particular woman at this particular time. The spirit offers two reasons: anger and heresy. The widow's sin of anger and the spirit's penetration of her body as a result are explained explicitly in Lurianic Kabbalah.

> The attribute of anger alone also is what prevents achievement entirely. . . . Any person who is angry, if he is a prophet, his prophecy leaves him, etc. . . . And here my teacher [Luria], may his memory be a blessing, took more care with anger than with all other transgressions . . . and he gave a reason for this, saying that, after all, all other transgressions do not cause [general] defect, but rather each and every transgressions causes a defect in a different organ, but the attribute of anger causes a defect in the entire soul and changes it entirely. And the matter is, when a man becomes angry, his sacred soul abandons him entirely and a soul from the side of the shell enters in its place.[31]

Nevertheless, the spirit's further account of the woman's heresy regarding the Exodus story and God's miracles in general falls into an entirely different area. The hypothesis that the women's deviation points to the new winds blowing, in Europe in particular, in the early modern period has substance to it. Rabbi Naphtali Bacharach, author of the 1648 work *Emek haMelech* (Valley of the King), which offers one of the earliest versions of the Safed dybbuk story, writes in his introduction that such heresy came into the world "because they accustomed themselves to the falsehoods of philosophy and occupied themselves with the culture of strangers, and certainly Rabbi Shimon bar Yochai and Rabbi Yitzhak Luria, may he be remembered for a life in the next world, will judge them in the next world."[32]

Beyond these great historical and cultural developments, it behooves us to consider the helplessness of the widow who needs to keep her house alone, without help, without the support of a husband or family, when every act, such as lighting a fire, demands huge efforts and becomes the source of disappointment and frustration. In the milieu of sixteenth-century Safed, she had to accept the doom of her widowhood and loneliness without complaint. Her anger shows that she did not accept it. She is angered by how bitter her fate is, and she vents her anger by crying out in despair, "May it be for the Satan!" Because she is not an educated or wealthy woman, as the story indicates, it seems likely that revolutionary ideas had not reached her from overseas and influenced her. Rather, she was expressing personal distress. Can an omnipotent God, who took her out of Egypt, not save her from her bitter fate? If he cannot do something so small, how can he have done so great a deed? If that is the case, the story of the Exodus, like the other tales of miracles ostensibly performed by God, must be fictions. The reason a spirit entered this woman is that she permitted her existential plight to affect her religious faith. Lying on her bed before the entire public, with a spirit speaking through her, she no longer belongs, either to the community around her or to its collective norms, which maintain its balance as a traditional society. It is only when Hayyim Vital forces himself on her (mentally) and impels her to recant the declaration she made before the entire community that she can reestablish her ties to the community. But how long will it last? The story does not tell us.

The importance of this event for the Safed community of the time and for Vital himself (its protagonist and apparently the first to tell it) is made clear by the story itself: "Then all the people who were there, a very large crowd, wept a great deal because the fear of judgment fell on them, and there was a great [moral, religious] awakening in that country from that affair." In other words, ghost stories of this sort are principally intended to elicit reverence and repentance and to bolster the faith of the members of the community in God's presence among them in their daily lives. The author of *Hemdat Yamim*, one of the most important and widely read ethical works to appear after the Safed era, offers an abbreviated version of the story, adding at its conclusion:

> May all women hear and see all that happened to her, and convey it to all women that they not do as she did in her unclean heart, to disdain the miracle, heaven forfend, but instead to believe in God, creator of the heavens, who stretched them over the earth. . . . [May] a person prevail and sound his voice loudly and in great awe in this story of the miracle, and make their hearts tremble that they may fear him and believe in God and his wonders. . . . They have said that women are more punctual in performing the commandments than men, [and thus] the onus lies on their husbands who have been negligent and perform all the commandments by rote . . . and therefore they should perform before them [their wives] all the details of the [Passover] Seder and read the Haggadah with great reverence and good intention, to instill faith in their [women's] hearts.[33]

In other words, the story has, above all else, a didactic purpose. It is meant to serve as an educational example for women, to warn them against following in the footsteps of this evil and bad-hearted woman who dared doubt the deeds of the creator. Likewise, it is meant to teach husbands (who are, of course, always stronger in their faith) that they must educate their wayward women.

Nevertheless, as in previous cases, here too it behooves us to pay attention to what this story is telling us inadvertently. The account overtly stresses that many people were present at the event described and that they can all testify that it actually took place and that it was effective in strengthening their faith and that it caused them to mend their ways. But the marginal elements of the story tell us something about the public atmosphere in Safed. When word of this exceptional event got out, curious people from all over the city crowded into the widow's tiny bedroom (how large could the room of a poor widow be?), at her door, and in her yard, so that they could watch the astounding sight—a woman helplessly writhing in pain on her bed, crying out in her misery, as a rabbi and mystic stands at her head and recites incantations, shouts out orders and instructions, and also performs actions that are not mentioned in this account but that are well documented in others, such as burning sulfur close to her nose so that she inhales the thick smoke (sometimes causing death) so as to force the spirit to leave her body.

Another incident that took place in Safed in 1571 is recounted in what is known as the Falkon Letter, a document written by Eliyahu Falkon and signed by other sages of Safed who were present. The event transpired in the presence of dozens of men who were crowded into a room.

> And they pleaded with him [the spirit that had possessed the woman] by means of the aforementioned oaths and the aforementioned smoke, and by means of names [of God] that the spirit exit via the large toenail on one of her feet. And then it [the spirit] showed us that it was leaving that way, as they said to it, by means of the movements in which it raised and lowered her legs one after the other at great speed, over and over again. And with that movement that it was doing with such great force the coverlet that was over her legs and thighs fell off, and she was exposed and shamed herself before everyone, and they would approach her to cover her thighs, and she did not feel it at all. And those who knew her knew how modest she was, and now she had lost all her modesty, all because she was as if dead and gone . . . but despite all this they did not believe her [that the spirit had exited through her toenail] and she shouted to her father-in-law and her grandmother, "Why are you letting them burn me [because they set a fire before her nostrils], because it

has already gone out and they do not believe me" . . . and then it became known that the spirit exited via that place [her vagina] and caused bleeding when it left . . . and along with the confusion throughout the city, Jews and Turks, who crowded in together, to see this thing that was awe-inspiring and wondrous to all, they kept the matter quiet out of fear of the Gentiles (who would want to burn her [as a witch]) . . . and eight days later the poor woman died as a result of the spirit who would not leave her be, and they say that he strangled her and left along with her soul.[34]

The eroticism and violence is evident. A woman thrashes about in a bed with dozens of men crowded around her, watching her body's uncontrollable shaking baring her intimate parts. They threaten her and shout that she must accept their practices and beliefs. In utter seriousness, they discuss and debate whether the spirit has left her, and if so from where—her toe or her vagina—and demand to see evidence of it—that is, they want to see the place it left from. Is her toe swollen? Are there blood spots between her legs? The woman's pain and suffering are not mentioned in the moral sermon with which the letter opens, nor in the testimony that comes at its end.[35]

Another case of possession took place twenty years later in Damascus, where Hayyim Vital ended up after leaving Safed. I mentioned this case in Chapter 2 when addressing the rivalry between Vital and Rabbi Ya'akov Abulafia, a rivalry that began in Safed and continued in Damascus. The daughter of Raphael Anaf, one of the most respected members of the city's Jewish communities, fell into a state of great distress, and none of the magic workers and healers could help her. The voice of a man was then heard speaking from her mouth. Here, too, the spirit of a dead man speaks to Vital and his rival, Abulafia, revealing what is taking place behind the heavenly screen.

> Woe to you, sages of this generation, who do not bring the people to repentance. And here, I have also seen scandalous deeds among the sages of Egypt, for there is no wisdom

among them at all, and they destroy the city by distorting justice. And the men of Egypt have slave servants, and when the men leave their homes, the slaves lie with their wives.... Your [the men of Damascus] wives also dress arrogantly, with indecent jewelry, as well as the *piganis* [type of head covering] they wear on their heads, and their breasts are exposed and they fill the bosoms of their garments so that their breasts will seem large, and they walk wearing these *lizaris* and *nokavis* [thin and transparent garments] to show off their bodies, and they place perfumes in their bosoms to rouse the evil urges of men. And [they do] all this in the marketplaces and streets, to display their beauty to all the people.... And here forty-eight people engage in transgressions with Gentile women and married women and homosexual acts, as well as other transgressions.... They lie with Gentile women, and the heretical daughter of Comeiru engages in harlotry with Yehoshua Koriat and others. And RBY and RY Mugyeras lay with Natan Kulif and now gave him his daughter but still fornicates with him ... and Raphael Kulif and his son Michael commit a number of transgressions with Jewish and Gentile women. And here on the night of the previous Sabbath, TH, who is called a sage in the Sephardi synagogue, lay with a Gentile woman in Gobar. And then we asked who was there then on the oven that is there? And it transpired that it was Avraham, because he and his wife would sleep there with a Gentile woman who was the landlady. And the wife of Meir Peretz and her daughter are entirely prostitutes who lead many to sin, and Rabbi David Gauzinan sinned much because he left his modest wife here and married a prostitute woman in Egypt, and because of his sins his wife and daughter-in-law, who were modest, died. And in Egypt he transgresses with prostitutes and has lost everything.[36]

If we believe that it was the spirit of a dead man who spoke from the body of a young virgin, then she served as a vehicle for conveying these important messages to the many people who were present and through them to the entire community. But it seems more reasonable to suppose that Raphael Anaf's young daughter intermixed the sexual fantasies of an adolescent girl with rumors and gossip that reached her in one way or another. Even if these things are the product of Hayyim Vital's feverish imagination, they testify to an atmosphere, to the tense presence of sexual fantasies in the life of the communities of Safed and Damascus.

As with the previous incident of the widow in Safed, this event is deliberately public. The more people present, the greater its effect and the more other people will be influenced. In the Damascus possession event, the spirit commands Hayyim Vital to summon all the city's sages to the girl's house. Her family, neighbors, and a multitude of curious onlookers stand on the neighboring roofs. Others watch through the windows. This case of possession thus marks the blurring of boundaries between the private and the public. The most intimate of scenes, a teenage girl or widow lying on her bed in great distress, turns into a show watched by a huge audience. Their plights and most intimate fantasies turn into a public text that the entire community "reads" and interprets. I have already noted that intrusion into the private realm of sexuality—the nature of sexual relations between husband and wife, means of achieving sexual satisfaction, and even erotic hallucinations and fantasies—reached its acme in cases of demonic possession. These stories give manifestly carnivalesque expression to the eruption of primal urges. It is very much like the descriptions penned by François Rabelais, as Bakhtin reads them. A young woman lies on her bed; dozens of men stand around her shamelessly watching her convulse, her dress rising and falling over her thighs as her private parts are bared. How do they react? Is it simply with sacred awe of the spiritual revelations they hear and a passion for repentance? Or do they respond with uncontrollable laughter, sexual arousal, and an outburst of primal urges?

These accounts bring to the surface another aspect of unparalleled importance and interest—the blurring of boundaries between the sacred and the wanton, the pure and the defiled, the divine and the mundane. We have already seen this in the tales adduced at the beginning of this chapter. The tales of possession bring this subject to its climax. The goal of these stories, once again, is to prove the existence of spirits and souls, to bolster belief in reincarnation, and thus to reinforce belief in the next world and divine punishment and reward, beliefs whose role is to govern daily life and the life of both the community and the individuals within it. Indeed, we do not have even a single possession tale that does not stress the huge impact it had on its audience and its success in prompting people to repent and change their ways. Yet, as we have seen, the spirits who speak at these events reveal a world full of sexual transgression, passions, adultery, and licentiousness. Beyond all this, the event itself is laden with symbols and passions of an almost orgiastic character. It is here that the blurring of boundaries between the sacred and the profane, between social norms and their subversion, between the private and the public, reached a height that is difficult to imagine in a puritanical society with such mystical ambience as that which prevailed in Safed circa 1600.

6

And He Had Knowledge About Everyone

And the wonders of Luria they tell, the basis of most of them is that he had knowledge about everyone what his soul had been in previous lives [*gilgul*].

—Leon of Modena, *'Ari Nohem*

Our Own Eyes Saw Terrifying Things

ONE OF THE FORMATIVE texts of the Safed myth, which first portrayed the town as a unique place and which was responsible for spreading word of it all around the Jewish world, is the four letters that Rabbi Solomon Shlumil of Dreznitz sent, in 1607, to his relatives in Bohemia after immigrating to Safed in 1602. These documents changed the image and history of the Upper Galilean mysterious city for contemporary European Jews. A passage from the first letter states:

> And had I come to announce his eminence, all the wonders, and the great deeds of Luria, may his memory be a blessing, before all of Israel in the land of glory, here in Safed, may it be built and established quickly in our day, which were told to me by my teacher and rabbi, Mas'ud Ma'arabi, may God protect and bless him, and from some of the rabbis and great scholars of the Land who poured water on his hands [studied directly under him] and who saw with their own eyes wondrous things from him that have not been seen in the entire land since the days of the *tanna'im*. Like Rashbi [Rabbi

Shimon bar Yohai], may he rest in peace, he had all the virtues such that he had knowledge of all the deeds of human beings and even their thoughts. He had knowledge of the wisdom that was in the countenance and soul of human beings and their incarnations and could say what evil men had been reincarnated in trees, stones, or in beasts and fowl, and he could say what transgressions a man had made from the commandments and the transgressions [he had committed] since his childhood, and he had knowledge of when amends had been made for this fault, and he had knowledge of the chirping of the birds and from their flight comprehended wonderful things, and this is like [the biblical verse, Ecclesiastes 10:20] "for a bird of the air shall carry the voice, and that which hath wings shall tell the matter." And he comprehended all this through his piety and abstinence and holy purity.[1]

It is hard to understand how we could not have noticed that this text, which has been read and examined so many times, contains a most significant internal contradiction. Shlumil, who in his first letter includes testimonies about the atmosphere and traditions of Safed as he felt and heard them during his years of residence there, speaks of "wondrous things from him that have not been seen in the entire land since the days of the *tanna'im*." In other words, in Safed Luria performed ("before all of Israel") wondrous and exceptional deeds. With his supernatural powers he performed deeds that elicited the awe of the people of Safed, who saw these acts with their own eyes. Shlumil records these explicit testimonies conveyed by people in Safed in his letter. And it is from this letter that European and Oriental Jewish communities formed their mythical image of Safed, centered on the figure of Luria and his miracles. But when Shlumil goes on to recount what these deeds were, the expression that gets repeated almost everywhere is "he knew": He knew about the reincarnation of evil people in trees and stones, beasts and fowl; he knew about the transgressions of each person from birth and the amends he had made for them; he knew the meaning of the chirping of the birds and their flight.

In writing that we have not noticed this contradiction, I have in fact done an injustice to the great and incisive early-seventeenth-century Venetian rabbi and scholar Leon of Modena (Judah Aryeh), quoted in the epigraph to this chapter.[2] His cautious choice of words displays his precision—he does not assert that Luria *performed* wonders but rather that *they tell* of such wonders. Leon says that he is presenting us with *stories* about Luria's wonders, not facts, because he did not believe that the wonders had indeed occurred. Writing in 1620, the Venetian sage perceived that in these stories Luria does not actually *do* anything. Instead, he "recognized," or in Shlumil's formulation, "he had knowledge of."

Thus at the foundation of the Lurianic myth lies a highly significant contrast between the claim that Luria performed awe-inspiring deeds that elicited the veneration of his contemporaries and the actual accounts of his deeds, which demonstrate that they involved no more than recognition or knowledge of a world hidden to others.

This is exceptional even from the point of view of comparative folklore. The trademark of saints' legends from the end of antiquity to the modern age is that holy men and women perform supernatural acts. They cure the sick, abrogate the laws of nature, rescue individuals and communities from various dangers, and make intensive use of magical powers (such as the use of the Tetragrammaton). Even the figure to whom Luria's students, as well as later generations, compared him, Rabbi Shimon bar Yohai, stands out in the Talmudic corpus for his magical powers and supernatural deeds. Almost all Jewish legends exalting medieval heroes—Rashi, Maimonides, Avraham ibn Ezra, Judah the Pious—include supernatural motifs in which these figures are depicted as able to change the normal course of events in a miraculous way.[3] To be somewhat less cautious than Leon was, I would say not that *most* of the original legends about Luria involve his knowledge or recognition of something but that they are *all* of this sort. Not a single legend told about Luria during his sojourn in Safed (or the fifty years around 1600 that this book is concentrated on; I am not speaking here about legends fashioned centuries later) recounts a miraculous deed. There are no stories of sick people lining up in front of his door so that he could cure them, or stories of threats to the Safed Jewish community that he averted or undid.[4]

This claim is reinforced by Rabbi Joseph Karo, who relates at the beginning of his intimate journal *Magid Meisharim* his potent desire to perform miracles like those performed by the great Jewish figures who had come before him.

> And so adhere always to the blessed name [God] and you will be favored to have miracles performed by you as they were performed by the ancients, and this people will know that there is a God in Israel, *for now there are no miracles, because the heavenly name is not sanctified, because the world does not see that miracles are performed by the wise men*, and when they see that they are performed by you, the name of heaven will be sanctified.[5]

Karo's language here is innocent, meaning that the center of interest is himself, not what is happening around him. He feels that he is not as saintly as the "ancients." He therefore must strive to achieve their level of sanctity so that he will be favored to perform miracles. His miracles will in turn bring the Jewish people to "know that there is a God in Israel." This common idea in medieval Judaism was known as "a memorial for his works" (Psalms 111:4). According to this idea, recognition of God's existence and his involvement in the world is produced by the manifestation of miracles in everyday life.[6]

Karo makes two claims of interest to the subject under discussion here. First, he does not even consider the possibility that another man—for example, Luria—might be able to achieve the spiritual level needed to perform miracles. Although this text was almost certainly written before Luria's arrival in Safed, Karo could refer to other famous miracle workers there. According to his self-estimation, if he himself were not to do so, the name of heaven would not be sanctified.

Second, Karo states clearly and explicitly that "now there are no miracles." In other words, the myth of Safed that later generations fostered and disseminated, that Safed had then been full of miracle-performing saints with Luria at their head, was utterly unknown to a man who lived in that town throughout its golden age and who ranks as the most preeminent of its scholars. Luria himself addressed this point directly, according to the testimony of his disciple Rabbi Hayyim Vital.

> [This is said] for a person who uses practical Kabbalah [mystical magic]. I will first comment on what its sin is. And these are the words of my late teacher, may peace be on his memory. I, the writer, Hayyim, asked my late teacher about the use of practical Kabbalah, which is forbidden in all the works of the recent masters of Kabbalah. And if so, how did Rabbi Ishmael and Rabbi Akiva, may peace be on them, in the *Pirkei Heikhalot* use names of awe for the matter of remembering and opening the heart? And he responded to me that in their time the ashes of the [red] heifer were available, and they would entirely purify themselves of all pollution, but we all are in a state of impurity caused by the dead, and there are no ashes of the heifer to purify us from impurity caused by the dead . . . and therefore we are not permitted in these times to use the holy names and one who uses them is liable for a great punishment, as I will write below.
>
> And another time my teacher, may peace be on his memory, responded to the same man in a different way, in this way: "Know that all the names [of God] and charms that can now be found written in books are in error, and even the names and charms that were tried and perfected by the experts have many mistakes. Thus it is forbidden to use them. But if we knew the names in their proper and true way, we too would be permitted to use them."[7]

Luria does not deny the validity and truth of Jewish magic—what Vital calls practical Kabbalah. He of course cannot dismiss the hundreds of ancient sources that mention the use of magic, from rabbinic through medieval to contemporary texts. But, as he always does, he frames magic as a theoretical possibility that cannot actually be manifested in his own time. At two different opportunities Luria offers two different explanations for the absence of magical powers from Jewish life of his time; one is the ritual pollution caused by dead bodies, which there is no way of purifying now, and the other is the ignorance of those who write holy names for use as charms. In both cases the conclusion is identical: There was no magic in his time in Safed. But tales, whether told deliberately or spontaneously, have a life of their own. Even though Luria himself explicitly denied reports of him performing miraculous deeds and even the very possibility that such deeds could be performed in his time, his fame as a wonder-working saint remains firmly ensconced to this day.

Yet, significantly, outside the general rumors attached to Luria's figure, the legends recounted in Shlumil's letters, which were the basis of the later Lurianic vitae *Shivkhei ha-'Ari* (Praises of the Ari [Luria]), make no mention of any miracles that he actually performed. This reinforces the conclusion I drew from other medieval legends about Jewish saints, such as those about Ibn Ezra, Maimonides, and Judah the Pious. In different and complex ways, the legends that sing their praises preserve a link to their authentic personalities and work. Despite the temptation to fashion magical legends around the figure of Luria, no such stories came into being in Safed in the years around 1600. This fact demonstrates that legends of Jewish saints of this time should not be seen as the products of unchecked fantasy and imagination. Rather, they are narratives that relate to the fundamental nature of their lives, stories that intricately interpret those lives while often remaining faithful to the actual facts about them.[8]

Luria Exorcises a Spirit

I ended Chapter 5 with a presentation of stories of possession, in which the spirits of the dead enter the bodies of women and men and act inside them. Of the three comprehensive and authentic reports that have survived from this period—in a report written by Rabbi Eliyahu Falkon, the story of the spirit in Safed, and the spirit that entered the daughter of Raphael Anaf in Damascus—two took place in Safed during the time of Luria and the third after his death. The Falkon report is our most extensive and important report of such a case and is signed by several of the most important scholars in Safed—but not Luria. In the second case, in which a spirit entered the body of a widow in Safed, Luria sent his student Rabbi Hayyim Vital to the woman's home rather than going himself, because "he did not have time to go with them." Luria avoided displaying his powers in public. He knew what was going on and instructed his disciple accordingly, but he himself did nothing—and this precisely in a place and at a time that we might expect him to demonstrate the "frightening" powers attributed to him.[9]

According to several accounts, Vital told of one case that seems to be an exception. A young man of 18, a yeshiva student, suffered horrible agonies, and Luria, seeing his misery, told his father, "Your son has a spirit within him and do not waste money on doctors." But the father claimed that the boy had a heart ailment (or, in another version, malaria). Luria spoke with the spirit, forcing him out of the boy's body and compelling him to promise not to torture him again. But the spirit made a condition: "This young man must not see the face of a woman for three days. If he violates this condition, I will kill him." Yet when the guards that had been placed over the student went out for a moment, his mother and aunt came to visit him, and when they kissed him "the spirit entered him once again and suffocated him." Luria and Vital feared that "the Gentiles will say that we killed him. The rabbi, may his memory be for life in the next world, made a miraculous leap with two staffs, and we went to Tiberias in a single moment . . . eight days later we returned to Safed."[10]

This story has all the characteristics of a saint's legend. It attributes supernatural powers and deeds to his hero, and it belongs to that small category of tales in which Luria acts as a real saint. But a comparison of this story to any other saint's legend in Jewish or other cultures shows just how different it is. In contrast to all other saints' tales, this one tells of a disastrous failure that compels Luria to flee Safed for his life, just like a common criminal fleeing the Ottoman authorities. This legend, even more than others, proves how different Luria is from the rest of the gallery of Jewish saints. And when he tries to act like other saints, he fails. This legend seems to be shouting at us that Luria's grandeur is not of this kind.

The Hidden World

There are innumerable examples of the phenomenon described here. In Chapter 2 I considered the Tale of the Oxen, concerning Rabbi Ya'akov Abulafia's journey to Egypt. In the story Luria knows in advance that on the return trip Abulafia will encounter the souls of men who had been reincarnated as oxen. Yet Luria does nothing—he offers no charm or incantation or devotion for the traveler to recite. He simply knows what will happen. In that same chapter I also adduced the legend about a calf that enters the study room of Luria's circle and places his forefeet on the table. Luria tells his disciples that they must purchase the calf at any price, slaughter him ritually, and eat its meat communally. The calf, he informs them, houses the soul of a ritual slaughterer who had caused the Jews of Safed to sin. Here, too, Luria does not *do* anything. He only *knows* something. As a result of this knowledge, he tells his students what to do, but his instruction does not include any act that takes it out of the realm of everyday life. In other words, Luria, once more, does not act like other saints.

Another such example was discussed in Chapter 3—the Tale of the Locusts. Here, Luria, sitting with his students outside the walls of Safed, knows that a huge swarm of locusts is on its way to the city to punish its inhabitants for not helping a poor man who was in dire straits. Once again, he takes no action. Yes, he instructs his students to collect alms for the poor man, but he uses no magic to avert the catastrophe.

> And once Luria told our teacher, Rabbi Yitzhak Cohen, to go to the village of Ein Zeitun, to the tomb of Rabbi Yehuda bar Ila'i, and convey to him his interpretation of a passage from the *Zohar*. And he commanded him not to speak with anyone and not to respond to anyone. Then he, may peace be on him, went and prostrated himself on the grave of Rabbi Yehuda bar Ila'i, may peace be on him, in the village of Ein Zeitun and did as he commanded him, and the holy *tanna* did not make any answer to him. Then he returned to his teacher and said, "Master, I went to the tomb of the *tanna* and I did as you commanded, and I received no answer from him." Luria, of blessed memory, responded to him, "And did I not see in a vision that you spoke with an Arab woman? Not only did she not greet you, but you went first and greeted her in such and such a place, and I commanded you not to speak with any person!" Then our venerable teacher Rabbi Yitzhak Cohen recalled that so it had been and confessed to him . . . and

> he also discovered the grave of Rabbi Kruspadai close to here, which had not been known, and there had never been any marker upon it, and it lies close to the bank of the river, and also the grave of Rabbi Pinhas Ben-Ya'ir, which no man had ever known, he, may peace be on him, revealed, and like these he revealed burial places of untold and innumerable *tanna'im* and prophets. And he used to say that because the *tanna'im* and saints who are from the hidden world, no markers were placed on them and their location was not known.... And when he went to the cemetery of Safed, may it be built and established quickly in our day, he would say here lies a certain pious man whose name is this, and here another pious man whose name is that, and they investigated after him and found that he had been directed to the truth, as if he had been there at their funerals.[11]

This is a typical account in Shlumil's letters, which I have cited only in part here. His third letter collects dozens of testimonies and traditions he heard from the inhabitants of Safed and disciples of Luria some three decades after the fact. They all consistently and insistently repeat the same claim: Luria knows. He does not cause things to happen; he does not intervene in mundane or divine events using supernatural knowledge or powers. Rather, he knows things that exist only in the hidden world, that are invisible to creatures of flesh and blood. For the most part, he does nothing with this knowledge. Sometimes, as in these examples, he tells one of his disciples to act in this world—to buy a calf and slaughter it, to give alms to a poor man. But this knowledge and the actions that derive from it have nothing in common with the magical deeds attributed to the saints, whether Christian or Jewish, in the saints' legends of the medieval and early modern period.

One important testimony in this regard, the reliability of which is testified to by the text itself, is related by Shlumil in his fourth letter.

> And a disciple of Luria, may his righteous memory be for a blessing, the scholar Rabbi Gedaliah Halevi, told me that in the time of Luria, may his righteous memory be for a

blessing, he would tell his disciples awe-inspiring and wonderful things that he saw each day time after time. He would position himself on a mountain that stood outside the town, and from there he saw the whole cemetery of Safed and saw hosts of souls that ascended from the graves to ascend to the divine paradise and the opposite as well, he saw myriads that descended in their place and these were the additional souls that are added to [the people of] Israel on the Sabbath. And out of all the confusion and mixing of the souls and hosts there, his eyes dimmed and could not see and he had to close his eyes, and yet he saw all the same things when his eyes were closed.

And also once Luria, of righteous memory, went to study Torah with his disciples in a field and he saw that sitting on all the trees were tens of thousands of souls, and also there was a stream close by and he saw that thousands and tens of thousands of souls were floating and teeming on the water. When he saw them, he asked what their nature was, and they answered him that they had heard about his saintliness, that he had it in his power to rectify them, and that they were souls who had been pushed outside the curtain [of the divine presence] for not having repented, and about the reincarnations they had gone through in this world. And the holy sage promised to do all he could to obtain their ascent.

And the sage related this afterward to his disciples because they had seen him ask and respond and did not know what about, and he told them the entire occurrence.[12]

This testimony is important for a number of reasons. First, it is reliable. The chain of transmission is direct and clear—from the event itself to the disciple who was present and heard Luria speak, to the oral account that Shlumil heard directly, to the written text. I do not mean to claim that the incident took place exactly as described. After all, more than a generation had gone by between the time of the event, 1571–1572 (Luria's arrival in Safed to his death there a year later), and Shlumil's letter, which was

"He would position himself on a mountain that stood outside the town, and from there he saw the whole cemetery of Safed and saw hosts of souls that ascended from the graves to ascend to the divine paradise and the opposite as well, he saw myriads that descended in their place."

written in 1607. Furthermore, it is hard to believe that Rabbi Halevi heard precisely this story and was not influenced by the burgeoning of Luria's reputation over the intervening thirty-five years. But the chain of transmission and the fact that the basis of the account is anchored in the spiritual milieu of Luria's Safed seem to be beyond doubt. The story's fascination lies in Luria's behavior. He closes his eyes, murmurs some words to himself, enters into himself, and utterly ignores the presence of his disciples. Such behavior greatly amplifies the mystery that his students sense in his company and the charismatic power that derives from that aura, as will be seen later. Furthermore, the absolute, unquestioning credence with which his disciples accept his report cannot but elicit our wonder. Some stories of this type include "proof" that Luria speaks the truth and possesses miraculous knowledge. But it is clear that such proofs are directed largely at people outside the community of believers. None of his disciples seek to verify their master's story. It is accepted, here and in nearly all similar stories, without any shadow of a doubt and without any demand for substantiation of any sort.

In any case, if we expected "awe-inspiring and wonderful things," as we are promised here, the promise is not kept. Again, Luria does not do anything, nor, as far as we know, does he keep his promise to do anything later. He simply has miraculous knowledge and perception of events "behind the curtain." He is not involved in any instance of supernatural action. Even the souls that gather around him to request that he rectify them do not receive this. Luria does not act; rather, he sees and knows.

Rabbi Halevi's story also demonstrates one more important point. In all the miracle stories about Luria, the world does not change. What changes is *perception* of the world. To the outside observer of the Safed cemetery, the stream at its feet, and the trees and stones surrounding it, nothing has happened. The world remains just as it was before Luria's miraculous manifestation within it. But after Luria reveals to his disciples what really has taken place, a huge change occurs in the way they *see* the world. After hearing their master, they sense no physical change in reality, but they will never again view the world as they did before. From this point on, they will observe the world around them through the prism of Luria's awareness. Not through his eyes, it should be stressed, as they do not see anything of what he spoke. Luria did not succeed in changing the world, nor did he seek to do so. Rather, he changed *their grasp of the world.*

Concealment, Mystery, and Charisma

Luria's knowledge of the "hidden world" is not just limited to the graves of saints, the souls of the dead, or the relations between the living and the dead. It also includes knowledge of the future. One such case comes as direct and reliable testimony from one of his disciples, Rabbi Yosef Sagis, as told by Hayyim Vital.

> I further heard about my teacher, may his memory be for a blessing, from the sage Rabbi Shlomo Sagis, may the Merciful One protect and bless him, that he once saw in a dream that his tefillin were defective, and he ordered new tefillin. And our teacher, may his memory be for a blessing, explained [the dream as meaning] that his wife was pregnant with a boy, whom she would miscarry, and then she would

afterward become pregnant once more with a boy who would live. And as he explained, so it came to be.[13]

This story places Luria in the company of other figures from Jewish tradition who interpreted dreams as predictions of future events. Luria hears an account of the dream from the dreamer and solves it using a symbolic language known only to him, and events that the dream predicts indeed come to pass.[14] The story's opening phrase, "I *further* heard," informs us that this element of Luria's reputation should be added to his miraculous knowledge of things "behind the curtain." It is not simply an interpretation of dreams, because that was not something Luria engaged in, but rather further testimony to his wondrous knowledge of what lay beyond the knowledge of other men. Note, however, that Luria makes no attempt to avert the coming evil. He was seen as a saint, not as a professional interpreter of dreams, and normally a saint would be expected not only to have knowledge of a coming catastrophe but also to know what could be done to prevent it. Luria, as in all the other cases adduced here, "knows" what is fated to happen but does nothing to save the family of his devoted disciple from this tragedy. This distinguishing mark removes the story from the genre of dream-solving stories and places it in the category of tales of Luria's miraculous knowledge of the world beyond this world.

One of the important means of enhancing the awe in which believers hold the higher powers that rule them is the *mysterium tremendum*, the awe-inspiring mystery. They have no explanation for the forces revealed to them, nor does the religious leadership seek to make exceptional phenomena easier to comprehend. On the contrary, it seeks to conceal them and to envelop them in an air—be it thin or thick—of mystery.[15] All the Lurianic legends cited here accord with this model. No attempt is made to explain, even in part, the source of Luria's miraculous knowledge. How could he know that a plague of locusts would soon descend on Safed and its environs? How did he know that his disciple disobeyed his command and spoke with an Arab woman? How could he have been aware of the burial places of ancient rabbis or the names of the dead buried in Safed's cemetery? The stories present all these as unquestionable truths. When Luria saw that "sitting on all the trees were tens of thousands of souls, and also there was a stream close by and he saw that thousands and tens of thousands of souls were floating and teeming on the water" (Shlumil's fourth letter), none of his disciples, nor the readers of Shlumil's letter, have any doubts about the matter. (The only exceptions are skeptics like Leon of Modena.) The audience for these dozens of legends is never given any explanation of Luria's miraculous knowledge. In fact, the mystery surrounding his knowledge enhances his holiness and the awe-inspiring nature of the forces whose witness and emissary he is.

> And sometimes he went with the initiates to the village of Meron and would sit on the place where Rabbi Shimon bar Yohai, may peace be on him, revealed the *Idra Rabba* [one of the sections of the *Zohar*] . . . and he would say that he saw a blazing fire around the initiates, but that it was not permitted for their eyes to see it, but only for him himself.[16]

Between Visible and Invisible

The demand that the miraculous way of knowing that Luria had been granted be concealed from his disciples led to constant tension between him and them. Luria's disciples tried to draw every scrap of information they could about the source of his powers out of him, even by theft or subterfuge, but without success. This tension persisted throughout Luria's sojourn in Safed. The revelation of the hidden was the principal cause of his early death, according to his inner circle of disciples. One of the most important and most enigmatic stories about Luria, known as the Tale of the Two Fawns, relates what happened.

> Our teacher Rabbi Hayyim [Vital], may the merciful one protect and bless him, asked Luria, of blessed memory, about the understanding of the *tosefta* [passage in the *Zohar*] of the Two Fawns. . . . Luria, of blessed memory, said, "On your life, Rabbi Hayyim, let me be in this matter, that I will not interpret it for you, and that it would be better for me and for you and the whole world, that there is a great secret here and they do not want me to reveal it." He [Vital] said to him, "You must

reveal it to me." Luria replied, "See that if I reveal it to you, you will in the end regret it with great regret and I warn you, but I am obligated and commanded not to keep from you anything that you wish to ask me. So I admonish you that you let me refrain from interpreting this *tosefta* for you." Rabbi Hayyim, may his Rock protect and maintain him, replied, "I want you to interpret it for me anyway." So he interpreted the *tosefta* for him and revealed secrets to him. And after revealing it, he said that the judgment had been handed down that Luria would die that very year as a punishment, "for having revealed this secret, and you yourself brought this harm on you, because if you had not pleaded with me so much, I would not have revealed it, and they would not have punished me from heaven. And I had already intimated to you several times, but you did not want to attend to my words."[17]

The kabbalistic background to this story has been discussed in depth by Yehuda Liebes, but what is important here are two other matters. First, this dialogue takes place, according to the account in Shlumil's letters, between Luria and Rabbi Hayyim Vital. That means that the narrator can only be Vital himself. (In later versions of this story, other disciples are also present.) The story thus reflects the heavy sense of guilt that Vital felt over his master's death—a guilt expressed so potently in the speech this story ascribes to Luria. Vital is accusing himself, openly and bluntly, of responsibility for the death of his teacher, whom he sees as the Messiah, son of Joseph.[18] Do Luria's words reveal something of the unconscious thoughts, his repression of a secret desire for Luria to die so that he could take his master's place? Does it show that Vital believed himself more worthy of leading the Jewish people to repentance and redemption? Vital seems to have felt such guilt for the rest of his life, and it offers one possible explanation of why he devoted his life, after Luria's death, to disseminating his master's teachings.

Another matter important to the current discussion is the fact that the tension between revealing and concealing that is so characteristic of Lurianic life is depicted in this legend as the tragic denouement of his life. The very reason Luria came into the world—to serve as a plentiful conduit for the transmission of divine secrets into the mundane world—is what causes his death. Luria's death is thus not a natural human death (in fact, he died in a cholera epidemic) but rather a cosmic event caused by spiritual weakness or his own sins and those of his disciples (the generation's transgressions). This resembles the death of other messianic figures, such as Yosef de la Reina, Shabbetai Zvi, and Jacob Frank.[19]

The common belief in Europe at the time maintained that "knowledge of what is above is dangerous" and should not be sought. European scholars and clergy of the sixteenth and seventeenth centuries believed that the pursuit of what lies beyond nature, such as metaphysics, astrology, magic, and knowledge of the future, came at great risk to the person involved and to society as a whole.[20] Although in Luria's case the danger awaiting him is not his own knowledge but his revelation of that knowledge to others, the final cause of his death is similar. It could well be that concealment was in the manifest interest of those scholars who sought to maintain their monopoly on such knowledge, while at the same time they sought to reinforce their social status and cultural authority. This is much like what Luria did.

But mystery is not a feature of all the sources that tell us about Luria. His disciples' writings offer several explanations for his miraculous knowledge, at least some of which have their source in things the master himself said. One of the most common manifestations of this astonishing knowledge is Luria's understanding of the calls of flying birds. Several times in their writings, Shlumil and Luria's disciples express great astonishment about this. For example, in his work *Sha'ar Ruach HaKodesh*, Hayyim Vital directly addresses it.

> In the wisdom of knowing the calls of the birds. The master, of blessed memory, had another [kind of] knowledge, in that he understood the chirping of the birds, and this is the meaning. Know that from the day the Torah was burned, as is known, by the nations of the world, for our many sins, its powers and secrets were given over to the *kelipot* ["shells," the Kabbalistic representation of evil]. And all of them, there is no creature in the world, even the unclean ones like beasts and animals and flying creatures and vermin, all of them have guardians assigned to them, and these angels know

the riddles and secrets of the Torah from that time. And these same guardian angels of these creatures or birds place in their mouths, in their calls and voices, profound secrets from the Torah, and one who understands their voices and calls can know some of the secrets of the Torah. And there are generations in which there are saints who understand them, and this is what I saw with my own eyes with my master, of blessed memory. So the guardian angels place these secrets and those worthy know and understand them, as noted. And know also, that all that is ruled from on high is declared in all the worlds, and especially in the mundane. Likewise all the transgressions that a person commits are all declared in this world by the divine court, and the emissary of the court that accompanies them. And the thickness and crudeness of the air does not permit the spiritual voice to pass and it is diminished within it. And indeed when the birds soar in the air, they cut through and slice the air and divide it by their soaring and flying, and then the voice of the herald passes through it.[21]

Apparently basing his interpretation on things he heard Luria say, Rabbi Hayyim Vital here explains the path taken by "profound secrets from the Torah" from the divine court, by means of the guardian angels. These heavenly voices are halted by the density of the air. But when the birds cut through the thick air, they score it with fissures through which the divine voice can descend to the mundane world. This para-scientific explanation removes the veil of mystery from Luria's miraculous knowledge, presenting him simply as a person who knows how to read the divine secrets through a natural process that can be explained rationally. On this account, Luria possesses no supernatural or miraculous powers but rather simply wisdom, a science like any other, which he knew how to apply.

This brings out another fundamentally important aspect of the Lurianic legend. The legend does not seek to interpret the wondrous phenomena that it presents. On the contrary, even when "rational" explanations are offered, as in the case of the calls of the birds, the legend ardently preserves an element of mystery. Any such explanations would, after all, muffle and, one might even say, eviscerate the awe that draws its strength from the unexplained mystery. Luria understood this psychic phenomenon well, and the constant tension between the hidden and the revealed that he maintained between himself and his disciples is easy to understand in this light. Moreover, it seems extremely likely that Luria's vast charisma, which lasted for many years after his death (Vital died about forty-eight years after Luria, and awe of his master was a feature of his character all that time), derived to a large extent from the mysterious aura that surrounded him. That mystery persisted because his disciples sensed that much more of their master was concealed from them than was evident.[22]

Were All the Seas Ink and All the Sky Parchment

One of the important components of the mystery that surrounded the figure of Luria was the fact that a sage of his stature wrote so little. Only a handful of texts that can be ascribed to him directly and several Aramaic liturgical poems for the Sabbath have survived. No more. His doctrine, as is well known, has come down to us through his teachings to his disciples, recorded, mainly, by Rabbi Hayyim Vital. It is difficult to evaluate where Luria's authentic teachings end and Vital's reworking and interpretation of them begin. This issue is no less complex than the question of how to distinguish which of the doctrines and arguments that Plato attributes to Socrates in his dialogues are actually ones taught or made by Plato's teacher.[23] The question of why Luria did not write down his teachings and thoughts caused his students sleepless nights during his lifetime. They did not hesitate to ask him.

> And indeed in one instance the sages of Safed once asked him, "Our Master, Candle of Israel, the Almighty gave Your Eminence so much wisdom, why should the Rabbi not compose a single good and illuminating work so that Torah not be forgotten by Israel?" He responded to them in these words: "Were all the seas ink and all the sky parchment and all the cane pens, they would not suffice to write down all my wisdom. And when I begin to reveal to you a single

secret from the Torah, so much plentitude multiplied within me, like a swift-flowing river, and I seek ploys, from where to open for you a thin small channel to tell you a single secret from the Torah, a tiny thing that you could bear, not to multiply for you more than your strength can bear and thus cause it all to be lost, like a baby choking because too much milk came for him. Therefore my advice is this, that you yourselves write down all that you hear from me, and it will remain for your memory and for the generations to come."[24]

This story, which makes several appearances in the Safed corpus, is of primary importance for understanding the way in which Luria's character is reflected in the legends. Here, too, Luria's claim regarding the great wisdom granted to him is not perceived by his disciples as pride or boastfulness but rather as an unquestionable truth. Luria's assertion that his wisdom is vast is presented here as another instance of the miraculous knowledge with which he had been endowed. But Luria truly grapples with the question only in the second half of the story, where he offers two different explanations. The first has to do with him, the second with his students. The second explanation is simpler and easier to understand; it is largely a didactic issue. Luria knows that his disciples, like a baby at his mother's breast, cannot drink from the profuse channel of his wisdom. They need a thin stream. Thus he counsels that they write down his teachings in accord with their ability to absorb them. If Luria himself were to write down his miraculous knowledge, his students would choke on its plentitude and would not be able to take in any of his wisdom.

The first explanation is more complex and more interesting, in that it contains an important and revealing element of personal confession. Luria admits that each time he tries to put his teaching into words, "so much plentitude multiplied within me, like a swift-flowing river, and I seek ploys, from where to open for you a thin small channel." In other words, his ideas come so profusely that he can find no way to order and verbalize them in a way that others could understand and plumb their depths. To put it another way, Luria here admits, if obliquely, that he suffers from some sort of communication disorder that arises from a curse of profusion. There is such a wealth of possibilities, worlds, and ideas, so many ways of thinking and creating, that he cannot focus on any one thing, on a single idea, to give it a clear formulation with an orderly line of thought from beginning to end—which would be the only way they could be put into writing. This confession directs us precisely to the subject to which this chapter is devoted: *Luria is a man of knowledge, not action.* He and his disciples are aware of the huge and astonishing abundance of his knowledge but recognize that when this abundance needs to be transferred into the dimension of action, from awareness into writing, he fails utterly. The same phenomenon notable in the miracle stories about Luria here manifests itself in his learning; he is unable to turn his miraculous abilities from potential into action.

When Luria speaks this way, we see his human side. Such an admission of weakness, even if indirect and vague, reveals a fascinating side not just of Luria's view of himself but especially of the way he shaped the persona he wished his disciples to see. Another important testimony relating to this has survived in another passage by Rabbi Hayyim Vital.

> And Rabbi Avraham Halevy, may his Rock protect and maintain him, also said that my master, of blessed memory, said to himself on the matter of comprehension, and that is that he should not engage in idle conversation and that he should rise at midnight and bewail his lack of knowledge and study the *Zohar* to gain proficiency without delving into its study, 40 or 50 leaves a day. And he should read the *Zohar* many times. And indeed my teacher, of blessed memory, told me, when I asked him how he came to have all his wisdom, he replied that he had worked very hard on this wisdom. And I told him that Rabbi Moshe Cordovero, of blessed memory, and I, Hayyim, also worked very, very hard at this wisdom. And he told me that the truth was that we [Cordovero and Vital] had worked very, very hard, more than the rest of the people of our generation, but we had not done as he had, because some nights he remained without sleep [studying] a single passage in the *Zohar*. And sometimes he would spend the six weekday nights in isolation,

studying a single passage of the *Zohar*. And most of the time he would not sleep at night at all.[25]

Luria instilled clear principles in his students, but unfortunately these instructions did not become part of the aura of myth that surrounded him in later generations. His knowledge and thinking, he maintained, were the result of study and hard work bordering on self-sacrifice. He did not come to his teachings easily, as a divine gift or revelation, but rather studied intensely day and night. The message he sought to pass on to his students was that they should not expect that there would be any shortcuts in their study. They had to work as he had, to know that the study of the *Zohar* was not a mystical experience but rather a difficult task requiring spiritual effort that cut a man off from the world around him and put him in a state of existential loneliness.

But the high point of the human dimension in testimonies about Luria appear in a comment from the same informant.

> Rabbi Yosef Sagis, of blessed memory, also told me, in the name of my teacher, of blessed memory, that they heard from him that there was nothing more necessary and proper for a man in the matter of comprehension as immersion [in the *mikveh*, the ritual bath], that a man should be pure at all times. And indeed I saw that my teacher, of blessed memory, during the six months of winter, did not immerse himself during most of them, because he was sickly and broken, and his mother would not permit him to immerse. And this is true and clear to me, and it was not at all because of this that his comprehension abandoned him.[26]

Luria taught and explained to his disciples the supreme importance of ritual immersion; it was a fundamental condition for achieving kabbalistic awareness and the understanding of the divine. The purity of the scholar depended on it, and without this there could be no real understanding or study. Had Rabbi Hayyim Vital left the testimony of Rabbi Yosef Sagis at that, the passage would have remained just one more of the homilies of moral wisdom and guidance that Luria's disciples heard from him. But Vital reveals a small truth here that may have been important for him: Luria himself did not immerse himself in the cold winter months in which the devotion of the true believer is tested, when performance of this precept is difficult and even dangerous. To immerse oneself in the *mikveh* in the hot summer months is no great virtue. Then why did Luria not immerse himself at all times, as he commanded his disciples and all Jews to do? Because he was "sickly and broken" (the latter term might mean that he had a hernia). Furthermore, his mother would not permit it! In contrast with the hundreds of stories about Luria that were told and retold, copied and recopied in work after work, this little report was never again cited, surviving only as a disregarded passage in Vital's book.

Furthermore, we learn from this passage that Luria had a period of eclipse in which "his comprehension abandoned him." Was this a passing incident or an ongoing one? Was it like the spiritual collapses experienced by Shabbetai Zvi, who lived not many years later—that is, akin to the manic-depressive episodes displayed by the "false" messiah? We cannot answer that question, because this report is the only one of its kind and offers no further details. Here we are not interested in Luria's mental or physical condition, or in his dependence on his mother in his adult years. Although these are of great importance in other contexts, they do not impinge on the question to which this chapter is devoted. The central point here is that the story corroborates what has already been shown regarding the disparity, if not the actual contradiction, between Luria's world of mystical belief, into which he drew his disciples, and the mundane world in which he lived. Here, too, as in the dozens of earlier stories cited, Luria's spiritual potential is enormous. He "knows" the source of the ritual power and force of immersion on which mystical understanding depends. But a huge gap separates this knowledge from the act of immersion itself. He himself did not immerse precisely when immersion would serve as evidence of true devotion.

These legends about Luria should not be viewed as biographical facts, even if, as noted, some of them can be legitimately used in a reexamination of his life. But that is not the main point. Their importance is the way in which they reflect and express the significance of the Safed myth for those who lived there in its golden age and for the generations that followed. The disparity or binary opposition between knowledge and action that characterizes the image of Luria in the legends about him casts a powerful and harsh spotlight on their most profound meaning.

That will be the subject of Chapter 7, the final rung in the ladder we have climbed into the Safed myth. It is a ladder firmly planted on the ground, or as the people of Safed then liked to say, "in the material world," but its top reaches far up into the heavens.

7

Life and Legend

> Here in Safed . . . the material days are sealed and pound like the sea on the Torah and on the service [of God].
>
> —Eleazar Azkari, *Sefer Kharedim*

Inconsistency Is in the Eye of the Beholder

THE QUESTION WITH WHICH I opened this book returns now in this final chapter, in the manner of wanderers through the labyrinth who take one turn after another only to find themselves back where they began. Astonishingly, none of the dozens of scholars and students of the writings of Safed's golden age have paused to consider Hayyim Vital's testimony about Luria's ritual immersion, recounted in Chapter 6. Yet anyone who seeks to understand the people of Safed not just as the giants who produced great kabbalistic and ethical works but also as human beings cannot afford to disregard the following account:

> Rabbi Yosef Sagis, of blessed memory, also told me [Vital], in the name of my teacher [Luria], of blessed memory, that they heard from him that there was nothing more necessary and proper for a man in the matter of [mystical] comprehension as immersion [in the *mikveh*, the ritual bath], that a man should be pure at all times. *And indeed I saw that my teacher, of blessed memory, during the six months of winter, did not immerse himself during most of them, because he was sickly and broken, and his mother would not permit him to*

immerse. And this is true and clear to me, and it was not at all because of this that his comprehension abandoned him.¹

But Vital himself contradicts this depiction of Luria as debilitated in body and spirit, subject to his mother at the age of 38, suffering from a severe psychological crisis ("his comprehension abandoned him"), in a first-person account of the death of his great teacher that he conveyed to his son Shmuel.

> And after the great bathing [the washing of Luria's body following his death], they led him to the place of immersion [the ritual bath], and they said to him, "Our master, we have done our duty, but we do not have permission for immersion, for the master told us to take him to the place of immersion, and the master would immerse himself, and now the master is in the place of immersion in the water." He immediately stood up straight in the water as if he were alive, bowed his head and immersed four times against the four letters of [God's] name. And after the immersion they dressed him in expensive clothes and declared, "There is no priesthood today!" And they led him from his home to the synagogue as they wept, to the point that tears flowed on the ground like a gushing river, and even the Gentiles who knew him wept for him and eulogized him.²

Do these two texts, from the same source, Luria's closest student, contradict each other? The contradiction would seem to be principally in the eye of the beholder of Safed's culture from the outside. Such an observer sees Safed through the prism of a different world, one that is measured and rational, one that divides that world's various aspects into preconceived categories. In that light, we find no contradictions between Shlumil of Dreznitz's account of Safed and that of Rabbi Moshe Alsheikh, which dates to about the same time, even though each describes a different Safed. Shlumil depicts an ideal and wondrous city in which all is illuminated and happy, a place where social harmony and economic prosperity both

[The gateway to the old *mikveh* of Safed.] "And after the great bathing they led him to the place of immersion . . . and now the master is in the place of immersion in the water. He immediately stood up straight in the water as if he were alive, bowed his head and immersed four times against the four letters of [God's] name."

prevail, where the life of the spirit is interwoven into material life. Alsheikh describes the same city as a place of darkness and abject poverty, of ugly rivalries, of great danger from within and without.[3] Or take another example adduced here: the wonder stories told of Luria. While Luria's students travel through Europe and the Orient spreading word of Luria's greatness and the wonders he performed, one of the most important rabbinic scholars of Italy, Rabbi Leon of Modena (Judah Aryeh), writes that he heard from a sage who had lived in Safed during Luria's time there and who had been close to him, Rabbi Ya'akov Abulafia, that none of the miracles and wonders ascribed to Luria actually happened and that Luria himself had rejected these rumors.[4] Again, this seems to be a bald contradiction. Either Luria performed miracles, or his students misled the public by spreading falsehoods. Such a view of dozens of ostensibly "contradictory" events that arise from the world of Safed arranges believers against skeptics and rationalists. Every reality is complex and complicated, and Safed is no exception.

Existential Tension Resolves Opposites

In an effort to comprehend what is going on here in its full depth, we must, once again, see the phenomena described in this book not as contradicting one another but as coexisting in a state of existential tension. What I mean by this is that they exist side by side and within one another. Rather than being mutually exclusive, they are the best possible characterization of the multifarious reality in Safed circa 1600.

The tale of Luria in the *mikveh* is one of the best pieces of evidence for this, which is why I chose to begin with it. Its importance lies, first, in the fact that the two ostensibly contradictory testimonies come from the same person. Rabbi Hayyim Vital himself, Luria's closest student, relates that Luria avoided immersion in the *mikveh* during Safed's cold winters, when it involved discomfort or put his health at risk. But he also tells his son about Luria "coming back to life" so as to immerse himself in the *mikveh*—in other words, the precept of ritual immersion was so important to Luria that he went so far as to return from the next world to perform it.

The contradiction between these two accounts, provided by the same person, can be resolved in a variety of different ways. But I maintain that the deep divide in Vital's soul, as evinced in all the autobiographical texts he wrote that have come down to us, offers the most persuasive explanation. The obvious tension is between the ways in which Vital viewed Luria. Vital saw before him a merchant who had recently arrived from Egypt and who was trying to disseminate his mystical fantasies. The man was weak of body and broken in spirit, and his elderly mother told him what to do. Yet it was this same man who, as Vital saw it, had in his life realized the messianic ideal, a man before whom the gates of heaven opened wider than they had for anyone before him or would ever open for anyone afterward.

This means that there is no contradiction between Shlumil's description of Safed as he experienced it physically and that of Alsheikh, who experienced the terror of Safed's decline from greatness in the last quarter of the sixteenth century. Rather, the ideal city and the real one were at odds in the souls and lives of its inhabitants. The conflict was not just psychological; it also filled the "material days." Such is the case also in those testaments to Luria's miracle working that Leon of Modena rejected. It would be wrong to say that there was one group of people who believed in the miracles while others rejected them. That is a simplistic view that contributes little to the understanding of the subject. Safed's inhabitants and its devotees in the Diaspora did both simultaneously. They believed but also knew that reality could not be identical to their dream. In most of them the two positions coincided, producing the unrelieved tension that was so characteristic of the Safed myth.

The same is true of the dreams that I have examined over the course of this book. In almost all the dreams analyzed in Chapters 3 and 4, the dreamers see themselves in the daily activities of Safed or Damascus—in the rooms of their homes, in their yards, on nearby and familiar streets, at the neighborhood well. In an instant they are transported to a different world of dark depths, or glowing dwarfs appear from nowhere and then vanish, or they ascend magically to the heavens and paradise. These dreams display the same constant mental tension between the routine and the domestic on the one hand and the world of wonders beyond this world on the other. The dreamers, like the other characters who appear in the dreams, are torn between the two experiences and evince the tension immanent in them.

The huge figure of the first Adam, the giant lying along a Safed street, with his head resting by the door of Karo's home and his feet in the town market, enormous but weak and helpless, exemplifies the tension felt by the dreamer between the pure and the impure. Adam's body reaches from the home of Karo, seen as Safed's spiritual spine, to the material and physical marketplace. The pure and impure reside side by side, and neither can exist without the other.

I devoted Chapter 6 to Luria's miraculous knowledge. I noted that the principal supernatural trait attributed to him in the tales about him is his knowledge of the hidden world that lies behind the visible world. Luria locates the graves of saints in places where nothing is evident in reality, sees the souls of the dead hovering in trees, converses with dead spirits, animals, and inanimate objects in which the souls of the dead have been reincarnated. But despite this wondrous vision, nothing changes in reality, except for knowledge of the unseen. For the disciples gathered around Luria, the world around them looks just as it did before their master appeared in it. In actuality, nothing has happened, but for them reality will never revert to what it was before they heard their master's teachings. From this point on, they see the world through Luria's consciousness, not necessarily through his eyes, for they in fact see no change.

Luria did not change the world, nor did he even try to do so. What he did do is change our *awareness* of the world. To put it another way, he granted the visible and the hidden world the same level of actuality, the same ontological standing. Dozens of legends about Luria have tried to persuade their listeners and readers of this. In fact, it seems as though a significant part of Luria's mystical system is based on this view of the spiritual. It trains believers to scrutinize the elements of daily reality, knowing that what they see is not all of reality but only that part of it that is visible, which is less significant. The more significant reality can be seen only through their teacher and with the mystical vision he opened for them. It may well be that mystics who preceded the Safed era also fashioned their spiritual worlds in this way, but when this mentality became habitual in increasingly broadening communities, its social and historical implications became much more important.

Because these two realities are equally "present," there can be no contradiction between actual and fantastic reality. Both have equal place in the minds of Luria's disciples, and they passed it on to the generations that followed. In short, there is no contradiction here but rather tension between two entities that exist alongside each other (because the disciples do not themselves see the hidden reality; they only know of it from what their master tells them). It is as though the disciples are saying, "True, I don't see any of it, but our faith in our teacher is so great that his words are no less actual for us than what we see without our eyes." It is like the tension in the soul of the emperor in the story by Hans Christian Andersen; he does not see or feel any clothing on his body, but his faith in his tailors, or the mental imperative associated with this faith, is stronger than his faith in his vision and his body's sense of touch. The same is true here; in the legends about Luria, mental tension, which would seem to be the most salient characteristic of Safed's culture at this time, is expressed in a powerful way.

It may well be that the most poetic and purest formulation of this tense reality comes from Rabbi Eleazar Azkari, one of the leading Safed moral teachers of Luria's time, in the passage I have used as an epigraph for this chapter: "Here in Safed . . . the material days are sealed and pound like the sea on the Torah and on the service [of God]." Azkari refers to that same duality of life "here in Safed." On the one hand, there are the material days, that is, the week's six profane workdays. But these days also "pound like the sea on the Torah and on the service [of God]." In other words, the profane days are not empty or open to everything. They are sanctified, designated for Torah and service—for the study of Torah and devotion to God. Note in particular the beautiful and precise simile used here: "pound like the sea." Behind the mundane world another spirituality pounds or surges like the sea. Like the sea, which is always there even if we are not consciously aware of it at every moment, the eternal spiritual world is present among us at every moment. With this wonderfully pregnant idiom, Azkari succeeds in expressing the full significance of the tension that I have sought to portray here and elsewhere in this book.[5] The presence of both these kinds of days—the material and the spiritual—and the aspiration for and pursuit of days of unadulterated and total spirituality are what constitutes the fundamental tension at the foundation of the Safed phenomenon, in its fullest and most multifarious extent.

Family or Messiah?

In his first letter, Shlumil of Dreznitz writes that Luria is the Messiah ben Joseph, adding that

> from another event it seems that he is. Once, on the eve of the Sabbath, close to the arrival of the bride [i.e., the beginning of the Sabbath], he went outside the city of Safed with his disciples dressed in four white garments: a robe and capote and shirt and pants to welcome the Sabbath. They began the psalm "Ascribe to the Lord O divine beings" [Psalm 29] and the song sung for welcoming the Sabbath, and "A Psalm, a song for the Sabbath day" [Psalm 92] and "The Lord is king" [Psalm 93] with pleasant melodies. And as they sang the Rabbi said to his students, "My companions, would you like us to go to Jerusalem before the Sabbath and do the Sabbath in Jerusalem?" And Jerusalem

is more than twenty-five parasangs from Safed. Some of the students responded, "We would like that." Some of them responded by saying, "We will first go and inform our wives." Since they said they would go first to their homes, the Rabbi was overcome with a great fear and clapped his hands and said, "Woe to us that we did not have the merit to be redeemed, had you all responded unanimously that you want to go with great joy, all of Israel would immediately have been redeemed, as this was the hour of redemption, and because you turned it down the Exile has returned to its full power as a result of our many transgressions."[6]

Two hundred years later, in 1798, Rabbi Nachman of Bratslav decided to make a trip to the Holy Land.

And when his wife heard this, she sent his daughter to him to ask him how he could leave them, who would provide their livelihood? And [Rabbi Nachman] replied, "You will go to your in-laws; your big sister—someone will take her to be a little servant in his home who is called Nianke; your little sister—someone will take her into his home out of compassion; and your mother will be a servant-cook. And I will sell everything in my home for my travel expenses." And when his family heard this, they all wailed loudly for several days, and he had no compassion for them. . . . And he said, "I want to go to the Land of Israel, and I know how great the obstacles and impediments that I will have, beyond all measure. But as long as my soul is within me, as long as I have the breath of life, I will give my soul and use all my strength to go there."[7]

It hardly seems likely that Rabbi Nachman did not know the tale about Luria and his ascent to Jerusalem on the eve of the Sabbath. The story had been widely disseminated through Shlumil's letters and editions of *Shivkhei ha-'Ari* that had circulated widely in Central and Eastern Europe.

Nachman's behavior here, depicted as quite cruel, sounds much like Luria's response to his disciples in the story. It goes right to the heart of the tension I have pointed to: The messiah and the family represent two extremes of the same reality. Rabbi Nachman does not try to accommodate both poles and say what Luria's disciples said: First we will go tell our families, and then we will ascend to Jerusalem. He knows, deep down, that such a compromise is an illusion, and he thus disregards it from the start. Ascending to the Land of Israel, an act replete with messianic symbolism, comes before all else. Hence the blunt response to his daughter gives voice to his decision and avoids the error that Luria's students made.

A similar tension, in a similar context, can be found in another essential tale.

> Afterward Luria put these ten companions in confinement and placed the women and children on their own in the courtyard of the place of confinement. After some months a fight broke out among the women on the eve of the Sabbath, and the women told their husbands, and it went on to the point that the companions also fought. The Master, may peace be with him, always admonished them to display brotherhood and love among them always, peace, love, and brotherhood. And that day they transgressed against his precepts in their sins, and when evening came, he went out with the companions to welcome the Sabbath and returned to the synagogue upset and angry and sat throughout the prayer service in bereavement. And when our honored teacher [Rabbi Hayyim] saw him that way, he was aghast, because it was not his custom to be that way. After the congregation had concluded the prayers, Rabbi Hayyim went to him and said, "Our Master, why did I see you throughout the prayer service in bereavement and despondency?" Rabbi Yitzhak [Luria], may peace be with him, said to him, "Because during the welcoming of the Sabbath I saw Samael, and he recited this verse: 'Both you and your king shall be swept away' [I Samuel 12:25]. And from this it looks as if

the judgment of your many sins has been sealed. And it was sealed only because of the fight that there was today among the companions, for so long as there was peace among them, he had no entry point from which to accuse, and thus it happened because of our many sins." That same year the Heavenly Seminary asked for the soul of our teacher and master and the crown of our heads, and the lives of five of the companions.[8]

In this narrative Luria is well aware of the tension between the family and spiritual lives of the members of his fellowship. He therefore decides on a solution. He moves them into common living quarters where they will study together and where their families will also reside. It seems to be a good way of addressing the existential tension between the material days and the life of Torah. It may be appropriate, but it is not realistic, because these two realities cannot live together. Each breaks through to the territory of the other, disrupting both. The altercation among the women upsets their routine and draws in the disciples, who are not supposed to be disturbed by such "small" matters. The result is the disruption of the divine-messianic world as well, as Luria says. In both these tales the desired event—a messianic Sabbath in Jerusalem and joint living quarters for Luria's fellowship and their families—does not relieve the tension between the two realities. On the contrary, the tension is exacerbated by the proof that these two realities cannot be reconciled. The tension between them is an unassailable fact.

But these two tales are first and foremost messianic legends. In the first the narrator stresses that Luria is the Messiah ben Joseph, meaning when he does not ascend to Jerusalem with his disciples on the eve of the Sabbath, he fails as the Messiah, just as Yosef de la Reina did. In the second tale, Samael's appearance in the lodgings of the fellowship and his declaration that Luria and his disciples will die soon because of the human weakness revealed in their camp amplify even more the similarity with the story of Yosef de la Reina. (Recall that in the Tale of the Two Fauns, discussed in Chapter 6, Luria is sentenced to death for revealing secrets of the Torah to his disciples—that is, a different reason is given there for his death.) This similarity cannot be a coincidence. The tale of Yosef de la Reina, which was well known in Safed during Luria's time there, is a classic story about the incredible spiritual exertion made by its hero, who in the end surrenders to his own human weakness.[9] It is a legend that expresses, in an almost paradigmatic way, the tension that occupies us here, between actual human reality, with all its weaknesses, and the huge effort of the protagonist to overcome that weakness, to emancipate himself from his humanity and break through to the hidden divine messianic reality. Yosef de la Reina fails. So does Luria. What remains of their heroic attempts is the unresolved tension between the flawed human reality and the huge spiritual efforts to leave it behind.

The Messianic Age Is Here and Now

The question of Safed's messianism during this period is a controversial one. Some see the principal spiritual effort of Safed during its great era as focused on the effort to bring about the redemption, whereas others maintain that the messianic idea was marginal to its spiritual activity. Some maintain that the major thinkers of this period were extreme in their messianism, whereas others see them as ascribing to a "soft" or "weak" messianism. I will not grapple with the findings of the study of Safed mysticism, the rituals founded and practiced there, or the ethical theory that developed in Safed during this period. All these are connected to the vicissitudes of the messianic theme in Safed and have received considerable attention. The one body of evidence that scholars have not dealt with is the one to which this book is devoted: the legends of Safed. As I have shown throughout this book, these legends give expression to profound debates, the Safed landscape, dreams and fantasies, sexual relations, and the standing of figures, such as Luria and Vital, who represent the place and era. The legends of Safed are thus able to make a significant contribution to understanding the status of messianism in Safed's life.

From the start, messianism in Jewish history has exhibited tension between exile and redemption. In Christian doctrine the redemption is a-territorial and everywhere. In contrast, in Judaism there can be no redemption without the Land of Israel. The main test the Jewish messiah faces is always his ability to bring the Jewish communities of the Diaspora to the Holy Land. In the absence of such a territorial shift, there can be no messiah and no redemption. The incongruence and opposition between the dark, evil, impure, and oppressive exile and the Promised Land, where God's presence is felt at every moment, have always been the fuel of Jewish messianic hopes.[10] To put it another way, without the Exile there is no messianic vision. It is the Jews' presence in the Diaspora that provided one of the Jewish people's most vital creative forces, the aspiration for redemption.

However, the big difference is that Safed is located in the Land of Israel, not in the Exile. I just asserted that without the Exile there can be no redemption. The accounts of the Yemenite traveler Zechariah (Yahya al-Dahiri) and the new immigrant Shlumil of Dreznitz, with which I opened this book, show that Jewish life in Safed was conducted on a level that any Diaspora Jew could only dream of. The Jews in Safed were a majority and conducted themselves accordingly. The city was prosperous and no one lacked for anything. Its spiritual life realized the hopes of previous generations—both Torah scholars and simple Jews devoted their days and nights to Torah and good deeds and led pure and honest lives. Their lives were directed and led by great masters of the Torah. And all this on the soil of the Upper Galilee, in the eternal home of biblical heroes and the great rabbis of the Mishnah and Talmud. What was left to be desired? How could these people not believe that the messianic era was already underway in Safed? Could one imagine a greater contrast than that between the marvels of Safed and the darkness of the Exile? Rabbi Joseph Karo, the spiritual pillar of Safed during this period, made this feeling explicit.

> My beloved had a vineyard on a fruitful hill [Isaiah 5:1]. Because when God saw the poverty his people Israel [had endured] for more than 1,500 years, ejected from their land, from nation to nation and from one kingdom to another people through several exiles and several destructions, He remembered the covenant of their fathers and brought them back and gathered them from the far corners of the world, one from a town and two from a clan [Jeremiah 3:14], to the beautiful land [of Israel], and they settled in the city of Safed, may it be built and established quickly in our days. It

is more beautiful than all the lands, and its elders and leaders behaved properly and bore the burden of the poor and indigent . . . and always the respect for and awe of the Torah lay on the elders and leaders of the city, and they did nothing until they had consulted with the rabbinic sages and elders. They came and went at their word. And indeed, the vineyard of the God of Israel was beautiful and also pleasant, the vine bloomed, the pomegranates budded, and the heads of the seminaries and their students studied in their places without any adversary and without any danger. They did not hear the voice of the oppressor, he broke the ground, cleared it of stones [Isaiah 5:2] the nobles of the nation with the God of Abraham . . . Torah and light went out from there to all the Diaspora.[11]

There is no way to miss the messianic expressions that Karo chooses to use here, at the opening of his work *Avkat Rochel*. They evince the typical polarity between the Exile and the Land of Israel, using biblical verses that have always been taken to refer to the messianic age; daily life is depicted as subordinate to the light of the spirit, and the center of spirituality is the light unto the nations. All these serve as clear evidence of the sense, which the great teacher of the generation shared, that Safed was living, if not actually in the days of the messiah, then as close to them as possible.

This is the place to note the similarity between these depictions of Safed and those found in utopian literature. The sixteenth century is known as the cradle of the utopian idea and utopian writings. At the beginning of the century, in 1516, Thomas More published his *Utopia*, and toward the end of the century, in 1580, Philip Sidney's *Arcadia* appeared. Between the two, many works of literature and philosophy, in many European languages, addressed the subject. The connection between political and religious utopias—that is, the messianic era—has been the subject of studies of the era and genre.[12] The depictions of Safed written by Zechariah, Shlumil of Dreznitz, Joseph Karo, and many others of their time is clearly utopian and very much part of the utopian literature of sixteenth- and seventeenth-century Europe. Nevertheless, there is one fundamental difference that supports my claims about the messianic character of Safed: Whereas the utopian idea and the literature it produced speak of an imaginary world that does not in fact exist in any concrete time or place, the accounts of Safed speak of an actual place experienced by the authors. They offer the sense that the utopian-messianic world is not just a hope that lies in some undefined future and in some undefined place, as was the case with European utopias. Safed's utopia exists in the here and now.

Further, though not explicit, the use of the Hebrew language in Safed's day-to-day life was evidence of the messianic presence. It could be argued, of course, that the language was called into use because of the arrival of Jews from both the East and the West, with Hebrew being the only lingua franca to which all of them had access as a result of studying it from a young age and using it in prayers, to read from the Torah, and on other such occasions. But testimonies from both outside and inside Safed indicate that the phenomenon had more profound significance. The English traveler William Biddulph, to whom I referred briefly in Chapter 1 in a different context, visited Safed in 1600 and wrote:

> Most of the Iewes can read Hebrue, but few of them speake it, except it be in two places in Turkey, and that is at Salonica, formerly called Thessalonica, a City in Macedonia by the gulfe Thermaicus; and at Safetta in the Holy Land, néere vnto the sea of Galile: Which two places are as it were Vwersities or Schooles of learning amongst them, and there (honoris grati) they speake Hebrue.[13]

This testimony is reinforced by Safed's spiritual leaders' insistence on the use of Hebrew. For example, Rabbi Moshe Cordovero wrote, "'You shall keep My laws and My rules, by the pursuit of which man shall live' [Leviticus 18:5] . . . to speak the Holy Tongue with others always."[14] The charters of the fellowships that operated in Safed and its environs also stipulated that Hebrew was to be spoken within the fellowships all week and with all Torah scholars (i.e., anyone who knows Hebrew) on Sabbaths.

There would seem to be no better proof of the messianic sensibility than speaking Hebrew. As Safed's inhabitants saw it, because they were living full

Jewish lives and treading the soil of the Holy Land, the only thing needed to complete the messianic milieu was the Hebrew language. One hardly needed proof of the language's importance and divine origin. It is apparent from classical midrashim and mystical lore. In fact, the importance of Hebrew had always been recognized, but following the rabbinic period the ideal of using it was not put into practice. That was not the case in Safed circa 1600, however, when a real effort was made to turn Hebrew into a spoken language. Was it a success? According to the fragmentary records that have reached us, it seems as though the success was only partial. Hebrew was used largely within the mystical fellowships, in synagogue sermons, and perhaps also in conversations among Torah scholars. It is hard to find testimony of Hebrew being used in everyday life. But there can be no doubt that the initiative to do so grew out of a clear sense that the redemption could not be fully realized if Hebrew were not used as a spoken language.

The ordination initiative that took place in Safed, beginning in 1538 in the seminary led by Rabbi Ya'akov Beirav, also needs to be seen in this context. The Jerusalem rabbis were furious. The attempt to reestablish the rabbinic institution of ordination was aimed at reestablishing the Sanhedrin, in the belief that that institution was needed to prepare the Jewish people for the impending messianic era. Some of the men ordained were still alive and active in the last third of the sixteenth century, most centrally Rabbi Joseph Karo, and the fact that their authority derived, in part, from that ordination shows that they felt that the redemption was taking place in their time and during their lives.[15]

This sensibility finds clear expression in the legends—this time, tellingly, by what they leave out. Every reader of Jewish folk literature from the Bible up to the folktales of present-day Jewish communities knows that one of the central and most important themes in the stories of every era is the conflict between Jews and other nations. The conditions of Jewish life involved danger and tension between Jewish minorities and the non-Jewish majorities that were hostile, at least in the view of Jewish communities. There are hundreds of stories of conflict, and they play a variety of roles: They discharge tension, provide psychological support, offer practical and moral guidance; or they may help define identity or shore up faith. These stories generally center on a spiritual leader—the prophet Elijah in the Bible, Shimon ben

Shatah or Shimon bar Yohai in rabbinic literature, Maimonides and Abraham ibn Ezra in the Middle Ages, Maharal of Prague (Rabbi Judah Loew ben Bezalel) in the early modern period, or the Ba'al Shem Tov and Baba Sali in modern times. Through the supernatural powers with which they have been endowed, these figures save individuals and entire Jewish communities from the hands of the Gentile authorities or from Jew haters who seek to harm them.[16]

What is surprising about the legends of Safed from this historical perspective is the almost complete absence of tales about conflicts with Gentiles. There are virtually no stories of miraculous rescues of individuals or communities by holy men who are the protagonists of the stories. The central reason for this would seem to be the sense that there were no adversaries around, no hostile majority that was oppressing the Jewish community, no Jew haters attacking the members of the weak minority. Let me stress once again that it makes no difference whether this feeling was in accord with the historical facts or whether the Jews of the Galilee did indeed enjoy equal rights and the full protection of the Ottoman authorities. As far as cultural perceptions are concerned, the fact that such stories do not appear in the rich repertoire of this time and place tells us that this is how they felt and this is what they believed.

The absence of such legends is also important in another critical way. At the center of the messianic view formulated by Maimonides is the rabbinic assertion that "nothing distinguishes this world from the days of the Messiah except the [Jews'] enslavement to the [Gentile] kingdoms" (*b. Berakhot* 34b). The absence of stories of conflict with and hatred of the foreign nations within which the Jews of Safed lived indicates that the dread of "enslavement to the kingdoms," the most salient hallmark of the Exile, was not felt in this period by a broad swath of the Jewish population in that city. The fact that the members of Safed's Jewish community did not feel that they were under the thumb of foreign rulers—if they did, the feeling would have been expressed in the stories they produced—joins other evidence I have adduced showing that this community felt that it was living on the verge of the messianic era.

When, at the end of his life in Damascus, during the first two decades of the seventeenth century, Rabbi Hayyim Vital recalled Luria's era in Safed, he saw before him his teacher, the messiah of his generation. He recalled the intensity of spiritual life there, the closely bonded fellowship that surrounded Luria, their great promise to lead all the Jews of Safed through a process of repentance and return to God and a life of purity and brotherhood. He had failed to achieve all this in Damascus. For Vital, Safed in Luria's time was quite literally the messianic era, the closest any Jew would get in this world to the messianic ideal.

But this ideological-messianic world was chock-full of flaws and failures. In Chapter 1 we saw the harsh disputes between communities and individuals and the immoral conduct of sages toward the members of their communities. In a letter dating from these years, Rabbi Moshe Alsheikh wrote of moral decline, the lack of leadership, the pursuit of monetary gain, and foul poverty. In Chapter 5 we viewed sexual life in Safed's mythology. There I showed the fanaticism of Safed's sages when it came to sexual purity, as they faced sexual sinfulness of all kinds throughout the city. Was that the messianic age? Was that the redemption the Jews had looked forward to during their years of exile? Here we see another line of tension, perhaps the most intense, between Safed as the realization of the redemption and quotidian, mundane, human Safed. This mental fault line is clearly evident in a personality like Vital's, but it can also be seen in his older contemporary, Joseph Karo, his teacher Luria, and another member of his fellowship, Eleazar Azkari, and apparently in others of that time and place as well. It can also be seen in Safed society as a whole.[17]

On the one hand, the Jews of Safed lived, consciously or unconsciously, with the feeling that they, more than any other Jews of their time, were closer to the promised redemption in location, their actions, and their lives. Yet, on the other hand, they were also certain that the redemption could not come in the Safed they knew, a city full of defects, human weaknesses, horrible sinfulness, conflict, and animosity. This is not the familiar tension between the desirable and the actual, the redemption and the Exile, that has always been part of Jewish life. On the contrary, this is the tension between two actualities. The Jews of Safed were, after all, no longer in the Exile. They were as proximate to the redemption in place and time as any Jew could possibly be, yet how defective that redemption was! If that were the case, was the promised perfect redemption even possible? Consciously, of course, in their writings and prayers, they believed that the true redemption would certainly come. Yet how could they be so close to achieving the conditions that defined the messianic age when the world around them was so flawed?[18]

The foundational tension underlying the Safed phenomenon is most exemplified by the messianic phenomenon. The presence of the ideal, of religious fantasy, alongside and intertwined with the actual, mundane, profane world can offer a different explanation for the presence and absence of the messianic issue in Safed's culture. As we have seen, Safed's legends grant the fantastic, things that the eye does not see but the existence of which is certain, an equal standing with the world as it is perceived by the senses. This mentality, which may be the most important contribution to Jewish religious experience to come out of Luria's era, grants the redemption a dimension of actuality, of equal ontological status to everyday life. The local and historical conditions in which Safed's population lived contributed, perhaps for the first time since the origin of the messianic idea among the Jews, to a perception of the redemption as an actuality. The heavenly Jerusalem was replaced by the earthly Safed, with its alleyways, its many seminaries full of scholars, its synagogues packed with worshipers. Its stone houses created an ambience of a wondrous past, as did the sacred tombs in the landscape around the city and Mt. Meron on the close horizon. This was the messianic world itself. Maimonides' claim regarding the realism of the messianic age described in actuality the life of Safed and its inhabitants, but in a way quite different from what he had intended. Rather than the lack of the fantastic and the continuation of ordinary and political life, which is how Maimonides had viewed the messianic age, in Safed the mystical, which was the most actual thing there was in the Safed mentality, turned into the reality of life.

However, this actualization of the messianic fantasy was also the cause of the severe tension that emerged between one actual reality, the messianic (as it was conceived in Safed), and the other actual reality, that of the material days. The tension between them seems to have been the principal source of the mental crisis experienced not only by the scholars and ethicists whose works we know but also by the ordinary inhabitants who believed themselves to be living physically in a messianic reality. On the other side, the defective reality produced incessant tension, which seems to have been one of the factors in Safed's decline. But that same tension was also a powerful factor in the development of post-Safed Judaism, seen in such phenomena as the Sabbatean movement, Hasidism, and the new spirituality in modern Israel, for which Safed of today is one of the most important centers.

The Legend Speaks

Such is the importance of the Safed legends to which this work is devoted. Like every rich folk literature, the legends grew out of tension and crisis, and these are reflected in them better than in any other work to emerge from that era. My attempt to understand and interpret the legends reveals the full force of the tension characteristic of Safed as a whole, not just of its scholars and ethicists. The dozens of tales we have examined over the course of this book have demonstrated the nature and significance of this fundamental tension. As is always the case with folk narratives, Safed's legends were not written by a single person or by a small group; they are the product of Safed society at large. By that I mean that even if they were created by a person like Hayyim Vital for specific purposes, when they were adopted by larger layers of Safed Jewish community, they became their cultural possession and heritage. Here lies their importance. The legends do not "reflect" reality. They are not historical documents. Rather, they are a highly important element of the society that produced and adopted them, one that actively participates in the time's social and philosophical discourse. The legends teach us that Safed was never what it seemed to be from the outside. Safed was characterized by a complex network of tensions extending into all areas of life and most saliently by a fault line between the sense its inhabitants had of living in the days of the messiah and the wretchedness and defectiveness of the world they saw around them. They felt that the redemption was dissolving into the material days right before their eyes, and that was not the redemption they had dreamed of. The legends' depiction of Safed's intensive and ongoing spiritual life are expressions of its inhabitants' sense that they were living during the End of Days and during the material days at the same time. They worked for their livings, experienced social tensions, dealt with the vexations of being parents and other everyday concerns. But that was not how the messianic era was supposed to be. They were like people going off on a long-planned vacation who found, once the vacation began, that it did not fulfill their great expectations. The tension between their aspirations and the reality in which those aspirations were ostensibly realized was almost certainly a major cause of the fault line in Safed. Since the destruction of the Jerusalem Temple, no Jewish community of historical memory came so close to realizing the ideal of the End of Days. How does an ordinary person of flesh and blood, not a heavenly saint, cope with such a fault?

There are some grounds for seeing a similarity between the messianic era that some Jews believe we are on the verge of today (i.e., the State of Israel as the "first manifestation of the approach of the redemption") and Safed circa 1600. The tension and mental fault line that nearly every Israeli experiences today has its origin in the intolerable disparity between the ideal model of the Jewish State envisioned by the Zionist movement and the harsh, flawed, and ugly real world. True, that is not the view of all social and religious groups in Israel. Haredi extremists see today's Israel as part of the Exile in every way. That was the view voiced by the late Rabbi Eliezer Menachem Shach, the leader of the Lithuanian Haredi community, who said, "The Jewish people remain in the Exile until the arrival of the Redeemer, even today in the Land of Israel, and this is not the Redemption or the first manifestation of the approach of the Redemption."[19] But this utter negation comes to counter the positive assertion it rejects and shows just how powerful it is. For broad and central swaths of Israeli society, secular and religious, the State of Israel is not the Exile, just as Safed's inhabitants four centuries ago did not see their city as part of the Exile. Shach, like many others, sensed the tension built into current Israeli life. On the one hand, Israelis live in the Holy Land, in a sovereign Jewish (if not religious) state, a realization of the messianic ideal. Yet the sins of the state utterly contradict the view of what the redemption should be. Haredi Judaism is thus the exception that proves the rule regarding Israel today, showing just how much it resembles Safed around 1600.[20]

Today's Safed, 400 years after the events described in this book, can serve as a metaphor. A person who wanders the narrow streets of Safed's Old City today sees a place that is trying its best to preserve its medieval ambience. Today's city seeks to replicate the structure of the homes and courtyards as they were then, to reconstruct ruins, to gather up the remnants of the past—objects, books, manuscripts, memories, and people—and display them in public and private museums. Safed's alleyways and courtyards are full of men and women who belong to a variety of sects—Kabbalists, Hasidim, varieties of mystics, New Agers, the newly religious, and everything in between. Each sect has its special garb and its own prayer and ritual customs, and their members conduct family and communal lives that lie outside the norms of both religious and nonreligious Israelis. What they all have in common is that they live in substandard conditions, barely support themselves, and are detached from the daily life of modern Israel. They live in a "spiritual" world that they have created or borrowed from the outside (Eastern or Western ideologies), in anxious expectation, so they say, of the "revelation of the light," which they maintain will come in the near future.

Alongside them, Safed is a modern city in every way. It has banks, cinemas, restaurants, hotels, and cafés. There are housing projects on its margins and a road system and traffic jams. The rivalry between these two poles of the city's life is difficult and bitter, and its effects can be seen every day, in both local and national politics and in its religious hierarchy.

In fact, the two worlds overlap. The members of the mystical-religious sects make considerable use of the services offered by the modern city, and the city's nonreligious inhabitants partake, to no little extent, in the experience of the Old City, visiting the artists' quarter, walking its streets, and attending celebrations and festivals. But they live in these different worlds. A classic example of this conflict is the Breslov Hasidic neighborhood that was constructed in the heart of the Old City, on a site with a view of the city's ancient cemetery and Luria's *mikveh*. The neighborhood is built over half-ruined houses that are of critical archaeological and historical importance. The larger and mostly secular community waged a battle in the municipality to prevent the project from going up, a struggle that reverberated in Israel's national politics and among the city's inhabitants. In the end the Hasidim built their neighborhood, despite the furor of the city's veteran inhabitants, on one of the city's most beautiful and most valuable sites.[21]

Today's Safed is proof that the battle over Safed's myth has not ended and may in fact be at its height. The proponents of the myth are seeking to keep Safed "as it was." That is the struggle against the construction by the

The Breslov neighborhood in the heart of Safed: large modern buildings that ruin the character of the Old City.

Breslov Hasidim of large and modern buildings that clash with the character of old Safed. The Breslovers seek to restore Safed to its central place in the heart of mystical-messianic Judaism. They thus have no interest in the archaeological preservation of relics of the past (which is what Safed's nonreligious inhabitants want). Rather, they want to return the mystical-messianic world, in new form, to the center of life in the city.

At the beginning of this long leap we have taken from sixteenth-century Safed to modern-day Safed we saw the great differences between the depiction of Safed by Shlumil of Dreznitz and Rabbi Moshe Alsheikh. The disparity typifies the tension that has characterized Safed's mythology from the sixteenth century to the present day, between the view that sees Safed's legends as an actual reality that can and should be lived and the view that stresses the drab and pallid material days. What can be learned from this analogy between Safed of 1600 and the State of Israel in the twenty-first century? What is the best way to grapple with its implications so as to repair the world? I leave those questions to the historians and ethicists. As a folklorist, I have done my part.

Notes

Introduction

1. On Schechter's life and work, see Ben-Horon (2007) and Scult (1997). On some mystical accounts in Schechter's essay, see Wolfson (2016).
2. For example, Schechter stated: "Thus the Safed of the sixteenth century, at least, is free from all antinomian tendencies. . . . The Safed Jew of that period saw no antagonism of principle between Caro and Loria [Luria]. Caro was for him the authority, Loria the model. But just as Loria was amenable to the discipline of the Law, so was Caro not unresponsive to the finer impulses of love and admiration" (Schechter 1908, p. 279). The same ambience is expressed in the poetical and full of pathos 1950 essay of Zalman Shazar (the third president of the State of Israel), who describes Safed from a typical Zionist point of view. A different essay, by Izhak Ben-Zvi (the second president of the State of Israel), is by far more accurate and erudite and has scholarly importance even today (Ben-Zvi 1976).
3. On New Historicism, see the basic works of Veeser (1989) and Greenblatt and Gallagher (2000). Murfin (1989) summarizes the basic definitions of the discipline. Magid (2008, pp. 5–10) uses this approach as a tool for understanding central aspects of Safed mystical creativity.
4. On the legend as an anticanonical genre, Sandra Weber made an important observation (based on her intensive fieldwork among the native population in northwest Tunisia): "Folk poetics (folklore) is, by definition almost, anticanonical discourse, the discourse of resistance of small groups, be they communal, occupational, ethnic, or regional, to larger forces. . . . Folklore, in both form and content, is by definition communally centered and time tested. Thus it is an especially apt artistic medium through which to learn about community-shared concerns from the perspective of the culture members themselves" (Webber 1991, pp. xxiv; 8–9).
5. In 1962 Naphtali Ben-Menachem published the first comprehensive bibliography on Safed studies (compare to Yassif 2013). He enumerated 504 specific studies. From this bibliography, we can clearly see how Schechter's indications and insights developed into independent study branches.

6. Outstanding among these studies are Dan (1974), who included the Safed tales in the history of the Hebrew narrative prose of the Middle Ages and emphasized the importance of the *shevakhim*/praises, and Alexander (1992a), who examined Luria's legends with the folkloristic model of "biography of the culture hero." In this context I should mention also Wineman (1988), who studied stories from Safed's moral and educational literature. His insightful literary and mystical interpretation is of pioneering importance. On the other hand, the seminal works of Werblowsky (1962) and Fine (2003), who use the Lurianic praise legends extensively, do not treat them at all as literary or cultural artifacts but as historical documents—reliable or deniable. Also typical are Jacob Katz's observations; Katz points to the important achievements of Safed in "the fields of religious culture, in *halakha*, in moral literature and preaching, poetry, and especially in Kabbalah" (Katz 1984, pp. 87, 92). See also Werblowsky (1987). The creativity in the field of legend and folk narrative is not included. Even in her popular survey, Ronit Meroz (2003), one of the important scholars of Safed mysticism, enumerates the rich spiritual life in Safed and mentions the Kabbalah, moral theory, magic, rituals on saints' graves, but the legends are totally missing.
7. On the *shevakhim*/praises as a historical and literary genre in traditional Hebrew literature, see Dan (1986), Bar-Itzhak (1987), and Yassif (1999).
8. On the philological works of Meir Benayahu in this field, see Benayahu (1961) and especially Benayahu (1967). The main criticism of Benayahu's historical conclusions regarding the authenticity of Shlumil's letters was published by Tamar (1986) and Rabinowitz (1968). The ups and downs of this controversy are described by Tamar (1992).
9. Benayahu's positivistic approach considers the legends as a source of information. This could be best seen in the fourth part of Benayahu (1967), the central part of his work: "*Sefer Toldot ha-'Ari* as a Historical Source" (pp. 91–121). This part is dedicated to the question of the authenticity of the legendary traditions: Which tales reflect events that "really" happened, and which tales are no more than forgeries?
10. In an seminal study, Pachter (1994, pp. 39–68) concludes, based on the eulogy of Rabbi Shmuel Ozidah immediately after Luria's death, that the miracle legends of Luria were not known at all right after his death.
11. Hacker (1984, p. 104).
12. Some of the studies on Vital's personality and work are Benayahu (1987), Bos (1994), and Patai (1994, pp. 340–64). On the book of recipes and household instructions, see Buchman (2001) and Buchman and 'Amar (2007), both of

which use an original autograph of Vital preserved in Ms. Mussayof 228, held in the Ben-Zvi Institute.

Chapter 1

1. On Shlumil of Dreznitz (using the Yiddish name of the town; Dreznitz is now Straznice in the Czech Republic), his letters, and their influence, see Cahana (1923, vol. 2), Benayahu (1967, pp. 41–60), and Tamar (1986, pp. 138–40).
2. The letters were published and known for the first time as "Kitvei shevach yekar u'gdulat ha-'Ari z"l" (Praises of the Greatness of Luria, of Blessed Memory), in Rabbi Yosef of Kandia's *Sefer Ta'alumot Khokhma* (Book of Wisdom Secrets) (Basel, 1628). They were published again from the same source in Cahana (1923, pp. 215–18). Since these letters were first known, they have been published in dozens of publications, in different formats known as *Shivkhei ha-'Ari* (Praises of the Ari [i.e., Luria]). Benayahu (1961) published a full bibliography of editions and translations to almost all Jewish languages. Since this publication, dozens of other editions have been published.
3. The account of Zechariah's travels is taken from Ya'ari (1976, p. 200). On Karo's schools and dominant position in the learned world of Safed, see Benayahu (1991, pp. 153–86) and the recent comprehensive biography of Karo by Altshuler (2016).
4. Azkari (1601, p. 2a). Azkari was one of the central moral teachers in Safed of that time. He wrote Yedid Nefesh (soul's friend), the canonical chant for the Sabbath, and the ethical book *Sefer Kharedim* (Venice, 1601). On Azkari, compare Pachter (1981), David (1993, pp. 158–59), and additional studies listed there.
5. Pachter (1994, p. 90).
6. Alsheikh's letter was published in a critical edition by Pachter (1994, pp. 92–107).
7. Simcha Assaf (1940) published a letter from 1604–1605 that laments the difficult economic situation of Safed during those years, as well as the lack of personal security of its Jewish citizens. Assaf also points to the controversy between this letter and those written during the same period by Shlumil of Dreznitz (pp. 136–38). Shraga Abramson published another anonymous short letter written in the same year, which says, "I would like to inform his honor that I prefer to stay in Russia and teach Torah to the Jews than to come to the Land of Israel, as by now the Land of Israel is very confused, God save us and all his people. When God will grant him good old age, and when he'll be old, [only] then come joylessly to the Land of Israel, as in any place that a man occupies himself with Torah and the commandments, there is the Land of Israel" (Abramson

1988, p. 20). For a detailed description of the decadence of Safed in the same years that Shlumil's letters were written, see Simonsohn (1962). Ya'ari (1958) published another memoir of a bookseller in the same venue.

8. The descriptions of the Christian travelers to Safed are found in Ish-Shalom (1963). David (1993, pp. 114–17) describes the difficult position of the Portuguese community, which had to struggle with their image as Marranos, converts to Christianity during the executions in Portugal. They even established a special fellowship of repentance in order to atone for their former deeds.
9. Rozen (1980, pp. 93–94). See also Ben-Zvi (1966) and Lamdan (1997). David (1992, pp. 112–24) provides testimonies for the strong intercommunal tensions between Provençal, Hungarian, and other Jews, because each community held fanatically to its traditions and customs. See also the helpful chart of these communities David draws (p. 126).
10. The economic structure and social tension in Safed and environs of that time have been described by Kna'ani (1934), Avitzur (1962), Hacker (1984), A. Cohen (1981, 7: 198, 248–50), Tamar (1986, pp. 124–30), David (1993, pp. 109–10), and Ben-Nae (2007, pp. 247–70).
11. Karo, *Avkat Rokhel*, sec. a (Karo 1859, pp. 1–2). In addition, Eliyahu de Vidas, in his *Sefer Reishit Khokhma*, an important moral book from Safed, writes, "That scholars are not engaged in work and they are supported by the rich of this generation, is supported (morally) by authorities . . . and these scholars are called 'sabbath' even during the weekdays, as they have no jobs except the burden of Torah and commandments. [Thus] the illiterates have the duty to support and feed them" (De Vidas 1579, p. 158).
12. Eberlein's controversy has been largely studied. See Benayahu (1963), Hacker (1984), and Altshuler (2016, pp. 382–84).
13. On the centrality of Rabbi Ya'akov Beirav and his house in Safed since 1524 and his attempt to renew the rabbinic ordination, see Dimitrowsky (1963), Katz (1951), Benayahu (1960), David (1993, pp. 148–50, 180–82), and additional works listed by David.
14. On Mitrani's criticism of the customs of Safed pietists, see C. Horovitz (1987). On Mitrani's debate with Karo on matters of Halakha and authority, see Benayahu (1991, pp. 9–98). Menachem Habavli's words are quoted in Dimitrowsky (1962, p. 67n167).
15. Benayahu (1967, p. 219). Benayahu refers to the source of this story as a Yemenite manuscript and claims that it reflects an authentic event (p. 110). On other variants of the story, see Lichtenstein (2007, pp. 341–51).

16. The quotation from *Sefer Hasidim* is from Hershler (1984, p. 145, no. 60). It is based on a maxim phrased in the Babylonian Talmud, *Berachot* 6b.
17. On the fellowships, see Scholem (1940a), Benayahu (1995), Meroz (1987), Tamar (1986, pp. 95–100), and Pachter (1987). Pachter suggests that Safed's ethical literature determined the rules of those fellowships, a view supported by documents in Fine (1984), Huss (2004), and Idel (1998b).
18. The story is quoted from *Sefer Hemdat Yamim*, *Shabat* 55a. On Najarah and his poetry, see Shazar (1950a, pp. 224–31), Mirsky (1962), Yahalom (1982), and Be'eri (1990, 1992, 2007).
19. Vital (1954, p. 34, sec. 1, 25).
20. Katz (1984, pp. 52–101); and from another point of view, Zak (1976). Rabbi Yosef Ashkenazy, one of Luria's best disciples, expressed the loathing of Safed kabbalists toward philosophy in sharp terms. See Scholem (2008b). Hacker (1987) gives a more comprehensive view on these debates.
21. Vital's story appears in his collection of dreams, Vital (1954, no. 16). The Luria legend is from Benayahu (1967, pp. 169–71) and other sources mentioned therein. Other sources tell about similar incidents between Luria and Karo (Benayahu 1967, pp. 217–19) and between Luria and Rabbi Avraham Galanti (pp. 219–24). This tension is transferred also to the next generation of Luria's and Karo's disciples, Vital and Rabbi Joshua bin Nun (*Sefer Ta'alumot Khokhma*, 1629, p. 12b).
22. *Sefer Ta'alumot Khokhma* (Yosef of Kandia 1629, p. 47a). Katz (1984, p. 92) presents another incident where Luria turned to Karo with a halakhic question and Karo answered with superior attention. On Karo as a kabbalist, see Werblowsky (1962, pp. 140–47) and Elior (1996). Altshuler (2016) dedicates the main part of her discussion to Karo as a mystical figure. Halamish (1988) presents the influence of mystical tendencies on Karo's halakhic rulings.

Chapter 2

1. This version of the legend appears in *Sefer Hemdat Yamim* (Algazi 1763, ch. 3, pp. 19b–20c). Other versions of the tale are gathered in Benayahu (1967, pp. 232–34).
2. On the economy of the Jewish community of Safed, which was dependent on support from the rich Jewish communities around the Mediterranean, see Chapter 1 and Ya'ari (1951, pp. 233–55), Benayahu (1959; 1962), and Hacker (2002).
3. On Rabbi Ya'akov Abulafia's nickname "the Egyptian," see Benayahu (1967, p. 114). A summary of the few details known about Abulafia is presented in David (1993, p. 180) and Benayahu (1991, p. 320).

4. On the involvement of Luria in the Jewish community of Egypt, see Benayahu (1985), David (1992; 1993, pp. 183–84), Shochetman (1983), and Fine (2003, pp. 19–40).
5. Such a harmonistic approach to Karo's character is presented in Benayahu (1991). Other important studies reveal the tensions that are the basis of Karo's spiritual achievements: Werblowsky (1962), Pachter (1988), and Altshuler (2016).
6. This quote and the following quotes from Leon of Modena are from his 'Ari Nohem (De Modena 1968, pp. 222, 233–34). On Leon of Modena's thought, see Safran (1987).
7. On the relationships between the European interest in the supernatural and Safed mysticism, see Chajes (1997) and the rich studies listed therein.
8. The controversy regarding whether or not Rabbi Israel Saruk was Luria's disciple starts with a well-known paper by Scholem (1940b) and is described by Meroz (2002).
9. Benayahu (1967, pp. 160–61).
10. This version of the legend appears in the Constantinople printing of Toldot ha-'Ari (Benayahu 1967, p. 233).
11. Scholem (1955, p. 85). See also Benayahu (1967, pp. 114–15).
12. Tishbi's studies on Hemdat Yamim are collected in Tishby (1993, 2: 365–418; 1994, pp. 108–68). The most recent study of the question is Fogel (2001), who contests Tishbi's claims and strongly suggests that the author of Hemdat Yamim was not a forger and that he quoted in truth his sources.
13. Folklorists have suggested and studied the development of the legend from the memorat, for example, Von Sydow (1948, pp. 60–85, 127–45), Van Gennep (1917), and Dégh (1965).
14. This quotation and the following two are from Sefer haHezyonot (Book of Visions) (Vital 1954, pp. 24–35). Reviews of the modern edition of Sefer haHezyonot are Tamar (1982; 1984a; 1984b).
15. Vital (1954, pp. 19–36). See also Benayahu (1967, pp. 290–95) and Nigal (1983, pp. 74–76 and variants quoted therein). Studies on the dybbuk are rich and varied, and I mention here only the ones relevant to our discussion: Newman (1998) presents the full theoretical range of the possession phenomenon. Chajes (2003b) deals directly with the texts discussed here; however, he exaggerates somewhat in presenting European influence as a major factor of these phenomena in Safed culture. See also the useful collection of studies by Goldish (2003) and a useful list of these events in early modern Jewish history by Zfatman (1982; 2015, esp. the rich bibliography).

16. These accusations appear in *Sefer haHezyonot* (Vital 1954, pp. 57–58). The rich and influential Sephardic community influenced other synagogues not to accept Vital as their rabbi and preacher.
17. Rabbi Benjamin Saruk's dream appears in *Sefer haHezyonot* (Vital 1954, pp. 128–29).
18. *Sefer haHezyonot* (Vital 1954, pp. 89–97).
19. Ibn Shahin (1977, pp. 48–52). For variants and studies, see Lipsker (2009).
20. *Sefer haHezyonot* (Vital 1954, pp. 92–94).
21. *Sefer haHezyonot* (Vital 1954, p. 32).
22. *Sefer ha-Gan* (1606, pp. 9b–10a). The acronym "cows" is discussed in Benayahu (1967, p. 114). On the affinity between German Pietism and Safed customs, see Fine (2003, pp. 180–86).
23. On the beard and its restrictions, compare Ginzberg (1902), E. Horovitz (1994), and Zimmer (1996, pp. 43–71).
24. Rabbi Judah he-Hasid, *Sefer Gematriyot*, facsimile of a manuscript written in Safed in 1853 (Judah the Pious 1998, p. 4a).
25. *Sefer Hemdat Yamim* (Algazi 1763, ch. 3, 19b).
26. A description of Safed sidelocks is given by Schechter (1908, p. 300).
27. Rabbi Ya'akov bar Tzemach, *Nagid u-Metzaveh* (Zemach 1712, p. 48b). Elimelech Horovitz (1994) publishes this manuscript, and brings from here additional information on the meaning of the beard for contemporary Jewish culture. He coins it as "the beard ritual that developed in Luria's circle" (pp. 138–39). Compare to Zimmer (1996, p. 51).
28. The basic discussion on *mirabilia* in Christian Europe is Le Goff (1988, pp. 27–46) and the comprehensive studies listed in Rotman (2016). Shyovitz (2017) concentrates mainly on this phenomenon among the German Pietistic circles. On the return of the dead to the world of the living in order to strengthen religious beliefs, see Petzoldt (1968) and Gurevich (1988, pp. 104–52).
29. The complete essay is reprinted in Scholem (1976a, pp. 334–51). Meroz (1992) studies the transformation into animals. According to Lurianic Kabbalah these "emendations," as given by Luria to Abulafia, are essential for ascension to higher levels of spirituality; see Fine (1986).
30. On the *tikkun* and its place in Lurianic Kabbalah, see Fine (2003, pp. 167–80, 187–219).
31. On the Tale of the Tanna and the Dead Man, see Lerner (1988) and Kushelevsky (1994).

32. The text of the binding contract of Luria's disciples is published in Z. Rabinowitz (1940) and has been studied in depth by Scholem (1940a). See also Benayahu (1995).
33. The legend appears in *Sefer Hasidim* (Wistinetzki and Freimann 1924, no. 63) and Wineman (1985, pp. 93–96).
34. In a comprehensive study, Schmitt (1998, pp. 93–122) discusses the Wild Hunt motif from both historical and folkloristic points of view. Orderic Vitalis's testimony appears in Chibnall (1968–1980, 4: 237–51).
35. The early-fourteenth-century anthology *Sefer ha-Zichronot* is a relevant testimony. See Yassif (2001, pp. 99–103 and the bibliography on this theme on pp. 462–66).
36. On the concept of purgatory in motion, see Schmitt (1998, p. 113). A possible equivalent to this concept in Jewish culture is the term *kaf ha-kelah* (literally, "the hollow of the sling"), in which the dead man's soul is thrown from tribulation to tribulation, so that its sins will be purified and to prepare it for entering hell. This is an essential part of the tale of the spirit that entered the body of the widow in Safed (discussed in Chapter 5) and in Nigal (1983, pp. 67–69). For more discussion on the concept, see Meroz (1992, pp. 219–21).
37. The dead ask the living to pray for them so that they will be able to depart from the convoy. See Schmitt (1998, pp. 110–13).
38. The ties of the Wild Hunt traditions to local historical events are discussed in Schmitt (1998, pp. 39, 99–110). Similar motives in the appearance of the dybbuk events in Safed are suggested by Chajes (2003b, pp. 124–58).
39. Azkari (1601, p. 1b). On Azkari and his place in Safed, see the discussion in Chapter 1.
40. This tale appears in *Sefer Kharedim* (Azkari 1601, p. 42a) and in another version told by Galanti (Benayahu 1967, pp. 111–12). Idel (1984) points to another legend told almost thirty years before Luria arrived in Safed, about an ox or a lamb taken to slaughter that tries to escape by hiding in a house. Compare to Werblowsky (1962, pp. 223–24).
41. The running of bulls in the streets has been known since the Middle Ages, much earlier than today's bullfight. The historical and cultural developments of the phenomenon are detailed in Mitchell (1988, pp. 126–68) and the vast scholarship presented in Mitchell (1991).
42. On the religious-ritual character of the bullfight, see Pitt-Rivers (1993) and Mitchell (1988, pp. 136–37).
43. On the bull as an ancient fertility symbol, see A. De Vries (1974, pp. 68–70) and Cirlot (1988, pp. 33–35). On the impressive presentation of bull symbols since

antiquity, see Conrad (1957), who defines the bullfight as a "symbolic drama" (pp. 183–94).
44. The concept of the bull and the ox as representing the contrast between nature and culture is discussed in Ritvo (1992). The Spanish proverb referring originally to the bullfight is discussed in Douglass (1984) and Mitchell (1988, 132–35).
45. On the bull as a father symbol, see the convincing examples that Conrad (1957) discusses throughout his book. The father as provider, as fertilizer, as guard, is, according to Conrad, an explanation for the bull's centrality since antiquity.
46. Werblowsky (1962, pp. 223–24); Idel (1984, p. 127); Meroz (1992).
47. The tale of the bull in Castile is told again in *Hemdat Yamim* (Algazi 1731, p. 56a), but this time together with the tale of the dog who bit the slandering woman (discussed in Chapter 5). Both are presented as incarnations of the sinners into animals, and both are connected to sexual sins.

Chapter 3

1. For the rich corpus of studies on theory of the legend, see Dégh (1965; 2001), Tangherlini (1990), and Oring (2008).
2. Benayahu (1967) presents dozens of documents from the seventeenth and eighteenth centuries on Safed legends as authentic testimonies that were transmitted generation after generation by Luria's disciples. In his *Sefer Divrei Yosef*, Yosef Sambari, the seventeenth-century historian, also integrated the Safed legends into his historical narrative as reliable facts. The Israel Folktale Archives, established in 1955 by Dov Noy, is home to dozens of Safed stories and Lurianic legends collected from narrators in Israel since the 1950s that testify to the fact that Safed legends are still alive in Jewish collective memory.
3. Dan (1986); Alexander (1992a); Bar-Itzhak (1987); Yassif (1999, pp. 321–42).
4. Yosef of Kandia (1629, pp. 39a–39b).
5. The close-up is even stronger in another version of the story that Shlumil tells in his fourth letter: "And he [Luria] told him [his student]: go to that alley, to that house, and there you'll find a poor man, his name so and so, and give him charity" (Assaf 1940, p. 130).
6. So it is already in midrashic literature. In the midrash on Exodus (*Shmot Rabba* 13:6), the Egyptian plague of the locusts is a warning so that the Egyptians will repent their sins against the Israelites.
7. Zoran (1997, p. 17).

8. For example, Joel 1–2 and as a common metaphor in Judges 6:5 and 7:12, Jeremiah 46:23, and Psalms 109:23. See Bodenheimer (1956, 2: 320–27). The present story was shaped according to the narrative in Exodus 10:19.
9. From another version of the tale, given in Benayahu (1967, pp. 172–73).
10. Benayahu (1967, p. 173).
11. Yosef of Kandia (1629). The version of the seventeenth-century historian Yosef ben Yitzhak Sambari (1994, pp. 338–39) is different from this one. However, it seems that all the later versions, including that in *Toldot ha-'Ari*, were based on the oral version Shlumil heard and recorded in his letter.
12. Yassif (1999, p. 482); Verman and Adler (1993–1994); Elstein 1982.
13. Cahana (1923, p. 223).
14. An insider's detailed explanation of the theology behind the holy graves cult is given in Vital's *Sha'ar Ruach haKodesh* (Vital 1988a, p. 109, 4th introduction). He gives the kabbalistic background of the cult and a minute deciphering of the customs taking place during the cult. On some of the great number of studies on this theme, see Ben-Ami (1984, pp. 39–46, 69–79), the rich bibliography in Wilson (1983, pp. 359–67), and Holm (1994). On the connection between the cult of the Moroccan Maraboutes and that of sixteenth-century Safed, see Fine (2003, pp. 259–99). Shoham-Steiner (2004) discusses the negative approach of medieval Jewish religious leaders to the cult of the holy graves. Reiner (1988, pp. 228–32) gives examples of holy sites and "ziarah spaces" outside the Land of Israel that were centers of pilgrimage in the fourteenth and fifteenth centuries. Compare also Meri (2002, pp. 214–50). The halakhic aspects of the cult are presented in Lichtenstein (2007).
15. The fourth part of Vital's *Sefer haHezyonot* is dedicated to the pilgrimages of Luria and his students to the holy graves in and around Safed. Of special interest is Vital's enumeration of the graves from Safed to Tiberias in his *Sha'ar haGilgulim* (Vital 1988b, pp. 181–85, 37th introduction). It seems to be the most detailed description of the holy graves traditions that emerged from Luria's group. On the elitist aspect of their attitude to the cult (in contrast to its folk-religion aspect among other cultures), see Huss (2003; 2004), who presents the kabbalistic-learned attitude of Luria and his disciples to the cult.
16. The continuous bonding between the living and the cemetery of Safed since the sixteenth century is well documented and interpreted in Bernstein (2001), on the holy grave of Alsheikh. Another type of connection between the living and the dead in Safed of that period is discussed in Chajes (2003b) and Fine (2003, pp. 259–99).

17. On the possible Sufic influence on the Jewish cult of the holy graves, see Fenton (1994) and Lichtenstein (2007, pp. 358–63).
18. Ben-Ari and Bilu (1987), from an anthropological perspective, point to the relationship between the "naturalization" of the inhabitants of the "development villages" in the Negev and the Galilee in modern Israel and the "discovery" of new holy graves in these villages, and the development of *ziara* cults and rituals there.
19. Cordovero's *Sefer Geirushin* (Cordovero 1602, ch. 11, p. 4a–4b).
20. Werblowsky (1996, p. 61). Werblowsky denies the "romantic approaches" to the *gerushin* ritual, and so does Kimelman (2003, pp. 20–22).
21. Cordovero's *Tomer Dvora* (Cordovero 1872, ch. 9, p. 26b). Compare Cordovero's work with the important discussion of Scholem (2008c).
22. The influence of the encounter of the kabbalists with the Land of Israel is described in many studies and surveys, for example, Kimelman (2003, p. 22) and Pachter (1994, p. 22). On the thought of Cordovero on this issue, see Huss (2003, pp. 238–40) and Pachter (1991, pp. 296–98), who emphasizes the importance of the environment of the Galilee for the development of the kabbalistic moral literature.
23. For example, the *Tikun Khatzot* (midnight emendation), as described by Idel (1998a, pp. 162–63, 311–14).
24. Zak (1991, p. 340). Huss (2002; 2003) discusses the essential ties between the speculations of the *Zohar* and the place—The Land of Israel. "The shift from text-oriented portable sanctity to the veneration of the relic and its locale" is an important process that was observed by Giller (1994, p. 149).
25. Shlumil's fourth letter (Assaf 1940, pp. 127–28). In *Pri Etz Haim* Vital adds to this story that on Sabbath eve all the souls are ascending on high and that there are souls who ascend from the earthly Eden and others who are descending so that they can participate with the righteous during the Sabbath (Vital 1803, ch. 8, p. 95b).
26. Vital, *Sha'ar haGilgulim* (Vital 1988b, 8th introduction and 22nd introduction). See also Wineman (1985).
27. Benayahu (1967, p. 234 and discussion on pp. 111–13).
28. Full versions of the encounters related in the preceding paragraphs are given in Sambari's *Sefer Divrei Yosef* (Sambari 1994, pp. 336–54) and Benayahu (1967, pp. 183–88).
29. Benayhu (1967, pp. 236 [the source is Shlumil's third letter], 199–200); Sambari (1994, p. 346). Compare also Vital's explanations of this phenomenon in his

Sha'ar haGilgulim (Vital 1988b, introduction 22). It is important to understand that Vital applies reincarnation as an animate or inanimate object to the severity of the sin, whereas the legends, which are intended for larger audiences, do not make suggest it.

30. Vital's *Sha'ar Ruach haKodesh* (Vital 1988a, p. 23). A full theoretical explanation of this idea is given by Hayyim Vital himself (pp. 22–23 [ch. 3]).
31. For some of the many studies that deal with the theoretical and historical background of animism, see Tylor (1958), Cocchiara (1981, pp. 384–89), Evans-Pritchard (1965), and J. De Vries (1977).
32. Freud (1913b, pp. 72–91).
33. This phenomenon is well described in two scholarly collections of studies that deal with African and Asian agricultural societies: Lehman and Myers (1993) and Marwick (1982). On the affinity between agricultural life and the development of religious beliefs, see the comprehensive approach of Eliade (1978, pp. 29–55), and on magical rituals with an agricultural basis in sixteenth-century Italy, see Ginzburg (1992a; 1992b).
34. Zak (1991, p. 322).
35. Yassif (1985, pp. 77–104). On the great collection of Berechia's fables from the twelfth century, see Berechia ha-Nakdan's *Mishlei Shu'alim* (ha-Nakdan 1967).
36. Shmuel's words are quoted in Vital's *Sha'ar haGilgulim*, 36th introduction (Vital 1988b, p. 125). Regarding these questions, see the discussion in Tamar (1984a) and the comprehensive overview of the editing of Vital's work by his son, in Avivi (2008, 2: 674–701).
37. Vital, *Sefer haHezyonot*, 2: 25 (Vital 1954, p. 61). According to Werblowsky's interpretation, Adam symbolizes Rabbi Joseph Karo, who is in need of Vital's kabbalistic knowledge (Werblowsky 1996, p. 144).
38. Vital, *Sefer haHezyonot*, 2: 3 (Vital 1954, pp. 77–78).
39. Vital, *Sefer haHezyonot*, 2: 10 (Vital 1954, p. 52–54). Ben-Zvi (1966, pp. 30–32) describes the personality of Ya'akov Guizo, a monk and ascetic who lived in the surroundings of Safed. It might be that Vital was referring to Guizo or his likes.
40. Vital, *Sefer haHezyonot*, 1: 21 (Vital 1954, p. 16).
41. On the centrality of this caravansary in the life of Safed of the time, see Ben-Zvi (1966, pp. 26–29), David (1993, pp. 106–7), and Heid (1955).
42. Vital, *Sefer haHezyonot*, 3: 12 (Vital 1954, p. 79).
43. On the close relationships between dreams and fairy tales, see Chapter 4.
44. In another dream, when Vital was only 18 years old, a fortune-teller told him that, when he will be 24 years old, many thoughts will come to him about

leaving the life of speculation and two paths will face him: the road to heaven and the road to hell. On these speculations in Vital's early life (especially choosing between halakhic and mystical studies), see Katz (1984, pp. 94–96).

45. Vital, *Sefer haHezyonot*, 3: 13 (Vital 1954, pp. 89–91).
46. Vital, *Sefer haHezyonot*, 3: 13 (Vital 1954, pp. 89–91).
47. Röhrich (1991, pp. 206–7) describes the phenomenon in which particular details from dreams or fairy tales that materialize in real life become elements that are used to strengthen the "trustfulness" of the narrative.
48. The dream is recounted in Vital, *Sefer haHezyonot*, 2: 5 (Vital 1954, pp. 42–47).
49. This incident is told again, in detail, in Vital, *Sefer haHezyonot*, 4: 6 (Vital 1954, p. 139). Here, the weeping is continued in the dream itself and is considered as a means for the ascension of the soul.
50. Here we discover another minor detail about Vital's life: that his hair turned white at an early stage of his youth. In addition to his short frame and his bodily weakness, he looks old at an early stage of his life.
51. Carroll (1958, p. 146).
52. For the vast literature on this theme, see Warner (1976) and Rubin (2009). On the penetration of Marian motifs into the Kabbalah (especially relevant regarding Vital), see Green (2002), Limor (2006), and Schäfer (2002).
53. Karo, *Magid Meisharim* (Karo 1879, pp. 3–4). On this revelation, see the detailed discussion in Werblowsky (1996, pp. 130–32) and, more recently, Altshuler (2016, pp. 122–38 and *passim*).
54. For some of the vast scholarship on the genre, see Zfatman (1993; 2010) and Bar-Itzhak (2001).
55. Pachter (1991, pp. 310–16).
56. Similar geopsychological observations, which connect real space, cosmic space, and dreams, are suggested by Tuan (2001).
57. Lévi-Strauss (1960; 1963); Doty (2000, pp. 266–96).

Chapter 4

1. On *Sefer haHezyonot*, see the detailed discussion in Chapter 3. See also Idel (1998a, pp. 166–67) and Rozen and Witztum (1992).
2. On general definitions and studies of the fairy-tale genre, see Lüthi (1976; 1984) and the seminal studies and bibliography in Ben-Amos (1981).
3. On the relationship between dreams and fairy tales, see Röhrich (1991, pp. 205–7), Hølbek (1987, pp. 206–9), and Alexander (1995). Bettelheim (1977) points to the dissimilarities between dreams and fairy tales, especially the fact that,

although dreams cannot be controlled by the dreamer, the fairy tale is strictly controlled by generations of storytellers and is a fully "conscious" expression.
4. Freud (1913a; 1966).
5. Vital, *Sefer haHezyonot*, 3: 48 (Vital 1954, pp. 114–16).
6. Vital, *Sefer haHezyonot*, 3: 24 (Vital 1954, p. 98–100).
7. Vital, *Sefer haHezyonot*, 3: 24 (Vital 1954, pp. 98–99).
8. On the sources of this legend, see Yassif (1999, pp. 54–55, 92–96, notes 25–27).
9. In another dream in *Sefer haHezyonot* (3: 69), Shmuel dreams that he sees a young and handsome Arab who has on his forehead a third eye "shining as the sun." The young Arab tells him to warn his father about his failure to make the Jewish community of Damascus repent. However, a psychoanalytic approach might see the third eye on the face of a handsome young Arab as a homoerotic yearning (see Nacht 1959, *s.v.* eye). However in this dream, as in the previous one, erotic motifs are mingled with religious ones, as can be expected from a young man whose religious-communal ideals are threatened by his sexual craving.
10. Vital, *Sefer haHezyonot*, 3: 25 (Vital 1954, pp. 100–102).
11. On the image of Shabbetai Zvi, see Scholem (1967, vol. 1, opening page). On Shimon bar Yohai and Luria as messianic figures, see Liebes (1990) and Tamar (1970).
12. For the basic definitions and characteristic of the genre, see Lüthi (1976; 1984), Ben-Amos (1981), and the seminal collection of studies by Bottigheimer (1986).
13. The spatial elements of Safed legends were discussed in Chapter 3.
14. On earlier Jewish fairy tales, see Yassif (2004, pp. 136–65), Zfatman (1979), and Zlotnik et al. (1947).
15. Nachman of Bratslav, *Sefer Chayei Moharan* (Sternhertz 1874, ch. 4, pp. 301–2). Other dreams of Rabbi Nachman's are recounted in Sternhartz's edition on pp. 301–20. For a collection of Nachman's dreams from various sources, see Shteinman (1951, pp. 163–68) and Green (1979, pp. 166–69). On dreamlike motifs in Rabbi Nachman's tales, see Wiskind-Elper (1998, pp. 159–60). The new and most comprehensive collection of Rabbi Nachman's tales and dreams is the scholarly edition by Mark (2014). This dream appears there on p. 301.
16. "Despite its doubtless connection to the unconsciousness, folktale narration is indeed a conscious art" (Röhrich 1991, p. 206).
17. For a multitude of studies and historical surveys on surrealistic literature, see Nadeau (1989) and Caws (2004).
18. Zipes (1983; 1999); Grätz (1996).

19. Oron (1987); Grözinger (1992); Bar-David (1993); Rimer (1972).
20. Vital, *Sefer haHezyonot*, 2: 36 (Vital 1954, pp. 66–68).
21. *Sefer Zerubavel*, as copied into the manuscript of *Sefer ha-Zichronot*, in Yassif (2001, pp. 427–28).
22. On Hayyim Vital as Messiah, son of Joseph, see Tamar (1984a).
23. Text and sources in Yassif (1979).
24. On this widespread motif, see Lindahl et al. (2000, pp. 45–50 ["Arthurian Lore"], 959–63 ["Sword"]). The medieval Hebrew translation of the romance does not include this episode (Leviant 1969).
25. Arbesman (1961); Weinstein and Bell (1982, pp. 105–7); and the detailed website www.sangalgano.info/spade_en.html.
26. Idel (1985) points to the similarity of this dream and the meeting between Shlomo Molcho and the pope.
27. In contrast, in his own dream, Kalev (not Vital himself!) saw Hayyim Vital "in a red silk gown and in my hand a drawn sword ready to take vengeance from the Gentiles" (*Sefer haHezyonot*, 3: 34 [Vital 1954, p. 107]).
28. The word should be *talsam* or *talisman*, an enchanted object. Lindahl et al. (2000, p. 10) note that the word *tilsam* was used also in Arabic, or *telesm* in Greek-Byzantine, meaning a statute or other magic object hidden in the wall and protecting the home or the city.
29. Vital, *Sefer haHezyonot*, 2: 44 (Vital 1954, pp. 72–73). The skull as a magic object was known already from rabbinic literature related to the teraphim that Rachel stole from her father's house. On this, see Mandel (1894), Ben-Yechezkel (1965, pp. 695–96), Krauss (1894), and Dan (1978).
30. The incident is described by Idel (1993).
31. On Armilus, see the wide perspective opened by McGinn (2000). On Abulafia as an anti-messiah, compare in Chapter 2.
32. On the vast literature about the medieval romance, both historical and poetical, see Krueger (2000) and Heng (2003).
33. The garden dreams in Vital, *Sefer haHezyonot*, 2: 5 and 3: 42 (Vital 1954, p. 42).
34. Vital, *Sefer haHezyonot*, 1: 17 (Vital 1954, pp. 9–10).
35. This phenomenon has been described and documented in Zaleski (1987).
36. The language of the contract of Luria's fellowship, signed by his students after his death, reads, "We, the after signed, agreed to be in one commune, to be devoted to God and be busy with his Torah day and night, as will lead us our teacher and master, rabbi and godly scholar, our Rabbi Hayyim Vital. And we shall learn with him the true wisdom [Kabbalah], and we shall be loyal [to him]

and keep in secret everything he will tell us, and we shall not burden him by asking too many of the things he does not want to tell us, we shall not reveal to others any secret we shall hear from him . . . and even what we heard from our master, blessed be his memory [Luria] we shall not disclose without his approval." Quoted in Z. Rabinowitz (1940, p. 125). On the historical and ideological background of the contract, see Scholem (1940a).

37. According to Vital, "Because of quarrels and gossip I left it [Safed]. And if I would not have left, it is possible that the redemption would have come in my time. And now all the people who wanted my destruction are dead" (*Sefer haHezyonot*, 3: 53 [Vital 1954, p. 242]); see also Benayahu (1952).
38. On the garden as messianic yearning, see Rosenberg (1990).
39. Röhrich (1991, pp. 88, 90). An interesting support for this interpretation is another dream: "In the beginning of the month of Shevat, Rabbi Kalev dreamt that he saw me in the street and my stature was very tall, taller than all the other people. And everyone was amazed as I am really of short stature. And Rabbi Kalev told them, 'Whoever wants to see King Saul [who was a tall person] will see him, as he is he [Vital is Saul], as Saul also was taller than all the people'" (Vital, *Sefer haHezyonot*, 3: 61 [Vital 1954, p. 125]).
40. Rotenberg (2002, pp. 157, 167).

Chapter 5

1. The central medieval narrative about the transition of Torah study centers is the "legend of the four captives" and the seminal study of Gershon Cohen (1960–1961). Other texts from that period were collected in the early-fourteenth-century *Sefer haZichronot* (Yassif 2001, pp. 312–13). An in-depth study of another well-known foundation legend can be found in Zfatman (1993, pp. 111–58) and, for early modern texts, Bar-Itzhak (2001).
2. Shlumil of Dreznitz, fourth letter (Assaf 1940, p. 128).
3. Idel (2005a) notes the connection between the ascension of the souls of the righteous after their death and the pillar of fire and suggests, "In some parts of the *Zohar* the pillar recurrently serves as a conduit for the ascent of the souls of the deceased righteous from a lower paradise to a higher one" (p. 101). Idel also quotes a long discussion of Rabbi Moshe Cordovero on the pillar of fire (pp. 116–19). The question of whether the pillar was constructed of fire or smoke is discussed in Lenowitz (2003, pp. 201–3).
4. Luria told Vital that he had sexual relations with his wife only on weekdays after midnight, so that he wouldn't have nocturnal seminal emissions (Biale 1997).

Luria's horror of seminal emission directed him to form special means to prevent it (Vital 1988a, p. 23).

5. Shlumil's fourth letter (Assaf 1940, p. 125).
6. On Kabbalah and Eros, see Biale (1997, ch. 5), Liebes (1994), Wolfson (2005), Idel (2005b), and Magid (1996).
7. On the differences between early Kabbalah and Safed Kabbalah in their approach to erotic matters, see the discussion in Biale (1997) and the insightful observations of Werblowsky (1996, pp. 134–41).
8. Vital, *Sha'ar Ruach haKodesh* (Vital 1988a, p. 63). A larger discussion of the theme and how sexual sins interfere with the flow of the *sefirot* can be found on pp. 52–63. Another detailed discussion is found in De Vidas's *Sefer Reyshit Khokhma*, ch. 17. On this sin in the Talmudic period, see Satlow (1994).
9. Wolfson (1995, pp. 223–24n145) discusses the question of erotic fantasies in the mystical fellowships and whether those fantasies were translated into real deeds.
10. The legend is printed from a Yemenite manuscript and is copied in Benayahu (1967, pp. 224–25).
11. On the magical-medical effects of the male organ, see Benayahu (1967, p. 110). The story of Moses and Tziporah is studied in depth by Avishur (1980). Lenowitz (1998, pp. 133–34) interprets this story from a kabbalistic point of view and connects it to Lilith, who commits men to spill their semen. Thus Luria was looking for a man who was not under the power of Lilith, who was the main cause of the death of newborns.
12. *Sha'ar Ruach haKodesh*, yikhud 11 (Vital 1988a, p. 118).
13. Benayahu (1967, pp. 159–60) describes these supervisors of transgressions in Safed. On the controversy they aroused in the Safed community, see Lamdan (1998).
14. Lamdan (1998, p. 119–20) addresses the reality that the Jewish religious and moral norms in those lands paralleled those of the Muslims; every meeting between male and female was considered as having a sexual basis and no other explanation of the encounter between sexes could be accepted. She also stresses that the goal of moral purity allowed the Jewish societies in Palestine and Egypt to invade the privacy of the individual and that the tracking of and informing on neighbors and acquaintances were almost everyday deeds.
15. Benayahu (1967, pp. 173–74, 177–78, 199–200). The horror from sexual sins among the greatest religious leaders is attested by Joseph Karo himself in his journal *Magid Meisharim* (Karo 1879, pp. 13b–14a). On this, see also Werblowsky (1996, pp. 149–55).

16. Vital, *Sha'ar Ruach haKodesh* (Vital 1988a, p. 17a).
17. The "lore of [Divine] Visages" (*Torat haPartzufim*), or metoposcopy, was already known in the Middle Ages and expanded during the Renaissance, as studied by Fine (1986).
18. Azkari, *Sefer Kharedim* (Azkari 1601, p. 65a and discussion on pp. 64a–65a).
19. Benayahu (1967, pp. 237–38). Benayahu also presents other versions in his notes.
20. Cordovero, *Sefer She'ur Komah* (Cordovero 1882, ch. 38, p. 167).
21. This version, from *Hemdat Yamim*, is from the fourth book (Algazi 1731, ch. 4, p. 56a).
22. Relevant studies that deal with the same period in Europe and the Middle East are Clark (1997, pp. 106–34), Thomas (1971, pp. 97–100, 678–79), and Roper (1994). Other wide-ranging studies that deal with this theme in the early modern period and add other rich studies are, Couliano (1987) and Stephens (2002).
23. Naphtali Bacharach, *Sefer Emek haMelech* (Bacharach 1648, ch. 4, p. 11a), and Benayahu (1967, p. 184).
24. On the Lilith myth, see Yassif (1985, pp. 63–71) and the insightful interpretation of Von Stuckrad (2006).
25. Benayahu (1967, pp. 185–87).
26. On the Yiddish and Hebrew variants of the story and the changes it underwent over the centuries, see Zfatman (1987; pp. 103–8 are relevant to the Safed legend). A feminist interpretation of this tale type is suggested by Alexander (1992b) and Goodblatt (2000). A reading of the story from a social-economic point of view is suggested by Dauber (2008) and Yassif (1999, pp. 368–70) and additional studies therein.
27. In a revealing study Ben-Nae (2001) presents reliable evidence for sexual habits among Muslims and Jews in the Ottoman Empire. The fact that ten to twenty years elapsed between sexual maturity and marriage produced the opening for homosexual relationships between boys in those male-only institutions. On homoerotic tendencies in Lurianic Kabbalah, see Magid (2008, pp. 111–42).
28. Yosef of Kandia, *Sefer Ta'alumot Khokhma* (Yosef of Kandia 1629, pp. 49b).
29. Yosef of Kandia, *Sefer Ta'alumot Khokhma* (Yosef of Kandia 1629, pp. 49b–50b). Other variants appear in Benayahu (1967, pp. 191–96) and Nigal (1983, pp. 67–70). On the phenomenon of the dybbuk in general, see Chapter 3. The theme has gained much interest in the last decades, as can be seen from the rich studies of the phenomenon all over the world—Africa, Europe, and the East. In

Jewish studies, Bilu (1983) opened the way for psychological and anthropological interpretations of the theme. He opened the discussion also into the role of the woman in these stories/reports and the light it sheds on the status of women in Jewish society. This point of view was followed and deepened by Alexander (2001), Elior (2005; 2008), and Rapoport-Albert (2008). However, my discussion attempts to look at this theme from the point of view of Safed culture and mentality and the ways it reflects on the tense moral and social atmosphere of Safed around the 1600s. A story from 1325 that is amazingly similar to the story of the Safed widow, from medieval Europe, is presented by Schmitt (1998, pp. 149–52). This is also a lengthy report, in which a church servant investigated a ghost that possessed a widow. However, there, the ghost was that of her dead husband and the sin was also sexual. The investigator forces the ghost (the dead husband) to tell him and the other listeners of his deeds, and he tells them, as in the Safed story, at length and in detail.

30. Yosef of Kandia, *Sefer Ta'alumot Khokhma* (Yosef of Kandia 1629, pp. 49b).
31. Vital, *Sha'ar Ruach haKodesh* (Vital 1988a, p. 33).
32. Two influential books—Naphtali Bacharach's *Sefer Emek haMelech* and Menashe Ben-Israel's *Sefer Nishmat Chaim* (both published in the mid-seventeenth century)—present many examples of such dybbuk incidents as evidence for the existence of life after death as part of their opposition to the new ideas in Europe at that time, ideas that put scientific discoveries above religious beliefs. Such events, according to Ben-Israel, are the ultimate proof for the existence of God and the heavenly world and their involvement in our life and reality. These books have been discussed on different levels by Dan (1987) and, from a wider historical perspective, Chajes (2003a). On the European debates and realities, see Greyerz (2008) and Stephens (2002). Of special interest is Clark (1997), who discusses many such events of possession that took place all over Europe during this period.
33. *Hemdat Yamim*, pt. 3 (on Passover), ch. 6, p. 31d (Algazi 1731).
34. The Falkon Letter and its variants are recorded in Nigal (1983, pp. 61–65). A detailed discussion of the letter and its European parallels is suggested by Chajes (2003a, pp. 37–44).
35. Menashe Ben-Israel, *Sefer Nishmat Chaim*, ch. 10, copies the detailed testimony of Gedalya ibn Yahya about the Ferrara dybbuk from 1575. One of the odd things there is that Gedalya testifies that, when he arrived at the location of the girl who was possessed and saw her lying in a coma, with dozens of men gathered around her, he said to himself, "This is the day I prayed for, to know the

truth of body and soul"—these speculation are the real important matter. The misery of the suffering girl is even not considered by him.

36. *Sefer haHezyonot* (Vital 1954, pp. 32–34). The Damascus dybbuk and its sources are discussed in Chapter 2 (section "Spirits, Reincarnations, and Other Visions").

Chapter 6

1. Shlumil's first letter, published in Yosef of Kandia, *Sefer Ta'alumot Khokhma* (1629, p. 38a).
2. De Modena (1968, p. 222).
3. Among the first studies of saints' legends in Jewish culture are Dan (1986), Alexander (1992a) (she considers some of the legends about Luria to include miraculous deeds, with which I disagree), Bar-Itzhak (1987), and Yassif (1999, pp. 106–20, 321–43). In addition, compare to the fuller perspective in Raspe (2006) and the additional bibliography added there.
4. Dan (1974, pp. 240–45) suggests that knowledge is the main feature of Luria's legends. Fine (2003) sees in this supernatural knowledge a kind of therapeutic analysis, the aim of which is to cure sicknesses of the soul. This is why, I presume, he called his book *Physician of the Soul, Healer of the Cosmos*.
5. Karo, *Magid Meisharim* (Karo 1879, p. 3a).
6. The quotation is from Karo, *Magid Meisharim* (Karo 1879, p. 3a). The concept of "a memorial for his works" has been studied by Dan (1968, pp. 194–202). Of seminal importance is the text by Rabbi Judah the Pious published by Ta-Shema (1994) and recently Shyovitz (2017).
7. Luria's reference to practical Kabbalah is quoted in Vital's *Sha'ar Ruach haKodesh* (Vital 1988a, p. 41). Ben-Yisrael, in *Nishmat Chaim* (1652), presents an overview of the traditional approach of Jewish culture to the beliefs in the supernatural. This is part of his reactionary project against modern approaches in Judaism that attempted to base religious beliefs on rational foundations. On this topic, compare Chajes (2003a, pp. 120–38).
8. On the complex relationship between the biography of a saint and the legends told about him, see Yassif (2005) and the bibliography therein.
9. On the possession tales discussed here, see Chapter 5 (section "A Spirit Entered Her"). The major texts are assembled in Nigal (1983, pp. 61–66, 67–70, 74–76, and associated notes).
10. Benayahu (1967, pp. 252–53 and additional variants in the notes); Nigal (1983, p. 72). Sambari, in *Sefer Divrei Yosef* (Egypt, ca. 1673) tells another variant of

the legend, which attests to the existence of another widespread tradition in the Jewish communities in the Muslim countries.

11. Shlumil's third letter, in Yosef of Kandia, *Ta'alumot Khokhma* (1629, pp. 43b–44a).
12. Shlumil's fourth letter, published in Assaf (1940, pp. 127–28).
13. Vital, *Sha'ar Ruach haKodesh* (Vital 1988a, p. 15a). On the outstanding personality of Rabbi Sagis and a discussion of this tale from a different angle, see Scholem (2008b, esp. pp. 127–28).
14. On dreams and dreaming in Jewish tradition and outside it, see Idel (1998a, pp. 166–67; 2006), Rozen and Witztum (1992), Röhrich (1991, pp. 205–7), Hølbek (1987, pp. 206–9), Alexander (1995), Bettelheim (1977), Hasan-Rokem (1996), Kuyt (1999), Niehoff (1992), and Weiss (2011).
15. Otto (1959, ch. 1).
16. Bacharach, *Emek haMelech* (1648, p. 11a). On this work and its author, see Liebes (1993).
17. This legend is reported for the first time in Shlumil's third letter; Yosef of Kandia, *Ta'alumot Khokhma* (1629, pp. 45b–46a). Liebes (1992) attempted to rebuild Luria's sermon that is hinted at in the legend.
18. On Jewish messiahs who fail or die because of their human weakness, see Lenowitz (1998).
19. A comparison between the death of Luria and other heroes of Jewish myths, such as Moses, Jesus, rabbinic saints, and the Ba'al Shem Tov (Rabbi Yisrael ben Eliezer), is suggested by Galley (2003).
20. Ginzburg (1989) discusses the theme of the danger to know things of the above.
21. Vital, *Sha'ar Ruach haKodesh* (Vital 1988a, pp. 22a–23b).
22. Luria's charisma is discussed in Fine (2003, pp. 93–110). Fine considers Luria's charisma in a different way from what I suggest here. According to Fine, the source of Luria's charismatic power, in the eyes of his disciples, is the divine authority that Luria and his students applied to him, his knowledge of things that were hidden from any other human being, and his affinity for Elijah the Prophet and Rabbi Shimon bar Yohai. I see these features of Luria's personality as an outcome of his charisma, not as its origin. In his important biography of Luria, Fine ignores the powerful tension between reality and imagination, the known and the hidden, the human and the divine, that were so dominant in Luria's personality and deeds. This tension, which his disciples were well aware of, was the primary source of his proven charisma. The main reason for this disregard in Fine's book, in my mind, is omitting any reference to the legends

about Luria and their importance for understanding his personality and the way he was perceived by the Safed society after his death. Even the author of *Emek haMelech*, Rabbi Naphtali Bacharach, as early as 1648, acknowledged this tension as a basis of Luria's personality and action (e.g., p. 12a and throughout ch. 6).

23. On the original writings of Luria, see Scholem (2008a, pp. 240–61), Meroz (2002), and the careful encyclopedia entry by Scholem and Idel (2007). However, the most detailed and comprehensive discussion of this question is Avivi (2008, 1: 32–57, 1: 77–97, 3: 1109–30).
24. Shlumil's first letter, in Yosef of Kandia, *Ta'alumot Khokhma* (1629, p. 38a). A slightly different version can be found in Bacharach, *Emek haMelech* (1648, p. 10b).
25. Vital, *Sha'ar Ruach haKodesh* (1988a, p. 36).
26. Vital, *Sha'ar Ruach haKodesh* (1988a, p. 36). A further detailed discussion of this incident is discussed in Chapter 7.

Chapter 7

1. Vital, *Sha'ar Ruach haKodesh* (1988a, p. 36).
2. This is the version from *Toldot ha-'Ari* (Benayahu 1967, p. 204). Another version is a testimony that Ya'akov Tzemach (Zemach) heard from Shmuel, Hayyim Vital's son, who said he heard it "from the mouth" of his father, who remembered the event years later. A third version of the legend also appears in Benayahu (1967, p. 259).
3. On the opposing representations of Safed in the writings of Shlumil and Alsheikh, see Chapter 1, section "Wonderful, Wretched Safed."
4. The testimony of Leon of Modena is in his *'Ari Nohem*, discussed in Chapter 2, section "Of Oxen and Beards."
5. Azkari, *Sefer Kharedim* (1601, p. 3a). Another Safed moralist, Rabbi Eliyahu de Vidas, in his book *Reishit Khokhma* (1579, ch. 7), indicates the importance of sanctification in everyday life and how the material world has to be submitted to the life of Torah.
6. From Shlumil's third letter, in Yosef of Kandia, *Sefer Ta'alumot Khochma* (1629, p. 38b). Regarding the aspects of place and space in the legends, see Chapter 3, where I deal with this theme at length.
7. Malkiel (2007, pp. 45–47).
8. Shlumil's third letter, in Yosef of Kandia, *Sefer Ta'alumot Khochma* (1629, p. 46a).

9. The Yosef de la Reina legend was known in the circle of Luria's disciples, as attested by Vital, *Sha'ar haGilgulim* (1988b, ch. 66, p. 80a). On the legend and its historical significance, see Scholem (1990b) and Dan (1974, pp. 222-37).
10. The theme of exile and redemption is discussed with the relevant scholarship by Meroz (1988). On the approaches toward messianic redemption in Judaism, see Scholem (1976b; 1990c). Baras (1984) is also a good collection of studies on this theme. Schwartz (2005, pp. 28-45, 46-90) has compared the messianic idea of Maimonides and apocalyptic messianism. On the territorial aspect of Jewish messianism, see Ben-Sasson (1960) and Yuval (2001). Karo's controversial attitude toward messianism is discussed by Werblowsky (1996, pp. 126-32). The debate between the scholars of Kabbalah regarding the status of messianism in sixteenth-century Safed is discussed by Idel (1998b, pp. 162-73), who opposes Scholem and "his followers" and claims that messianism had no central role in Safed Kabbalah. I think that in this case his claims are not well founded, and my discussion of the legends points to the fact that messianism had indeed a central role in the spiritual mentality of Safed society of the time.
11. Karo, *Avkat Rochel* (1859, ch. 1, p. 1).
12. On utopian literature of the period, see Levin (1972), Leslie (1998), and Bloch (2000). On utopias in Jewish culture, see Scholem (1990a) and Gitelman (1992).
13. Biddulph (1608-1609, p. 75).
14. Quoted in Ish-Shalom (1944, p. 391).
15. For sources of this controversy, see Benayahu (1960). Ben-Sasson (1969, p. 289) confirms that one of the reasons for reestablishing the ordination in Safed was that, according to Maimonides, the new establishment of the Sanhedrin would pave the road for the messiah.
16. On this theme in Jewish folk literature, see Noy (1981) and Marcus (1978).
17. One typical characteristics of this period in Safed is the exposure of the intimate personal life of the major figures there. The three intimate journals of Joseph Karo, Hayyim Vital, and Eleazar Azkari reveal their most hidden fears, tensions, and inner conflicts. The dread from the temptations of Satan and the acute dangers that confront their aspiration for bringing the messiah in their own time have been noted already by Schechter (1908, pp. 210-22).
18. The existential tension turns into a psychological one: "That this strain should produce certain psychological phenomena more interesting to the pathologist than to the theologian, is hardly necessary to state" (Schechter 1908, p. 247).
19. Ravitzky (1993, p. 204).

20. The idea that the State of Israel is the beginning of the messianic redemption is studied in depth by Ravitzky (1993). For the same attitude of other Haredi leaders, see Ravitzky (1993, p. 205). On the other side, Zalman Shazar, the third president of Israel and a central Zionist thinker, describes sixteenth-century Safed as though it is a Zionist settlement, and Luria turns out to be, according to Shazar's interpretation, a proto-Zionist figure. See Shazar (1950, pp. 212–18).

21. I heard about the conflict over the building of the Breslov campus in Safed from two people who live its history and reality, Aryeh Lubowsky and Rivka Ambon, and from the vast exposure of the conflict in the daily newspapers. For example, see Eli Ashkenazi, "The Last Remnant of the Kabbalists' Quarter in Safed Is About to Collapse," *HaAretz* (September 6, 2007), p. 11. A similar procedure happened just some dozens of miles from there, in the pioneer Galilee settlement of Yavne'el. Sobel (1993) describes the penetration of a large community of Breslov Hasidim in the midst of this early-twentieth-century agricultural settlement and their (successful) attempt to change its secular atmosphere and turn it into "sacred community."

Bibliography

Primary Sources

Algazi, Ya'akov, ed. 1731. *Hemdat Yamim*. Smyrna. (Hebrew)
———, ed. 1763. *Hemdat Yamim*. Venice. (Hebrew)
Azkari, El'azar. 1601. *Sefer Kharedim*. Venice. (Hebrew)
Bacharach, Naphtali Hertz ben Elchanan. 1648. *Sefer Emek haMelech: Commentary on the Zohar and All of Luria's Books*. Amsterdam. (Hebrew)
Benayahu, Meir. 1967. *Sefer Toldot ha-'Ari: Its Versions and Historical Significance*. Jerusalem: Makhon Ben-Zvi (Hebrew)
Ben-Israel, Menashe. 1652. *Sefer Nishmat Chaim*. Amsterdam. (Hebrew)
Ben-Yechezkel, Mordechai. 1965. *Sefer ha-Ma'asiot*. Tel Aviv: Dvir. (Hebrew)
Berechia ha-Nakdan. 1946. *Mishley Shu'alim*. Ed. Avraham Meir Haberman. Jerusalem: Schocken. (Hebrew)
———. 1967. *Mishlei Shu'alim: Fables of a Jewish Aesop*. Trans. Moses Hadas. New York: Columbia University Press.
Biddulph, William. 1608–1609. *The Travels of Certaine Englishmen into Africa*. London.
Buber, Shlomo, ed. 1959. *Agadat Bereishit: Agadic Midrash on Genesis*. New York: Ktav. (Hebrew)
Cordovero, Moshe. 1602. *Sefer Geirushin*. Venice. (Hebrew)
———. 1872. *Tomer Devorah*. Warsaw. (Hebrew)
———. 1882. *Sefer She'ur Komah*. Warsaw. (Hebrew)
De Modena, Aryeh, Yehuda (Leon of Modena). 1968. *'Ari Nohem* (1638). Ed. Pnina Nave. Jerusalem: Mossad Bialik. (Hebrew)
De Vidas, Eliyahu. 1579. *Sefer Reishit Khokhma*. Venice. (Hebrew)
[Rabbi Eleazar of Worms?]. 1606. *Sefer haGan*. Venice. (Hebrew)
Hershler, Moshe. 1984. "*Sefer Hasidim le-R. Yehudah he-Ḥasid*: A New Edition and Variant from Manuscript." *Genuzot* 1: 125–62. (Hebrew)
Hillel, Ya'akov Moshe, ed. 1982–1988. *Shnot Haim: Biography and Praises of Our Teacher and Rabbi Haim Vital*. Jerusalem: Shuvi Nafshi. (Hebrew)

———, ed. 1998. *Shivei ha-Ari ha-Shalem*. Jerusalem. (Hebrew)
ibn Shahin, Nissim. 1977. *An Elegant Composition Concerning Relief After Adversity*. Ed. and trans. William M. Brinner. New Haven: Yale University Press.
Judah the Pious. 1998. *Sefer Gematri'ot*. Ed. Daniel Abrams and Israel Ta-Shema. Los Angeles: Cherub Press. (Hebrew)
Karo, Joseph. 1859. *Sefer Avkat Rochel*. Leipzig. (Hebrew)
———. 1879. *Magid Meisharim*. Vilna. (Hebrew)
Leviant, Curt, ed. and trans. 1969. *King Artus: A Hebrew Arthurian Romance of 1279*. New York: Ktav.
Levin, Benyamin M. 1928–1943. *Otzar ha-Geonim: Responsa of Babylonian Geonim and Their Commentaries According to the Talmudic Sequence*. Haifa.
Sambari, Yosef ben Yitzhak. 1994. *Sefer Divrei Yosef*. Ed. Shimon Shtober. Jerusalem: Yad Ben-Zvi. (Hebrew)
Shteinman, Eliezer, ed. 1951. *Collected Writings of Rabbi Nachman*. Tel Aviv: Knesset. (Hebrew)
Sternhertz, Nathan. 1874. *Sefer Chayei Moharan*. Jerusalem. (Hebrew)
Vital, Hayyim. 1803. *Pri Etz Haim*. Dobrovna. (Hebrew)
———. 1954. *Sefer haHezyonot* [Book of Visions]. Ed. Aharon Zeev Eshcoly. Jerusalem: Mossad Harav Kook. (Hebrew)
———. 1988a. *Sha'ar Ruach haKodesh*. Ed. Yehuda Zvi Brandwein. Jerusalem. (Hebrew)
———. 1988b. *Sha'ar haGilgulim*. Jerusalem. (Hebrew)
Wistinetzki, Yehuda, and Ya'akov Freimann, eds. 1924. *Sefer Hasidim* [According to the Parma Ms]. Frankfurt am Main: Mekitzei Nirdamim. (Hebrew)
Yosef of Kandia. 1629. *Sefer Ta'alumot Khokhma*. Basel. (Hebrew)
Zemach, Ya'akov. 1712. *Sefer Nagid u-Metzave*. Amsterdam. (Hebrew)

Secondary Sources

Abramson, Shraga. 1988. "A Letter from Safed from the Year 1607." *Kathedra* 48: 17–21. (Hebrew)
Alexander, Tamar. 1992a. "Saint and Scholar: Luria and Maimonides in Folk Narratives." *Jerusalem Studies in Hebrew Literature* 13: 29–64. (Hebrew)
———. 1992b. "Theme and Genre: Relationship Between Man and She-Demon in Jewish Folklore." *Jewish Folklore and Ethnology Review* 14: 56–61.
———. 1995. "Dreams in Folk-Literature." In Miriam Reimond, *Meetings in Dream*. Hod-ha-Sharon: Astrolog, 21–31. (Hebrew)
———. 2001. "Dybbuk: The Woman's Voice." *Mikan* 2: 165–190. (Hebrew)

Altshuler, Mor. 2016. *The Life of Rabbi Yosef Karo*. Tel Aviv: Tel-Aviv University Press. (Hebrew)

Arbesman, R. 1961. "The Three Earliest Vitae of St. Galganus." In Sesto Prete, ed., *Didascaline: Studies in Honour of Anselm M. Albareda*. New York: B. M. Rosental. 1–38.

Assaf, Simcha. 1940. "Letters from Safed." *Kovetz al-Yad* 3: 121–33. (Hebrew)

Avishur, Itzhak. 1980. "The Demonic Character of the Story of the Blood Bridegroom (Exodus 4:24–26)." *Eshel Be'er Sheva* 2: 1–18. (Hebrew)

Avitzur, Shmuel. 1962. "Safed as a Center of Wool Industry in the 16th Century." *Sefunot* 6: 41–70. (Hebrew)

Avivi, Yosef. 2008. *Lurianic Kabbala*, 3 vols. Jerusalem: Ben-Zvi Institute for the Study of Jewish Communities in the East. (Hebrew)

Baras, Zvi, ed. 1984. *Messianism and Eschatology*. Jerusalem: Zalman Shazar Center. (Hebrew)

Bar-David, Yoram. 1993. "Kafka and Rabbi Nachman: Between Prayer and Awareness of the Heart." *Am va-Sefer* 8: 139–56. (Hebrew)

Bar-Itzhak, Chaya. 1987. "Legends of the Saints as Genre in Folk Literature of Jewish Communities: According to a Sample of Oral Tales About Rabbi Israel Ba'al Shem Tov, Rabbi Haim Pinto, and Rabbi Shalem Shabazi." Ph.D. dissertation, The Hebrew University, Jerusalem.

———. 2001. *Jewish Poland: Legends of Origin*. Detroit: Wayne State University Press.

Be'eri, Tova. 1990. "'Olat Khadash by Rabbi Israel Najarah: Themes and Contents." *Asupot: A Yearbook for Jewish Studies* 4: 311–24. (Hebrew)

———. 1992. "Sephardic Elements in the Poetry of R. Israel Najarah." *Pe'amim* 49: 54–67. (Hebrew)

———. 2007. "Israel Najarah's Poems About His Poetry." In Ephraim Chazan and Yoseph Yahalom, eds., *Le'ot Zikaron: Studies in Hebrew Poetry and Jewish Culture—Memorial Book for Aharon Mirsky*. Ramat-Gan: Bar Ilan University Press. 397–418. (Hebrew)

Ben-Ami, Issachar. 1984. *Saint Veneration Among the Jews in Morocco*. Jerusalem: Magnes Press. (Hebrew)

Ben-Amos, Dan, ed. 1981. *Folklore Genres*. Austin: University of Texas Press.

Ben-Ari, Eyal, and Yoram Bilu. 1987. "Saints' Sanctuaries in Israeli Development Towns: On a Mechanism of Urban Transformation." *Urban Anthropology* 16: 243–72.

Benayahu, Meir. 1952. "Rabbi Haim Vital in Jerusalem." *Sinai* 30: 65–75. (Hebrew)

———. 1959. "Safed Envoys in the Time of Its Decline." *Otzar Yehudey Sefarad* 2: 77–81. (Hebrew)

———. 1960. "The Revival of Ordination in Safed." In S. W. Baron, B. Dinur, S. Ettinger, and I. Halpern, eds., *Jubilee Book for Isaac Beer for His 70th Birthday*. Jerusalem: Historical Society of Israel. 248–69. (Hebrew)

———. 1961. "Shivkhei ha-'Ari" [Praises of Luria]. *Areshet* 3: 144–65. (Hebrew)

———. 1962. "Ships Loaded with Wool and Money Sent by Constantinople Community To Help Safed." *Otzar Yehudey Sefarad* 5: 101–8. (Hebrew)

———. 1963. "The Consent of Safed to the Exemption of Torah Students from Taxes and the Attempt of Yehuda Aberlein to Annul It." *Sefunot* 7: 103–17. (Hebrew)

———. 1967. *Sefer Toldot ha-'Ari: Its Transformations, Editions, and Historical Significance*. Jerusalem: Ben-Zvi Institute. (Hebrew)

———. 1985. "Geniza Documents About Luria's Business and About His Family in Egypt." In M. Benayahu, ed., *Memorial Book for Rabbi Itzhak Nissim*. Jerusalem: Yad Harav Nissim. 4: 225–53. (Hebrew)

———. 1987. "Collection from the Cures and Remedies Book of Rabbi Haim Vital." *Korot* 9: 91–112. (Hebrew)

———. 1991. *Yosef Bekhiri: Studies in the History of Our Master Rabbi Joseph Karo*. Jerusalem: Yad Harav Nissim. (Hebrew)

———. 1995. "The Bonding Contracts of Safed and Egypt Kabbalists." *Asupot: Yearbook for Jewish Studies* 9: 129–60. (Hebrew)

Ben-Horon, Meir. 2007. "Schechter, Solomon." In *Encyclopedia Judaica*. Detroit: Macmillan Reference. 18: 113–14.

Ben-Menachem, Naphtali. 1962. "Publications on Safed: A Bibliography." *Sefunot* 6: 475–99. (Hebrew)

Ben-Nae, Yaron. 2001. "Homosexuality in Jewish Society in the Ottoman Empire." *Zion* 67: 171–200. (Hebrew)

———. 2007. *Jews in the Realm of the Sultans*. Jerusalem: Magnes Press. (Hebrew)

Ben-Sasson, Haim Hillel. 1960. "Exile and Redemption in the Eyes of the Generation of Spanish Exiles." In S. W. Baron, B. Dinur, S. Ettinger, and I. Halpern, eds., *Jubilee Book for Isaac Beer on His 70th Birthday*. Jerusalem: Historical Society of Israel. 216–27. (Hebrew)

———. 1969. *Chapters in the History of Jews in the Middle Ages*. Tel Aviv: Dvir. (Hebrew)

Ben-Zvi, Izhak. 1966. "The Musta'aravim: The Ancient Inhabitants of the Land of Israel." In Izhak Ben-Zvi, *Studies and Sources*. Jerusalem: Yad Izhak Ben-Zvi. 15–20. (Hebrew)

———. 1976. "The Golden Age of Safed." In Itzhak Ben-Zvi, *The Land of Israel and Its Settlement During Ottoman Rule*. Jerusalem: Yad Izhak Ben-Zvi. 169–87. (Hebrew)

Bernstein, Aharon. 2001. "The Holy 'Alsheikh Cave in the Old Cemetery of Safed: Guidelines for the Development of a Tradition." M.A. thesis, Tel Aviv University, Tel Aviv. (Hebrew)

Bettelheim, Bruno. 1977. *The Uses of Enchantment: The Meaning and Importance of Fairy Tales*. New York: Vintage.

Biale, David. 1997. *Eros and the Jews*. Berkeley: University of California Press.

Bilu, Yoram. 1983. "The Dybbuk in Judaism." *Jerusalem Studies in Jewish Thought* 2: 529–63. (Hebrew)

Bloch, Ernst. 2000. *The Spirit of Utopia*. Stanford, CA: Stanford University Press.

Bodenheimer, Shim'on. 1956. *Animals in the Bible Lands*. Jerusalem: Mosad Bialik. (Hebrew)

Bos, Gerit. 1994. "Hayyim Vital's Practical Kabbalah: A 17th Century Book of Secrets." *Journal of Jewish Thought and Philosophy* 4: 55–112.

Bottigheimer, Ruth B., ed. 1986. *Fairy Tales and Society: Illusion, Allusion, and Paradigm*. Philadelphia: University of Pennsylvania Press.

Buchman, Yael. 2001. "The Medical Notebook of Rabbi Haim Vital." *Kathedra* 99: 37–64. (Hebrew)

Buchman, Yael, and Zohar 'Amar. 2007. *Practical Medicine of Rabbi Haim Vital (1543–1620): Medicine in Eretz Yisrael and Its Environs*. Ramat Gan: Bar-Ilan University Press. (Hebrew)

Cahana, Avraham. 1923. *Sifrut ha-Historia ha-Yisra'elit* [Historiography in Jewish Culture]. Warsaw: Di Welt. (Hebrew)

Carroll, Lewis. 1958. *Through the Looking-Glass*. New York: Macmillan.

Caws, Mary Ann. 2004. *Surrealism*, rev. ed. London: Phaidon.

Chajes, Jeffrey Howard. 1997. "Judgments Sweetened: Possession and Exorcism in Early Modern Jewish Culture." *Journal of Early Modern History* 1: 124–69.

———. 2003a. *Between Worlds: Dybbuks, Exorcists, and Early Modern Judaism*. Philadelphia: University of Pennsylvania Press.

———. 2003b. "City of the Dead: Spirit Possession in Sixteenth-Century Safed." In Matt Goldish, ed., *Spirit Possession in Judaism: Cases and Contexts from the Middle Ages to the Present*. Detroit: Wayne State University Press. 124–58.

Chibnall, Marjorie. 1968–1980. *The Ecclesiastical History of Orderic Vitalis*, 6 vols. Oxford: Clarendon Press.

Cirlot, J. E. 1988. *A Dictionary of Symbols*. London: Routledge.

Clark, Stuart. 1997. *Thinking with Demons: The Idea of Witchcraft in Early Modern Europe*. New York: Oxford University Press.

Cocchiara, Giuseppe. 1981. *The History of Folklore in Europe*. Philadelphia: Institute for the Study of Human Issues.

Cohen, A. 1981. *The History of Eretz Israel Under Mamluk and Ottoman Rule (1260–1804)*, vol. 7. Jerusalem: Yad Itzhak Ben-Zvi. (Hebrew)

Cohen, Gershon D. 1960–1961. "The Story of the Four Captives." *Proceedings of the American Academy of Jewish Research* 29: 55–131.

Conrad, Jack Randolph. 1957. *The Horn and the Sword: The History of the Bull as Symbol of Power and Fertility*. New York: Dutton.

Couliano, Ioan P. 1987. *Eros and Magic in the Renaissance*. Chicago: University of Chicago Press.

Dan, Joseph. 1968. *The Esoteric Theology of Ashkenazi Hasidism*. Jerusalem: Mosad Bialik. (Hebrew)

———. 1974. "The Lurianic Tales." In Joseph Dan, *The Hebrew Story in the Middle Ages*. Jerusalem: Keter. 238–52. (Hebrew)

———. 1978. "Teraphim: From Popular Belief to a Folktale." *Scripta Hierosolymitana* 27: 99–106.

———. 1986. "Shvakhim Literature: East and West." *Pe'amim* 26: 77–86. (Hebrew)

———. 1987. "Manasseh ben Israel's *Nishmat Hayyim* and the Concept of Evil in Seventeenth-Century Jewish Thought." In Isador Twerski and Bernard Septimus, eds., *Jewish Thought in the Seventeenth Century*. Cambridge, MA: Harvard University Press. 63–76.

Dauber, Jeremy. 2008. "Thinking with Shedim: What Can We Learn From the 'Mayse fun Vorms'?" *Jewish Studies Quarterly* 15: 19–46.

David, Abraham. 1992. "Religious Law and Trade in *Toldot ha-'Ari*." *Jerusalem Studies in Jewish Thought* 10: 287–97. (Hebrew)

———. 1993. *Immigration and Settlement in the Land of Israel in the Sixteenth Century*. Jerusalem: Rubin Mass Ltd. (Hebrew)

Dégh, Linda. 1965. "Process of Legend Formation." In Georgios A. Megas, ed., *IV International Congress for Folk-Narrative Research in Athens: Lectures and Reports*. Athens: n.p. 77–87.

———. 2001. *Legend and Belief: Dialectics of a Folklore Genre*. Bloomington: University of Indiana Press.

De Vries, A. 1974. *Dictionary of Symbols and Imagery*. Amsterdam: North-Holland.

De Vries, Jan. 1977. *Perspectives in the History of Religions*. Berkeley: University of California Press.

Dimitrowsky, Haim Zalman. 1962. "The Debate Between Rabbi Joseph Karo and the Mabi't." *Sefunot* 6:71–123. (Hebrew)

———. 1963. "The School of Rabbi Ya'akov Beirav in Safed." *Sefunot* 7: 43–102. (Hebrew)

Doty, William G. 2000. *Mythography: The Study of Myths and Rituals*. Tuscaloosa: University of Alabama Press.

Douglass, Carrie B. 1984. "Toro muerto, vaca es: An Interpretation of the Spanish Bullfight." *American Ethnologist* 11: 242–58.

Eliade, Mircea. 1978. *A History of Religious Ideas*. Chicago: University of Chicago Press.

Elior, Rachel. 1996. "R. Joseph Karo and R. Israel Ba'al Shem Tov: Mystical Metamorphosis, Kabbalistic Inspiration, and Spiritual Internalization." *Tarbiz* 65: 671–709. (Hebrew)

———. 2005. "The Dybbuk: Between the Visible and the Hidden Worlds." *Jerusalem Studies in Jewish Thought* 19: 499–536. (Hebrew)

———. 2008. *Dybbuks and Jewish Women in Social History, Mysticism, and Folklore*. Trans. Joel Linsider. Jerusalem: Urim.

Elstein, Yoav. 1982. "A Hidden Midrashic Background: Reading in the Story 'A Tale of a Goat.'" In Hillel Barzel, ed., *Shmuel Yoseph 'Agnon: A Selection of Studies on His Work*. Tel Aviv: Am Oved. 521–32. (Hebrew)

Evans-Pritchard, Edward E. 1965. *Theories of Primitive Religion*. Oxford: Oxford University Press.

Fenton, P. B. 1994. "Influences Soufies sur le développement de la Qabbale a Safed: Le cas de la visitation des tombes." In P. B. Fenton and R. Goetschel, eds., *Expérience et écriture mystiques dans les religions du livre*. Leiden: Brill. 163–90.

Fine, Lawrence, ed. and trans. 1984. *Safed Spirituality: Rules of Mystical Piety*. New York: Paulist Press.

———. 1986. "The Art of Metoposcopy: A Study in Isaac Luria's Charismatic Knowledge." *Association for Jewish Studies Review* 11: 79–101.

———. 2003. *Physician of the Soul, Healer of the Cosmos: Isaac Luria and His Kabbalistic Fellowship*. Stanford, CA: Stanford University Press.

Fogel, Moshe. 2001. "The Sabbateanism of *Sefer Hemdat Yamim*: A New Evaluation." In Rachel Elior, ed., *He Khalom ve-Shivro: The Sabbatean Movement and Its Extensions*. Jerusalem: Institute of Jewish Studies. 365–422. (Hebrew)

Freud, Sigmund. 1913a. "Märchenstoffe in Träumen." *Internationale Zeitschrift für ärzliche Psychoanalyse* 1: 145–51.

———. 1913b. *Totem und Tabu: Einige übereinstimmungen im Seelenleben der Wilden und Neurotiker*. Vienna: Hugo Heller.

———. 1966. "Dream Symbolism." In Sigmund Freud, *The Works of Sigmund Freud*, trans. Chaim Izak. Tel Aviv: Dvir. 1: 98–113. (Hebrew)

Galley, Susanne. 2003. "Der Tod des Jitzchak Luria." In Susanne Galley, *Der Gerechte ist das Fundament der Welt*. Wiesbaden: Harrassowitz. 370–74.

Giller, Pinchas. 1994. "Recovering the Sanctity of the Galilee: The Veneration of Sacred Relics in Classical Kabbalah." *Journal of Jewish Thought and Philosophy* 4: 147–69.

Ginzberg, Louis. 1902. "Beard." In *Jewish Encyclopedia*. New York: Funk & Wagnalls. 2: 611–15.

———. 1960. *On Law and Lore*. Tel Aviv: Dvir. (Hebrew)

Ginzburg, Carlo. 1989. "The High and the Low: The Theme of Forbidden Knowledge in the Sixteenth and Seventeenth Centuries." In Carlo Ginzburg, *Clues, Myths, and the Historical Method*. Trans. John Tedeschi and Anne Tedeschi. Baltimore: Johns Hopkins University Press. 60–76.

———. 1992a. *The Cheese and the Worms: The Cosmos of a Sixteenth-Century Miller*. Baltimore: Johns Hopkins University Press.

———. 1992b. *The Night Battles: Witchcraft and Agrarian Cults in the Sixteenth and Seventeenth Centuries*. Baltimore: Johns Hopkins University Press. (Original Italian edition, 1966).

Gitelman, Zvi, ed. 1992. *The Quest for Utopia: Jewish Political Ideas and Institutions Through the Ages*. Armonk, NY: M. E. Sharpe.

Goldish, Matt, ed. 2003. *Spirit Possession in Judaism: Cases and Contexts from the Middle Ages to the Present*. Detroit: Wayne State University Press.

Goodblatt, Chanita. 2000. "Women, Demons, and the Rabbi's Son: Narratology and 'A Story from Worms.'" *Exemplaria* 12: 231–53.

Grätz, Manfred. 1996. "Kunstmärchen." *Enzyklopädie des Märchens*. Berlin: Walter de Gruyter. 8: 612–22.

Green, Arthur. 1979. *Tormented Master: A Life of Rabbi Nahman of Bratslav*. Tuscaloosa: University of Alabama Press.

———. 2002. "Shekhinah, the Virgin Mary and the Song of Songs: Reflections on a Kabbalistic Symbol in the Historical Context." *AJS Review* 26: 1–52.

Greenblatt, Steven, and Catherin Gallagher. 2000. *Practicing New Historicism*. Chicago: University of Chicago Press.

Greyerz, Kaper von. 2008. *Religion and Culture in Early Modern Europe, 1500–1800*. Oxford: Oxford University Press.

Grözinger, Karl Erich. 1992. *Kafka und die Kabbala*. Frankfurt am Main: Eichborn.

Gurevich, Aron. 1988. *Medieval Popular Culture: Problems of Belief and Perception*. Cambridge, UK: Cambridge University Press.

Hacker, Joseph. 1984. "A Historical-Halachic and Social Study of the Jezeeya Tax by Eretz Yisrael Rabbis in the Sixteenth Century." *Shalem* 4: 93–104. (Hebrew)

———. 1987. "The Intellectual Activity of the Jews of the Ottoman Empire During the Sixteenth and Seventeenth Centuries." In Isador Twerski and Bernard Septimus, eds., *Jewish Thought in the Seventeenth Century*. Cambridge, MA: Harvard University Press. 95–136.

———. 2002. "Safed in the Sixteenth Century: A Chapter in the Support of the Jews of Eretz Israel and Their Self-Rule." *Shalem* 7: 133–50. (Hebrew)

Halamish, Moshe. 1988. "Kabbalah in the Ruling of R. Joseph Karo." *Da'at* 21: 85–102. (Hebrew)

Hasan-Rokem, Galit. 1996. "A Dream Is One-Sixtieth of Prophecy." In Benjamin Zeev Kedar, ed., *The Folk Culture*. Jerusalem: Zalman Shazar Center. 45–54. (Hebrew)

Heid, Uriel. 1955. "Ottoman Documents on Safed Jews in the Sixteenth Century." *Jerusalem* [*Mekhkerey Eretz Yisrael*] 2: 128–35. (Hebrew)

Heng, Geraldine. 2003. *Empire of Magic: Medieval Romance and the Politics of Cultural Fantasy*. New York: Columbia University Press.

Hølbek, Bengt. 1987. *Interpretation of Fairy Tales*. FF Communications 239. Helsinki: Suomalainen Tiedeakatemia.

Holm, J., ed. 1994. *Sacred Space*. London: Pinter.

Horovitz, Carmi. 1987. "Notes on the Attitude of the *Mabit* to Safed Pietists." *Shalem* 5: 273–84. (Hebrew)

Horovitz, Elimelech. 1994. "On the Meaning of the Beard in Jewish Communities in the East and in Europe in the Middle Ages and Early Modern Period." *Pe'amim* 59: 124–48. (Hebrew)

Huss, Boaz. 2002. "Sacred Place, Sacred Time, Sacred Book: The Impact of the *Zohar* on Pilgrimage to Miron—Customs and Lag b'Omer Celebrations." *Kabbalah* 7: 237–56. (Hebrew)

———. 2003. "The Ritual of Holy Graves in Safed Kabbalah." *Machana'im* 14: 123–34. (Hebrew)

———. 2004. "The Zoharic Communities of Safed." In Zeev Gries, Haim Kreisel, and Boaz Huss, eds., *Shefa Tal: Studies in Jewish Thought and Culture*. Be'er Sheva: Ben Gurion University Press. 149–70. (Hebrew)

Idel, Moshe. 1984. "R. Yehuda Chaliwa and His Work *Sefer Tzafnat Pa'ane'ach*." *Shalem* 4: 119–48. (Hebrew)

———. 1985. "Solomon Molcho as a Magician." *Sefunot* 3: 193–219. (Hebrew)

———. 1993. "Reuveni and R. Haim Vital." In Aharon Z. Aeschkoli, ed., *The Story of David ha-Reuveni*. Jerusalem: Mosad Bialik. 36–39. (Hebrew)

———. 1998a. *Messianic Mystics*. New Haven, CT: Yale University Press.

———. 1998b. "On Mobility, Individuals, and Groups: Prolegomenon for a Sociological Approach to Sixteenth-Century Kabbalah." *Kabbalah* 3: 145–73.

———. 2005a. *Ascensions on High in Jewish Mysticism: Pillars, Lines, Ladders*. Budapest: Central European University Press.

———. 2005b. *Kabbalah and Eros*. New Haven, CT: Yale University Press.

———. 2006. *Night Kabbalists*. Jerusalem: Carmel Press. (Hebrew)

Ish-Shalom, Michael. 1944. "Toward a History of Everyday Hebrew." *Areshet: Yearbook of the Religious Writer's Organization* 1: 387–93. (Hebrew)

———. 1963. "Information About Safed in the Books of Christian Travellers." *Sefunot* 7: 206–25.

Katz, Ya'akov. 1951. "The Ordination Debate Between Rabbi Ya'akov Beirav and Rabbi Levi ben Haviv." *Zion* 16: 28–45. (Hebrew)

———. 1984. *Halacha and Kabbalah: Studies in the History of Jewish Religion, Its Divisions, and Social Relations*. Jerusalem: Magnes Press. (Hebrew)

Kimelman, Reuven. 2003. *Lekha Dodi and Kabbalat Shabbat: The Mystical Meaning*. Jerusalem: Magnes Press. (Hebrew)

Kna'ani, Ya'akov. 1934. "Economical Life in Safed and Its Environs in the Sixteenth and First Half of the Seventeenth Century." *Me'asef Zion* 6: 172–217. (Hebrew)

Krauss, Samuel. 1894. "Teraphim." *Am UrQuell* 5: 117–19.

Krueger, Roberta L., ed. 2000. *The Cambridge Companion to Medieval Romance*. Cambridge, UK: Cambridge University Press.

Kushelevsky, Rella. 1994. "The Tanah and the Wandering Dead: A Non-Jewish Legend?" *Bikoret u-Farshanut* 30: 41–63. (Hebrew)

Kuyt, Annelies. 1999. "With One Foot in the Renaissance: Shlomoh Almoli and His Dream Interpretation." *Jewish Studies Quarterly* 6: 205–17.

Lamdan, Ruth. 1997. "The Relationships Between the Communities in Safed After the Expulsion from Spain: A New Evaluation." *Pe'amim* 72: 75–83. (Hebrew)

———. 1998. "Deviations from Accepted Moral Norms in Jewish Society in the Land of Israel and in Egypt in the Sixteenth Century." In Isaiah Gafni and Israel Bartal, eds., *Sexuality and Family in History*. Jerusalem: Zalman Shazar Center. 119–30. (Hebrew)

Le Goff, Jacques. 1988. *The Medieval Imagination*. Chicago: University of Chicago Press.

Lehman, Arthur, and James Myers, eds. 1993. *Magic, Witchcraft, and Religion: An Anthropological Study of the Supernatural*. Mountain View, CA: Mayfield.

Lenowitz, Harris. 1998. *The Jewish Messiahs: From the Galilee to Crown Heights*. New York: Oxford University Press.

———. 2003. "A Spirit Possession Tale as an Account of the Equivocal Insertion of Rabbi Hayyim Vital into the Role of Messiah." In Matt Goldish, ed., *Spirit Possession in Judaism: Cases and Contexts from the Middle Ages to the Present*. Detroit: Wayne State University Press. 197–214.

Lerner, Miron Bialik. 1988. "The Tale of the Rabbi and the Dead Man: Its Literary and Halachic Transformations." *Asupot* 2: 29–70. (Hebrew)

Leslie, Marina. 1998. *Renaissance Utopias and the Problem of History*. Ithaca, NY: Cornell University Press.

Levin, Harry. 1972. *The Myth of the Golden Age in the Renaissance*. New York: Oxford University Press.

Lévi-Strauss, Claude. 1960. "Four Winnebago Myths: A Structural Sketch." In S. Diamond, ed., *Culture in History: Essays in Honour of Paul Radin*. New York: Columbia University Press. 351–62.

———. 1963. *Structural Anthropology*, vol. 1. New York: Basic Books.

Lichtenstein, Yehezk'el Shraga. 2007. *From Impurity to Sacredness: Prayers and Religious Artifacts in Cemeteries and Pilgrimage to Saints' Tombs*. Tel Aviv: Ha-Kibbutz ha-Meuchad. (Hebrew)

Liebes, Yehuda. 1990. "The Messiah of the Zohar: Toward the Messianic Figure of R. Shim'on bar-Yochai." In *The Messianic Idea in Jewish Thought: A Study Conference in Honour of the Eightieth Birthday of Gershom Scholem*. Jerusalem: Israel Academy of Sciences and Humanities. 87–236. (Hebrew)

———. 1992. "The Secret Sermon of Luria Before His Death." *Jerusalem Studies in Jewish Thought* 10: 113–69. (Hebrew)

———. 1993. "Toward the Figure, Writings, and Kabbalistic Thought of the Author of 'Emek ha-Melech.'" *Jerusalem Studies in Jewish Thought* 11: 101–37. (Hebrew)

———. 1994. "Zohar and Eros." *Alpa'yim* 9: 67–119. (Hebrew)

Limor, Ora. 2006. "Mary and the Jews: Story, Controversy, and Testimony." *Historein* 6: 55–71.

Lindahl, Carl, John McNamara, and John Lindow, eds. 2000. *Medieval Folklore: An Encyclopedia of Myths, Legends, Tales, Beliefs, and Customs*. Santa Barbara, CA: Booklist.

Lipsker, Avidov. 2009. "The Shining Rob." In *Encyclopedia of the Jewish Story*. Ramat Gan: Bar-Ilan University Press. 2: 291–302. (Hebrew)

Lüthi, Max. 1976. *Once Upon a Time: On the Nature of Fairy Tales*. Bloomington: Indiana University Press.

———. 1984. *The Fairytale as Art Form and Portrait of Man*. Bloomington: Indiana University Press.

Magid, Shaul. 1996. "Conjugal Union, Mourning, and Talmud Torah in R. Isaac Luria's Tikkun Hatzot." *Da'at* 36: xviii–xlv.

———. 2008. *From Metaphysics to Midrash: Myth, History, and the Interpretation of Scripture in Lurianic Kabbala*. Bloomington: Indiana University Press.

Malkiel, Eliezer. 2007. *A Travel to the Secret: In the Footsteps of Rabbi Nachman of Bratslav's Voyage to the Land of Israel*. Tel Aviv: Yedioth Ahronoth. (Hebrew)

Mandel, L. 1894. "Teraphim." *Am UrQuell* 5: 92–93. (German)

Marcus, Eliezer. 1978. "The Confrontation of Jews and Gentiles in Folktales of Jews from Muslim Countries." Ph.D. dissertation, The Hebrew University, Jerusalem. (Hebrew)

Mark, Zvi. 2014. *The Complete Stories of Rabbi Nachman of Bratslav*. Tel Aviv: Miskal–Yediot Ahronot Books; and Jerusalem: Bialik Institute. (Hebrew)

Marwick, Max, ed. 1982. *Witchcraft and Sorcery: Selected Readings*. Harmondsworth, UK: Penguin.

McGinn, Bernard. 2000. *Antichrist: Two Thousand Years of the Human Fascination with Evil*. New York: Columbia University Press.

Meri, Josef W. 2002. *The Cult of Saints Among Muslims and Jews in Medieval Syria*. Oxford: Oxford University Press.

Meroz, Ronit. 1987. "The Fellowship of Rabbi Moshe ben-Makhir and Its Regulations." *Pe'amim* 31: 40–61. (Hebrew)

———. 1988. "Redemption in Lurianic Discipline." Ph.D. dissertation, The Hebrew University, Jerusalem. (Hebrew)

———. 1992. "Selections from Ephraim Penzieri: The Sermon of Luria in Jerusalem and the Significance of Eating Food." *Jerusalem Studies in Jewish Thought* 10: 211–57. (Hebrew)

———. 2002. "The Saruk School of Kabbalists: A New Historical Interpretation." *Shalem* 7: 151–94. (Hebrew)

———. 2003. "Spiritual Life in Sixteenth-Century Safed." *Ariel* 157–58: 82–90. (Hebrew)

Mirsky, Aharon. 1962. "Poems of Nagar and Bar-Nagar." *Sefunot* 6: 259–302. (Hebrew)

Mitchell, Timothy. 1988. *Violence and Piety in Spanish Folklore*. Philadelphia: University of Pennsylvania Press.

———. 1991. *Blood Sport: A Social History of Spanish Bullfighting*. Philadelphia: University of Pennsylvania Press.

Murfin, Ross C. 1989. "What Is the New Historicism?" In Ross C. Murfin, ed., *Joseph Conrad, Heart of Darkness: A Case Study in Contemporary Criticism*. New York: St. Martin's Press. 226–36, 255–58.

Nacht, Ya'akov. 1959. *Female's Symbols*. Tel Aviv: privately published. (Hebrew)

Nadeau, Maurice. 1989. *The History of Surrealism*. Trans. Richard Howard. Cambridge, MA: Belknap.

Newman, Barbara. 1998. "Possessed by the Spirit: Devout Women, Demoniacs, and the Apostolic Life in the Thirteenth Century." *Speculum* 73: 733–70.

Niehoff, Maren. 1992. "A Dream Which Is Not Interpreted Is Like a Letter Which Is Not Read." *Journal of Jewish Studies* 43: 58–84.

Nigal, Gedalyah. 1983. *Dybbuk Tales in Jewish Literature*. Jerusalem: Rubin Mass. (Hebrew)

Noy, Dov. 1981. "The Confrontation Between Jews and Gentiles in Folk Legends of Yemenite Jews." In Shlomo Morag and I. Ben-Ami, eds., *Communal and Geniza Studies*. Jerusalem: Magnes Press. 229–95. (Hebrew)

Oring, Elliot. 2008. "The Legendary and the Rhetoric of Truth." *Journal of American Folklore* 121: 127–66.

Oron, Michal. 1987. "Kafka und Nachman von Bratzlaw: Erzählen zwischen Traum und Erwartung." In Karl Erich Grözinger, Stéphane Mosés, and Hans Dieter Zimmermann, eds., *Franz Kafka und das Judentum*. Frankfurt: Jüdischer Verlag. 113–21.

Otto, Rudolf. 1959. *The Idea of the Holy*. Trans. John W. Harvey. Harmondsworth, UK: Penguin.

Pachter, Mordechai. 1981. "Life and Personality of R. Eleazar Azkari in Light of His Mystical Journal and *Sefer Kharedim*." *Shalem* 3: 127–47. (Hebrew)

———. 1987. "The Beginning of the Kabbalistic Ethical Literature in Sixteenth-Century Safed." In Joseph Dan, ed., *Culture and History: In Memory of Prof. Inno Shaki*. Jerusalem: Misgav Yerushalayim, Center for Research and Study of Sephardi and Oriental Jewish Heritage. 77–94. (Hebrew)

———. 1988. "R. Joseph Karo's *Sefer Magid Meisharim* as an Ethical Work." *Da'at* 21: 57–83. (Hebrew)

———. 1991. "Eretz Israel in the Preaching and Ethical Literature of Safed Scholars in the Sixteenth Century." In Moshe Halamish and Aviezer Ravitzki, eds., *Eretz Israel in Jewish Thought of Middle Ages*. Jerusalem: Yad Izhak Ben-Zvi. 290–319. (Hebrew)

———. 1994. *From Safed's Hidden Treasures: Studies and Texts Concerning the History of Safed and Its Sages in the Sixteenth Century*. Jerusalem: Zalman Shazar Center. (Hebrew)

Patai, Raphael. 1994. *The Jewish Alchemists*. Princeton, NJ: Princeton University Press.

Petzoldt, Leander. 1968. *Der Tote als Gast: Volkssage und Exempel*. Helsinki: Academia Scientiarum Fennica.

Pitt-Rivers, Julian. 1993. "The Spanish Bull-Fight and Kindred Activities." *Anthropology Today* 9: 11–15.

Rabinowitz, Ze'ev. 1940. "From the Stoliner Geniza." *Zion* 5: 125–32. (Hebrew)

Rabinowitz, Zvi Me'ir. 1968. "On *Toldot ha-'Ari*." *Mo'aznayim* 26: 145–47. (Hebrew)

Rapoport-Albert, Ada. 2008. "On the Status of Women in the Sabbatian Movement." *Jerusalem Studies in Jewish Thought* 16: 183–91. (Hebrew)

Raspe, Lucia. 2006. *Jüdische Hagiographie im mittelalterlichen Aschkenas*. Tübingen: Mohr Siebeck.

Ravitzky, Aviezer. 1993. *Messianism, Zionism, and Jewish Religious Radicalism*. Tel Aviv: Am Oved. (Hebrew)

Reiner, Elchanan. 1988. *Emigration and Pilgrimage to the Land of Israel, 1099–1517*. Ph.D. dissertation, The Hebrew University, Jerusalem. (Hebrew)

Rimer, Yehudit. 1972. "Kafka and Rabbi Nachman." *Shedemot* 44: 95–101. (Hebrew)

Ritvo, Harriet. 1992. "Race, Breed, and Myths of Origin: Chillingham Cattle as Ancient Britons." *Representations* 39: 1–22.

Röhrich, Lutz. 1991. *Folktales and Reality*. Bloomington: Indiana University Press.

Roper, Lyndal. 1994. *Oedipus and the Devil: Witchcraft, Sexuality, and Religion in Early Modern Europe*. London: Routledge.

Rosenberg, Shalom. 1990. "The Return to Garden of Eden: Contributions to the History of the Idea of the Restorative Redemption in Medieval Jewish Thought." In *The Messianic Idea in Jewish Thought: A Study Conference in Honour of the Eightieth Birthday of Gershom Scholem*. Jerusalem: Israel Academy of Sciences and Humanities. 37–86.

Rotenberg, Mordechai. 2002. "If You'll Live: It Is a Legend." *Alpa'yim* 24: 150–70. (Hebrew)

Rotman, David. 2016. *Dragons, Demons, and Wonderous Realms: The Marvelous in Medieval Hebrew Narrative*. Be'er Sheva: Heksherim Institute. (Hebrew)

Rozen, Minna. 1980. "The Position of the Musta'rabs in the Intercommunity Relationships in the Jewish Settlements in Eretz Yisrael from the End of the 15th Century to the End of the 17th Century." *Kathedra* 17: 73–101. (Hebrew)

Rozen, Minna, and Eliezer Witztum. 1992. "The Dark Mirror of the Soul: Dreams of a Jewish Physician in Jerusalem at the End of the 17th Century." *Revue des Études Juives* 151: 5–42.

Rubin, Miri. 2009. *Mother of God: A History of the Virgin Mary*. New Haven, CT: Yale University Press.

Safran, Bezalel. 1987. "Leone da Modena's Historical Thinking." In Isador Twerski and Bernard Septimus, eds., *Jewish Thought in the Seventeenth Century*. Cambridge, MA: Harvard University Press. 381–98.

Satlow, Michael L. 1994. "Wasted Seed: The History of a Rabbinic Idea." *Hebrew Union College Annual* 65: 137–75.

Schäfer, Peter. 2002. *Mirror of His Beauty: Feminine Images of God from the Bible to the Early Kabbalah*. Princeton, NJ: Princeton University Press.

Schechter, Solomon. 1908. "Safed in the Sixteenth Century: A City of Legists and Mystics." In S. Schechter, *Studies in Judaism*. Philadelphia: Jewish Publication Society of America. 202–308.

Schmitt, Jean-Claude. 1998. *Ghosts in the Middle Ages: The Living and the Dead in Medieval Society*. Trans. T. Lavender Fagan. Chicago: University of Chicago Press.

Scholem, Gershom. 1940a. "The Binding Contract of Luria's Disciples." *Zion* 5: 133–60. (Hebrew)

———. 1940b. "Israel Sarug: Luria's Disciple." *Zion* 5: 214–43. (Hebrew)

———. 1955. "And the Mystery Is Not Solved." *Bekhinot* 8: 85. (Hebrew)

———. 1967. *Shabbetai Zevi and the Sabbatean Movement During His Lifetime*. Tel-Aviv: Am Oved. (Hebrew)

———. 1976a. *Elements of the Kabbalah and Its Symbolism*. Jerusalem: Mosad Bialik. (Hebrew)

———. 1976b. "Toward Understanding the Messianic Idea in Judaism." In Gershom Scholem, *Dvarim be-Goh*. Tel Aviv: Am Oved. 155–90. (Hebrew)

———. 1990a. "Memory and Utopia in Jewish History." In Gershom Scholem, *'Od Davar*, ed. Avraham Shapira. Tel Aviv: Am Oved. 187–98. (Hebrew)

———. 1990b. "Toward an Understanding of the Story of Joseph Dela-Reyna." In Gershom Scholem, *'Od Davar*, ed. Avraham Shapira. Tel Aviv: Am Oved. 249–62. (Hebrew)

———. 1990c. "Types of Redemption." In Gershom Scholem, *'Od Davar*, ed. Avraham Shapira. Tel Aviv: Am Oved. 243–48. (Hebrew)

———. 2008a. *Lurianic Kabbalah*, ed. Daniel Abrams. Los Angeles: Kruv. (Hebrew)

———. 2008b. "New Information on R. Yosef Ashkenazi, the 'Tana' of Safed." In Gershom Scholem, *Lurianic Kabbalah*, ed. Daniel Abrams. Los Angeles: Kruv. 125–86. (Hebrew)

———. 2008c. "What Is *Sefer ha-Geirushin?*" In Gershom Scholem, *Lurianic Kabbalah*, ed. Daniel Abrams. Los Angeles: Kruv. 187–90. (Hebrew)

Scholem, Gershom, and Moshe Idel. 2007. "Luria, Isaac ben Salomon." In *Encyclopedia Judaica*, 2nd ed. Detroit: Macmillan Reference. 262–67.

Schwartz, Dov. 2005. *The Messianic Idea in Jewish Thought of the Middle Ages*. Ramat Gan: Bar-Ilan University Press.

Scult, Mel. 1997. "Schechter's Seminary." In Jack Wertheimer, ed., *Tradition Renewed: A History of the Jewish Theological Seminary*. New York: Jewish Theological Seminary of America. 43–102.

Shazar, Zalman. 1950. "Your Watchers, Safed." In Zalman Shazar, *Kochvey Boker*. Tel Aviv: Am Oved. 185–294. (Hebrew)

Shochetman, Eliav. 1983. "New Sources from the Geniza on the Commercial Activity of Luria in Egypt." *Pe'amim* 16: 56–64. (Hebrew)

Shoham-Steiner, Ephraim. 2004. "Jews, Holy Tombs, and the Search for Healing Between East and West in the Middle Ages." *Pe'amim* 98–99: 39–66. (Hebrew)

Shyovitz, David I. 2017. *A Remembrance of His Wonders: Nature and the Supernatural in Medieval Ashkenaz*. Philadephia: University of Pennsylvania Press.

Simonsohn, Shlomo. 1962. "Safed Messengers in Mantua in the Seventeenth and Eighteenth Centuries." *Sefunot* 6: 329–54. (Hebrew)

Sobel, Zvi. 1993. *A Small Place in Galilee: Religion and Social Conflict in an Israeli Village*. New York: Holmes & Meier.

Stephens, Walter. 2002. *Demon Lovers: Witchcraft, Sex, and the Crisis of Belief*. Chicago: University of Chicago Press.

Tamar, David. 1970. "Luria and Vital as Messiah, Son of Joseph." In David Tamar, *Studies in the History of the Jews in the Land of Israel and Italy*. Jerusalem: Rubin Mass. 115–23. (Hebrew)

———. 1982. "Notes to *Sefer ha-Hezyonot*." *Sinai* 91: 82–86. (Hebrew)

———. 1984a. "The Dreams and Messianic Visions of R. Hayyim Vital." *Shalem* 4: 211–29. (Hebrew)

———. 1984b. "The Greatness of R. Hayyim Vital." In S. Israeli, R. Singer, and Y. Raphael, eds., *Festschrift in Honor of R. Joseph Dov Soloveichik*. Jerusalem: Mossad Harav Kook. 2: 1297–1311. (Hebrew)

———. 1986. *Studies in the History of the Jewish People in Eretz Israel and Italy*. Jerusalem: Rubin Mass. (Hebrew)

———. 1992. "Misunderstandings and Criticisms." *Sinai* 95: 184–87. (Hebrew)

Tangherlini, T. R. 1990. "'It Happened Not Too Far from Here': A Survey of Legend, Theory, and Characterization." *Western Folklore* 49: 371–90.

Ta-Shema, Israel. 1994. "The Treatise *Zecher 'Asah le-Nifla'otav* by Rabbi Yehuda the Pious." *Kovetz al-Yad* 12: 123–46. (Hebrew)

Thomas, Keith. 1971. *Religion and the Decline of Magic*. Harmondsworth, UK: Penguin.

Tishby, Isaiah. 1993. *The Study of the Kabbalah and Its Offspring*, 3 vols. Jerusalem: Magnes Press. (Hebrew)

———. 1994. *Netivei 'Emunah u-Minut*. Jerusalem: Magnes Press. (Hebrew)

Tuan Yi-Fu. 2001. "Cosmos Versus Hearth." In Paul C. Adams, Steven D. Hoelscher, and Karen E. Till, eds., *Textures of Place: Exploring Humanist Geographies*. Minneapolis: University of Minnesota Press. 319–39.

Tylor, E. B. 1958. *Religion in Primitive Culture*. New York: Harper.

Van Gennep, Arnold. 1917. *La formation des Legends*. Paris: Flammarion.

Veeser, H. Aram, ed. 1989. *The New Historicism*. New York: Routledge.

Verman, M., and S. H. Adler. 1993–1994. "Path Jumping in the Jewish Magical Tradition." *Jewish Studies Quarterly* 1: 131–48.

Von Stuckrad, Kocku. 2006 [1999]. "Constructing Femininity: The Lilith Case." books.google.co.il/books/about/Constructing_Femininity.html?id= gQPlGwAACAAJ&redir_esc=y (accessed July 31, 2018).

Von Sydow, Carl Wilhelm. 1948. *Selected Papers on Folklore*. Copenhagen: Rosenkilde & Bagger.

Warner, Marina. 1976. *Alone of All Her Sex: The Myth and the Cult of the Virgin Mary*. New York: Vintage.

Webber, Sabra J. 1991. *Romancing the Real: Folklore and Ethnographic Representation in North Africa*. Philadelphia: University of Pennsylvania Press.

Weinstein, Donald, and Rudolph M. Bell. 1982. *Saints and Society: The Two Worlds of Western Christendom, 1000–1700*. Chicago: University of Chicago Press.

Weiss, Haim. 2011. *All Dreams Follow the Mouth: A Reading in the Talmudic Dreams Tractate*. Or Yehuda: Kinneret, Zmora-Bitan, and Dvir. (Hebrew)

Werblowsky, R. J. Zvi. 1987. "The Safed Revival and Its Aftermath." In Arthur Green, ed., *Jewish Spirituality II: From the Sixteenth-Century Revival to the Present*. New York: Crossroad. 7–33.

———. 1996 [1962]. *Joseph Karo: Lawyer and Mystic*. Jerusalem: Magnes Press. (Hebrew)

Wilson, Stephen, ed. 1983. *Saints and Their Cults*. Cambridge, UK: Cambridge University Press.

Wineman, Aryeh. 1985. "The Dialectic of *Tikkun* in the Legends of the Ari." *Prooftexts* 5: 33–44.

———. 1988. *Beyond Appearances: Stories from the Kabbalistic Ethical Writings*. Philadelphia: Jewish Publication Society.

Wiskind-Elper, Ora. 1998. *Tradition and Fantasy in the Tales of Reb Nahman of Bratslav*. Albany: State University of New York Press.

Wolfson, Elliot R. 1995. *Circle in the Square: Studies in the Use of Gender in Kabbalistic Symbolism*. Albany: State University of New York Press.

———. 2005. *Language, Eros, Being: Kabbalistic Hermeneutics and Poetic Imagination*. New York: Fordham University Press.

———. 2016. "Asceticism, Mysticism, and Messianism: A Reappraisal of Schechter's Portrait of Sixteenth-Century Safed." *Jewish Quarterly Review* 106: 165–77.

Ya'ari, Avraham. 1951. *Messengers of the Land of Israel*. Jerusalem: Mosad Harav Kook. (Hebrew)

———. 1958. "A Bookseller in Sixteenth-Century Safed." In Avraham Ya'ari, *Mekhkrei Sefer: Chapters in the History of the Hebrew Book*. Jerusalem: Mossad Harav Kook. 154–62. (Hebrew)

———. 1976. *Travels in the Land of Israel*. Ramat Gan: Masada Press. (Hebrew)

Yahalom, Joseph. 1982. "R. Yisrael Najara and the Renaissance of Hebrew Poetry in the East After the Expulsion." *Pe'amim* 13: 96–124. (Hebrew)

Yassif, Eli. 1979. "The Story of Yo'av's Heroism: Characterization of the Hebrew Heroic Story in the Middle Ages." *Yeda-Am* 19: 17–27. (Hebrew)

———. 1985. *The Tales of Ben-Sira in the Middle Ages*. Jerusalem: Magnes Press. (Hebrew)

———. 1999. *The Hebrew Folktale: History, Genre, Meaning*. Bloomington: Indiana University Press [Hebrew original, 1994].

———. 2001. *Sefer haZichronot, That Is, The Chronicles of Jerachme'el: A Critical Edition*. Tel Aviv: Tel Aviv University Press. (Hebrew)

———. 2004. *The Hebrew Collection of Tales in the Middle Ages*. Tel Aviv: Ha-Kibbutz ha-Meuchad. (Hebrew)

———. 2005. "The Medieval Saint as Protagonist and Storyteller: The Case of R. Judah he-Hasid." In Rachel Elior and Peter Schäfer, eds., *Creation and Re-Creation in Jewish Thought: Festschrift in Honor of Joseph Dan*. Tübingen: Mohr Siebeck. 179–92.

———. 2013. "Safed (12 sections)." Oxford Bibliographies Online, Oxford University Press, 2013. www.oxfordbibliographies.com/view/document/obo-9780199840731/obo-9780199840731-0030.xml.

Yuval, Israel I. 2001. "Between Political and Utopian Messianism in the Middle Ages." In D. Ariel-Yoel and M. Leibovich, eds., *The Battle of Gog and Magog: Messianism and Apocalyptics in Judaism in the Past and Present*. Tel Aviv: Yedioth Ahronoth. 58–76. (Hebrew)

Zak, Bracha. 1976. "The Attitude of Rabbi Shlomo Alkavetz to Philosophical Inquiry." *Eshel Be'er Sheva* 1: 288–306. (Hebrew)

———. 1991. "The Land of Israel in the Thought of R. Moshe Kordovero." In Moshe Halamish and Aviezer Ravitzky, eds., *The Land of Israel in Jewish Thought of the Middle Ages*. Jerusalem: Yad Izhak Ben-Zvi. 332–41. (Hebrew)

Zaleski, Carol. 1987. *Otherworld Journeys: Accounts of Near-Death Experience in Medieval and Modern Times*. New York: Oxford University Press.

Zfatman, Sara. 1979. "Maysehbukh: The Character of a Genre in Old Yiddish Literature." *Ha'sifrut* 28: 126–52. (Hebrew)

———. 1982. "Exorcism of Spirits in Seventeenth-Century Prague." *Jerusalem Studies in Jewish Folklore* 3: 7–32. (Hebrew)

———. 1987. *The Marriage of a Mortal Man and a She-Demon*. Jerusalem: Akademon Press. (Hebrew)

———. 1993. *Between Ashkenaz and Sefarad: Toward the History of the Jewish Story in the Middle Ages*. Jerusalem: Magnes Press. (Hebrew)

———. 2010. *From Talmudic Times to the Middle Ages: The Establishment of Leadership in Jewish Literature*. Jerusalem: Magnes Press.

———. 2015. *Jewish Exorcism in Early Modern Ashkenaz*. Jerusalem: Magnes Press. (Hebrew)

Zimmer, Isaac. 1996. "The Head Sidelocks: Jewish Identity Card?" In Isaac Zimmer, *'Olam ke-Minhago Noheg': Society and Its Customs*. Jerusalem: Zalman Shazar Center. 43–71. (Hebrew)

Zipes, Jack. 1983. *Fairy Tales and the Art of Subversion*. New York: Heinemann Educational.

———. 1999. *When Dreams Came True: Classical Fairy Tales and Their Tradition*. New York: Routledge.

Zlotnik, Yehuda Leib, and Raphael Patai. 1947. *Ma'she be-Yerushalmi, Which Was Copied by R. Abraham ben Maimon*. Jerusalem: Folklore and Ethnography Institute. (Hebrew)

Zoran, Gavriel. 1997. *Text, World, Space: Ways of Organizing the Space in Textual Narrative*. Tel Aviv: Ha-Kibbutz ha-Meuchad. (Hebrew)

INDEX

Abramson, Shraga, 245n7
Abulafia, Ya'akov
    conflict between Vital and, 53–57, 69–71, 82, 154, 192
    depiction of, in *Sefer haHezyonot*, 113
    and Dybbuk of Damascus, 52, 53–54, 57, 192–93
    in Eliahu Amiel's dream, 120–21, 122
    and Tale of the Oxen, 39–43, 46–49, 58, 63, 66–68, 76
    and Tale of the Radiant Robe, 56–57
    and Wild Hunt tales, 77
Adam, Vital's dream of, 110–13, 130, 225, 254n37
Agnon, S. Y., 128
Akiva, Rabbi, 120, 121, 138, 201
Alexander, Tamar, 244n6
Alkabetz, Shlomo, 97, 98–99, 107, 120, 121
Alsheikh, Moshe, 11, 15–18, 31–34, 127, 222–23, 224
Alterman, Nathan, 150
Amiel, Eliahu, 55–56, 120–22
Anaf, Raphael, 29, 51, 53–54, 192–94
anger, 188
animals
    reincarnation as, 175–79
    as wandering souls, 101–3, 105

animism, 105–7, 108, 114
Arabian Nights, The, 159
Armilus, 152–54
army, procession of dead, 71–77
Arthur, King, 151
Ashkenazy, Yosef, 247n20
Assaf, Simcha, 245n7
Aveiro, Pantaleão de, 18
Avraham, son of Maimonides, 145
Ayelet Ahavim (Alkabetz), 98–99
Azkari, Eleazar, 14–15, 78–82, 120, 173–74, 221, 226–27, 245n4

Bacharach, Naphtali, 189, 264n22
barefoot, walking, 97–98, 99
bar Yohai, Shimon, 99, 143
beard, mutilation of, 58–63, 66
Beirav, Ya'akov, 23, 43, 174
Ben-Ari, Eyal, 253n18
Benayahu, Meir, 3–4, 42, 49, 244nn8–9, 251n2
Ben-Menachem, Naphtali, 243n5
Ben-Nae, Yaron, 260n27
Ben-Zakkai, Yohanan, 120, 121
Ben-Zvi, Izhak, 243n2
betrothal, of demoness, 181–85
Bettelheim, Bruno, 255–56n3
Biale, David, 258n4, 259nn6–7
Biddulph, William, 18, 234

287

Bilu, Yoram, 253n18, 261n29
bird calls, understanding of, 212–13
Book of Zerubavel, 148, 150, 152, 154
Breslov Hasidim, 241–42, 266n21
bulls, 80–82
burial customs, 163–64

Christian travelers, 18, 246n8
chronicats, 50
Cohen, Nisim, 54–55, 155–56
Cohen, Yitzhak, 88, 204–5
Cordovero, Moshe
    in Eliahu Amiel's dream, 120, 121
    and *gerushin* ritual, 97, 98, 99
    and legend of Luria's successor, 161–62, 165
    on mystical quality of Israel, 107
    on reincarnation and sexual transgressions, 176–77, 178
    on speaking Hebrew, 234
cult of holy graves, 95–97, 130, 252nn14–15. *See also* pilgrimage
Dan, Joseph, 244n6
David, Abraham, 246nn8–9
dead. *See also* dybbuk; reincarnation; spirit(s)
    return of, to world of living, 63–65, 156–58
    tales of procession of, 71–77
Delmedigo, Joseph Solomon, 185–90
demonic, sexual transgressions and the, 180–85
demon kings, dream of, 134–37
de Vidas, Eliyahu, 246n11
Diaspora, 94, 130, 225, 231–32
discord, in Safed, 16–18, 19–31
donations, solicitation of, 39–43

donkey, 103
dream(s). *See also* Sefer haHezyonot (Vital)
    connection between fairy tales and, 134–37, 255–56n3
    of Eliahu Amiel, 120–22
    garden motif in, 155–59
    of Hayyim Vital, 109–17, 122–28, 130, 133, 148–55, 225, 254–55n44
    of Hayyim Vital's wife, 156–59
    Luria's interpretation of, 208–9
    of Rabbi Kalev, 258n39
    of Rabbi Nachman of Breslov, 145–46
    of Rachel the Ashkenazit, 117–20
    of Shmuel Hayati's wife, 156
    of Shmuel Vital, 134–36, 137–48, 154–55, 256n9
dybbuk, 103, 185–91, 260–62nn29,32, 35. *See also* spirit(s)
Dybbuk of Damascus, 29–31, 51–54, 57–58, 248n15

Eberlein, Rachel (the Ashkenazit), 117–19
Eberlein, Yehuda, 22–23
Eberlein controversy, 22–23
economy, of Safed, 16–18
Eden, Garden of, 123–26, 127, 156–57
Efrayim, 141–43, 145
Egypt
    banning from heaven and travel to, 57–58
    fund-raising trip to, 39–43
Eleazar of Worms, 58–60, 62–68
Elijah, Prophet, 122–25

288 · Index

Emicho, Count, 75
Encierro, 80–81
Eros, and Kabbalah, 145
erotic symbols, 139–40, 145, 164–69, 180–85, 191–94. *See also* sex and sexuality
Excalibur (sword), 151
Exile (personal), 97–99, 130
Exile, 128, 228, 231–33, 236, 240
Exodus, 187, 188–89, 251n6

fairy tales. *See* folk- and fairy tales
Falkon Letter, 191–92, 202
family, tension, 227–31
famine, in Safed, 16–18
field, going into, 98–99
Fine, Lawrence, 244n6, 263–64n22
finger, of demoness in forest, 181–85
fire, pillar of, 161–63, 258n3
Fogel, Moshe, 248n12
folk- and fairy tales
    components and subcategories of, 85
    connection between dreams and, 134–37, 255–56n3
    development of, 50
    elements in Hayyim Vital's nightmares, 148–55
    elements in Shmuel Vital's dreams, 137–48
    and enchanted garden dream motif, 155–59
    as means of mental survival, 159–60
    of Rabbi Nachman of Breslov, 145–48
folk culture, 164, 181, 185
folklore, anticanonical nature of, 2, 243n4

fowl, in wandering soul tale, 101–2
Freud, Sigmund, 106, 134
frog, in wandering soul tale, 105
fund-raising trips, 39–43
future, Luria's knowledge of, 208–10

Galanti, Moshe, 43, 120, 167, 177–78
Galanti, Yedidya, 44, 46
Galilee, as semiotic space, 94–99
garden, enchanted, 155–59
Gedalya ibn Yahya, 261–62n35
Gehazi, 138–39, 147, 155
Gentiles
    conflict with, 236
    hair as visual distinction between Jews and, 60–63, 66, 67
gerushin, 97–98, 99, 130
goat, in wandering soul tale, 101
God, in Vital's dream, 124, 126
graves, cult of holy, 95–97, 130, 252nn14–15
Guizo, Ya'akov, 254n39

haBavli, Menachem, 24
Hacker, Joseph, 6
Halakha
    tensions between masters of Kabbalah and, 31–37, 43
    Vital's inner conflict concerning Kabbalah versus, 127
Halevi, Gedaliah, 100, 205–8
Halevy, Avraham, 216
Haredi Judaism, 240
Hayati, Shmuel, dream of, 156
"Hazut Kashah (Difficult Vision)" (Alsheikh), 15–18
Hebrew, 234–35

Index • 289

Hibat Zion movement, 98
holy graves, cult of, 95–97, 130, 252nn14–15
Horovitz, Elimelech, 60, 249n27
Huss, Boaz, 253n24

ibn Susan, Isachar, 20–21
Idel, Moshe, 258n3
immersion, ritual, 217–18, 221–22, 224
impotence, 122, 125
Isaiah (Prophet), 140
Israel Folktale Archives (Dov Noy IFA), 251n2

Joab, 150–51
Jonah, 120
Judah ben Samuel of Regensburg, (Judah the Pious), 3, 58–60, 61, 71–72, 74–75, 77–79
Judah the Prince, Rabbi (Yehuda ha-Nasi), 120, 121
Judaism, disputes concerning, 20–22, 24–25

Kabbalah
 anger in, 188
 disputes concerning, 24–25
 and emergence of cult of holy graves, 96–97
 erotic symbols in, 145, 164–69
 establishment of Luria's school in Safed, 161–64, 165
 and *gerushin*, 98
 Luria on, 201–2
 reincarnation in Lurianic, 64–66
 repentance in Lurianic, 75–76
 tensions between masters of Halakha and, 31–37, 43
 Vital's inner conflict concerning Halakha versus, 127
kaf ha-kelah, 250n36
Kalev, Rabbi, 141, 258n39
Karo, Joseph
 claims to be prophet, 27
 in Eliahu Amiel's dream, 120, 121
 and messianism of Safed, 232–33
 on miracles, 200–201
 pleads for guidance from Luria, 43
 and social and religious tension in Safed, 21, 22, 23
 and tensions between halakhists and kabbalists, 34–37, 43
 vision of, 126–27
 in Vital's dream, 124, 126–27
Katz, Jacob, 244n6
Kitvei Shevah yekar uGedulat haAri, 87–89

Lamdan, Ruth, 259n14
land and landscapes. *See also* space and place
 and enchanted garden dream motif, 155–59
 encounters with, 107–8, 120–29
 in Hayyim Vital's dreams, 148–50, 152, 154
 in Rabbi Nachman's dreams and fairy tales, 146, 147–48
 Safed as mythical, 110–13, 115–18
 in Shmuel Vital's dream, 141–42, 144–45, 146, 147–48
Leon of Modena (Judah Aryeh), 39, 44, 45–46, 197, 199, 223

Levi, Gedaliah, 157
Liebes, Yehuda, 211, 256n11, 259n6, 263nn16–17
locusts, 94, 251n6. *See also* Tale of the Locusts
Luria, Isaac
   Abulafia's relationship with, 69
   on anger, 188
   charisma of, 207, 214, 263–64n22
   clairvoyance of, 208–10
   confrontation with Safed religious leadership, 25–29
   contract of fellowship of, 257–58n36
   death of, 8, 211–12, 222, 230
   and deciphering of exceptional events, 179
   and demonic sphere, 180–82
   depiction of, 112–16
   early life of, 86
   in Eliahu Amiel's dream, 56
   and exile of *Shekhinah*, 97–98
   exorcises spirit, 202–3
   as father figure, 82
   knowledge of, 170, 172–73, 174, 203–8
   Leon of Modena on, 39
   on magical powers, 201–2
   and "The Marriage of a Man and a Demoness," 181–82, 183, 184–85
   as Messiah ben Joseph, 227–28, 230
   in messianic story, 91–92
   miracles performed by, 197–99
   and ritual immersion, 217–18, 221–22, 224
   sex and sexuality in legends concerning, 169–75
   in Shmuel Vital's dream, 143
   sidelocks of, 62
   social position of, 39–49
   source of mysterious knowledge of, 212–13
   study of, 216–17
   successor to, 161–64, 165
   and Tale of the Locusts, 87–91, 129
   in Tale of the Oxen, 66–68
   and Tale of the Spirit, 186
   tension between disciples and, 210–14
   tensions between halakhists and kabbalists, 31–36, 37
   in Vital's wife's dream, 157, 158–59
   and wandering tales, 100–105, 108
   writings of, 214–16

magic, 40–47, 106, 201–2. *See also* miracles
Magid Meisharim (Karo), 126, 200–201
Maimonides, 238
Marriage of a Man and a Demoness, 181–85
Meir, Rabbi, 120, 121
Meri, Josef, 96
Meron, Mt., 25–29
Meroz, Ronit, 64, 244n6
Messiah, coming of, 51–54, 55
messianism, 231–39
mikveh (ritual bath), 217–18, 221–22, 224
mirabilia, 64, 74. *See also* miracles
miracles
   contradicting accounts of Luria's, 223–24
   Karo's desire to perform, 200–201
   of Luria exorcising spirit, 202–3

miracles *(continued)*
    and Luria's clairvoyance, 208–10
    and Luria's knowledge, 170, 172–73, 174, 203–8
    performed by Luria, 197–99
    tension between hidden and revealed, 210–14
Mitrani, Moshe, 22, 24, 116
moral norms, 259n14
Moses (biblical), 113–15
mouse, as wandering soul, 102–3, 108
Musta'arabim, 20–22, 27
mysterium tremendum, 209–10
myth, 114–24, 128

Nachman of Braslov, 145–48, 228–29
Najar, Musa, 141
Najarah, Israel, 28–31
near-death experience, 156–58
neo-animism, 105–7, 114, 128–29
New Historicism, 2, 6
nocturnal emissions, 125, 161–62, 163, 165–67, 174, 258–59n4

Og (biblical), 139, 147, 155
ordination of rabbis, 235
Oriental gardens, 159
Ottoman regime, 22–23
oxen. *See* Tale of the Oxen
Ozidah, Shmuel, 244n10
Pachter, Mordechai, 129, 244n10
path jumping, 93, 121
pilgrimage, 27, 55–56, 95–96
pillar of fire, 161–63, 258n3
Pisso, Jacob, 51–53
place. *See* land and landscapes; space and place

poverty, 16–18
prayer, disputes concerning, 20–21
Puah, Avraham, 175–79
Purim customs, 20–21

Radiant Robe, tale of, 56–57
Rashbi, *hilula* of, 25–28, 29
Rauter, Ludwig von, 19
ravens, as wandering souls, 102
redemption, 231–33, 235
reincarnation, 44–45, 63–66, 78–79, 101, 175–79, 254n29
Reiner, Elhanan, 96
repentance and rectification
    and Dybbuk of Damascus, 51–54
    in Tale of the Oxen, 41, 42, 65–66, 68
    in Tale of the Tanna and the Dead Man, 68–69
    in wandering soul tales, 100–101
    and Wild Hunt tales, 71–77
Reubeni, David, 154
Röhrich, Lutz, 255n47, 256n16
Romano, Menahem, 53
Rotenberg, Mordechai, 133, 159–60
Rozen, Minna, 20–21

Safed
    Azkari on, 14–15
    burial customs in, 163–64
    centrality of, in Vital's mind, 113–19
    Christian travelers to, 18, 246n8
    conditions in, 15–18, 245n7
    contradicting depictions of, 222–23, 224–25
    discord and strife in, 16–18, 19–31
    discovery and documentation of legends of, 5

duality of life in, 226–27
as launching pad to realm of myth, 114–24, 128
legends of, as local, 86–87
messianism of, 231–39
outsiders' views of, 18–19
public atmosphere in, 191
Schechter's study of, 1–2
scholarship on, 2–4, 243–44nn5–6
sexual morality in, 169–75
Shlumil's encounter with, 11–13
significance of legends of, 5, 24–29
tension and crisis in legends of, 31–37, 239–40
"Safed in the Sixteenth Century" (Schechter), 1–2
Sagis, Yosef, 208–9, 217
saint legends (*shevakhim*), 3
Sambari, Yosef, 251n2
San Galgano, 151–52
Sanhedrin, 235
Saruk, Binyamin, 55
Saruk, Israel, 44, 45–46
Schechter, Solomon, 1–2, 243n2
Schmitt, Jean-Claude, 72, 75, 76
Scholem, Gershom, 48–49, 65
Sefer Gematriot (Judah the Pious), 61
Sefer haGan, 58–60, 62–68
Sefer haHezyonot (Vital), 50–51, 55, 56–57, 58, 82–83, 109–20, 133, 134–38
Sefer Hasidim (Judah the Pious), 71–72, 74–75, 77–79
Sefer Hemdat Yamim, 49–50, 58, 61, 62, 190
Sefer Kharedim (Azkari), 78–82, 173–74

Sefer Ta'alumot Khokhma (Delmedigo), 185–90
Sefer Toldot ha-'Ari (Benayahu), 3–4
seminal emissions, 125, 161–62, 163, 165–67, 174, 258–59n4
Sephardim, and social tension in Safed, 20–22
sex and sexuality. *See also* erotic symbols
  homosexual, in male-only institutions, 184, 260n27
  Kabbalah's concept of, 164–69
  in Lurianic legends, 169–75
sexual purity
  and Luria's successor, 161–64
  and moral norms, 259n14
  and saving Jewish lives, 167
sexual transgressions
  and conflict between Vital and Abulafia, 53, 57–58
  connection between demonic sphere and, 180–85
  and possession by spirits, 185–95, 261n29
  punishment for, 175–79
  surveillance over, 170–71, 175–77
Sha'ar haGilgulim (Vital), 252n15
Sha'ar Ruach haKodesh (Vital), 165–66, 168–69
Shabbetai Zvi, 143, 218
Shach, Eliezer Menachem, 240
shaving, prohibition against, 58–63, 66
Shazar, Zalman, 243n2, 266n20
Shekhinah, exile of, 97–98
shells, vanquishing, 98
shevakhim (saint legends), 3
Shivkhei ha-'Ari, 86, 91–93, 202

Shlumil, Solomon, of Dreznitz
  depiction of Safed, 222–23
  drawn to Safed, 86
  first encounter with Safed, 11–13, 17–18
  legends of Safed recorded by, 5, 8, 24
  letters of, 94–95, 205–8, 245n2
  on Luria as Messiah ben Joseph, 227–28
  on Luria's miraculous deeds, 197–99, 205–8
  as oldest source of legends about Luria, 85
  on Safed's burial customs, 163–64
  Tale of the Locusts, 87–91, 94
  and tensions between halakhists and kabbalists, 34–37
  wandering soul tale, 100–101
Shul'el, Isaac, 22
sidelocks, 41–42, 48, 62–63, 67, 68
skull, in Hayyim Vital's dream, 152–53
sleep, 33–34, 36, 40. *See also* dream(s)
Sobel, Zvi, 266n21
space and place. *See also* land and landscapes
  Galilee as semiotic sphere, 94–99
  mediating, 130
  mythical, 108–27, 129–30
  and Tale of the Locusts, 87–91, 129
spirit(s). *See also* dybbuk
  exorcised by Luria, 202–3
  sexual transgression and possession by, 185–95, 261n29
  wandering, 100–108
sword, in Hayyim Vital's dream, 149–52

Tale of a Man from Worms, 182–84
Tale of the Goat, 93
Tale of the Jerusalemite, 182, 183
Tale of the Locusts, 87–91, 94, 129, 204–5
Tale of the Oxen, 39–84
Tale of the Radiant Robe, 56–57
Tale of the Spirit, 185–91
Tale of the Tanna and the Dead Man, 68–69, 75
Tale of the Two Fawns, 210–12
taxes
  Alsheikh on, 16
  as source of tension, 22–23
telfas (magic), 153
three demon kings, dream of, 134–37
Tishbi, Yeshayahu, 49–50, 248n12
tree, 140
Tylor, E. B., 106
Tzemach, Jacob, 62

"University" of Safed, 18
utopian literature, 233–34

visions, of Joseph Karo, 126–27. *See also* dream(s); *Sefer haHezyonot* (Vital)
Vital, Hayyim. *See also Sefer haHezyonot* (Vital)
  appearance of, 255n50
  complexity of, 6–7
  conflict between Abulafia and, 53–57, 69–71, 82, 192
  and discord in Safed, 25–26
  dream of wife of, 156–59
  dreams of, 109–16, 122–28, 130, 133, 148–55, 225, 254–55n44

and Dybbuk of Damascus, 29–31, 51–54
in Eliahu Amiel's dream, 120–21
on exorcism performed by Luria, 203
on holy graves cult, 252n14
impotence of, 122, 125
knowledge of *Sefer haGan*, 60
leaves Safed, 258n37
in legend of Israel Najarah, 28–29
on Luria's mysterious knowledge, 172–73, 208–9, 212–13
on Luria's study of *Zohar*, 216–17
personal identity of, 160
and possession, 192–94
Rabbi Kalev's dream of, 258n39
on reincarnation, 254n29
on ritual immersion, 217–18, 221–22, 224
on Safed during Luria's time, 236–37
Sha'ar haGilgulim, 252n15
Sha'ar Ruach haKodesh, 165–66, 168–69
in Shmuel Vital's dreams, 137–43
on sidelocks, 62
social standing of, 70–71
and Tale of the Oxen, 5, 49–51, 58
and Tale of the Spirit, 186–87, 188, 189

in Tale of the Two Fawns, 210–11
and transmission of Luria's teachings, 214
in wandering soul tale, 103
and Wild Hunt tales, 77
works of, 8
Vital, Shmuel, 44, 105, 109–10, 134–48, 152, 154–55, 256n9
Vital, Yosi, 141
Vitalis, Orderic, 72, 74–75

Walchelin, 72–73
walking barefoot, 97–98, 99
Weber, Sandra, 243n4
Weblowsky, Zvi, 97, 244n6
wedding ring, and demoness, 181–85
wheat seeds, 137–40
widow, 186–91
"Wild Hunt, The," 72–78
Wineman, Aryeh, 72, 244n6
Yosef de la Reina, 230–31

Zak, Bracha, 99, 107
Zaltman, Moshe, 59–60
Zechariah (Yahya al-Dahiri), 13–14, 36
Zerubavel, Book of, 148, 150, 152, 154
Zfatman, Sara, 183
Ziara (pilgrimage), 96
Zoran, Gabriel, 90